What are people saying about
Harvard Can't Teach What You Learn from the Streets

"Sam's real world and practical approach to teaching investment methodology creates a fundamental knowledge base for anyone considering a career in real estate investing. As a 20+ year industry veteran leading both acquisition and property management teams, *Harvard Can't Teach What You Learn From The Streets* will be required reading for my first year team members to augment their educational coursework with real world considerations."

—**Stephen Mitchell**, EVP of Asset Living, a multi-generational family business that is currently ranked the 5th largest property management company in the United States by NMHC

"Sam Liebman has created a manifesto for anyone who wants to up their game, not only in the Real Estate space but in business in general…if you're looking to achieve a higher level of excellence in business by becoming remarkable…this will inspire you, along with focusing your efforts on suc-cess while building real wealth! Simply put…it's a great read!"

—**Tim Sabean,** CEO of Sabean Media and former SVP of the Howard Stern Channels

"*Harvard Can't Teach What You Learn From The Streets* is the most comprehensive and practical book on real estate I have ever read. The book provides the perfect game plan for learning how to build lasting wealth through real estate. I will be strongly recommending the book to my clients and friends. Great job Sam!"

—**Richard "Big Daddy" Salgado** is the CEO of Coastal Advisors LLC, and correspondent for Fox News, ESPN, the NFL Network, and Bloomberg

D1591258

"**This is the book you never knew you needed....**What if you could take a masterclass in real estate with a true master? Sam Liebman brings us just that—street smarts instead of book smarts—breaking down the real estate game in an easy-to-understand, step-by-step workbook. Pick up your copy of *Harvard Can't Teach What You Learn from the Streets*. Whether a newbie or a veteran, dog ear it, mark it up. Sam cuts through the mystery of buying, maintaining and managing Real Property. Sometimes hilarious, but always on point, this is a must have in every real estate professional's library."

—**Brad Szollose,** Serial Entrepreneur,
Award-winning author of *Liquid Leadership*

"The most practical book on real estate I've ever come across. Sam takes you on a rarely seen insider's view of the real estate industry, and teaches the skills you need to amass wealth over time. Not a get rich quick book---this is a get smart quick book. A real-life study of the business through the eyes of a master player. A must read for anyone seriously looking to improve their skills in the game."

—**Joel Schechter,** retired CEO of Honora
Pearl and QVC on-air personality (former)

"Sam Liebman effortlessly produces enviable results with his masterpiece tome, *Harvard Can't Teach What You Learn from the Streets*. In this riveting book, you learn many little-known, step-by-step life and business strategies to accomplish getting to the top. It's better than any how to do it book - Liebman's life and career is about utilizing the most effective and uber-practical strategies to excelling not only in real estate, but in any foray you embark on. This page turner will help catapult you into the elite stratosphere of high achievers. A book that will become an instant top bestseller!"

—**Ian Halperin,** *NYT* Bestselling author
and award winning filmmaker

"Harvard Can't Teach What You Learn from the Streets follows my per-sonal mantra of **quality over quantity**. The books content is so strong that it's one-stop shopping for anyone who wants to learn the real estate business. Funny, witty and extremely informative. *It's* a first round draft pick."

—**Mike Tannenbaum**, ESPN NFL Front Office Insider,
Executive VP of football operations
for the Miami Dolphins (former) and General
Manager for the New York Jets (former)

"Harvard Can't Teach What You Learn from the Streets provides the perfect game plan for success in the real estate business."

—**Neil O'Donnell**, Pro-Bowl
NFL Quarterback (former)

"This book is essential reading for anyone entering or already in the real estate industry. A great playbook for real estate and business in general."

—**Marvin Washington**, Medical Cannabis entrepreneur
and NFL Superbowl Campion (former)

"Sam Liebman is an incredibly knowledgeable businessperson who has had great success in his career. To have the opportunity to learn many of the things Sam has learned over the years is something everyone who wants to be successful in real estate will value. What makes this business book unique is the fact that in addition to being informative, Sam was able to make it an enjoyable read. *Harvard Can't Teach What You Learn From The Streets* is a book everyone must have for their business library."

—**Ken Cage**, CEO of IRG Group the world's premiere
Airplane Repossession company and Star of the
Discovery Channel's hit TV show, Airplane Repo

"Sam's book is a candid and effective blueprint for running a successful real estate business. From the title forward, his straightforward, real-world approach makes this a compelling and invaluable must read for any real estate professional. Sam's knowledge extends beyond just real estate and his approach to business is something that any entrepreneur can learn from. This book should be on every business person's list to read."

—**Thomas M. Sparico**, Entrepreneur & Venture Capitalist, Managing Partner of Brand New Matter, Named Inventor on 100+ Patents, Founding Team of Priceline.com

"Sam Liebman has written a delicious as well as digestible guide to real estate where he shares his deep insights…similar to a famed chef featuring the nuances of their epicurean talents via a cookbook—A MUST READ for the seasoned real estate professional as well as anyone desiring to learn what a CAP rate is. My cap or is it chef's hat off to Sam!"

—**Donna Drake**, The Donna Drake Show: Live it Up! Award-winning creative artist, writer, producer, actor and influencer

"Sam Liebman has had an incredibly successful career in the real estate space. His book, *Harvard Can't Teach What You Learn From the Streets* offers incredible insight to the essentials for business success. His techniques are proven and he has the results to back it up. His principals and concepts are targeted toward real estate but can be utilized in a multitude of different businesses as well. After you finish this book you will have additional insights that are essential in the business world."

—**Bill Porricelli**, Music & Entertainment Industry Executive, SVP for Paul McCartney's MPL Communications Inc. (former)

"*Harvard Can't Teach What You Learn From The Streets* brings to attention and answers many questions that should be asked and answered before making any real estate or business decisions. Sam clarifies the fundamentals of real estate effortlessly; I earned another degree after this great read!"

—**Mark MK,** Singer/Performer, Media Maven, collaborator and performer with John Legend, Flo Rida, Snoop Dogg, and Sean Paul

HARVARD
CAN'T TEACH
WHAT YOU LEARN
FROM THE STREETS

**The Street Success Guide to
Building Wealth through
Multi-Family Real Estate**

SAM LIEBMAN

MADE FOR
SUCCESS

Made for Success Publishing
P.O. Box 1775 Issaquah, WA 98027
www.MadeForSuccessPublishing.com

Distributed by Made for Success Publishing

First Printing

Library of Congress Cataloging-in-Publication data
Liebman, Sam
    HARVARD CAN'T TEACH WHAT YOU LEARN FROM THE STREETS: The Street Success Guide to Building Wealth Through Multi-Family Real Estate

            p. cm.

LCCN: 2021949108
ISBN: 978-1-64146-652-3 (*paperback*)
ISBN: 978-1-64146-653-0 (*ebook*)
ISBN: 978-1-64146-654-7 (*audiobook*)

Printed in the United States of America

For further information contact Made for Success Publishing
+14255266480 or email service@madeforsuccess.net

ACKNOWLEDGEMENTS

THERE'S NO WAY in a million years I would have reached my full potential without the love, support, and devotion of Korey, my beautiful wife of 30 years. Korey, you are the engine that keeps our family going. (I just buy the gas LOL).

To my children Chelsey and Michael: you are my world. I love you guys and mom more than anything in it. To my sister Susan, I love you and am so glad you're in my life. To my cousin Jerry and his wife Nancy, I love you guys, and I'm so glad we reconnected. To my father-in-law and mother-in-law, Howard and Jeanette Arkin. How many son-in-law's can truly say they love their in-laws? I can. To my brother and sister in-law, Larry and Andrea Glick and Camryn and Austin, my niece and nephew; love you guys.

To Neil Tepper, my surrogate brother, partner, and best friend since college. You covered all my weaknesses as we both chose to travel the same road to success together. We were the perfect complement to each other. I value our love and friendship tremendously.

To Annette Sciarrone, Neil and I sincerely appreciate your hard work and dedication year after year as a member of our team. We hit the "employee lotto" when we hired you over 35 years ago.

A special thanks to my actress friend Bonnie Loren. Without your constant support and non-stop urging to fulfill my various creative endeavors I would never have written this book. I will always remember you constantly saying, "Sam, you're very talented. You just don't know it."

To my Alma Mata, Brooklyn College and the best teacher I've ever had, Professor Robert Minors. Thank you for changing my educational life.

Special thanks to L. Robert Lieb, founder of Mountain Development Corp. You took me under your wing and exposed me to a business world I would have never been privy to without you.

Another special thanks to the late James Kinsey of the Kinsey Corp. Jim was first a client, then a friend, and then a partner. Together, we purchased over 20 properties in Manhattan that we subsequently renovated and improved, resulting in over tripling their value.

To Daniel Perla, my friend and partner. Together we built The Crossing 23rd Condominium, a ground up 21-story luxury high-rise's with a $100 million sellout. I will always remember the day when we structured the deal on a napkin at the local diner.

To Elizabeth Hamilton and Brad Szollose, who were instrumental in getting me my book deal with Made for Success Publishing. My sincere thanks.

To my publisher, Made for Success, without your tireless organization, time and support this book would not be what it currently is. A special thanks to Scott Wilson, Katie Rios and DeeDee Heathman who worked closely with me in perfecting my manuscript.

To my close friends Howard and Robyn Jaslow, Glen and Suzanne Paragament. Kenny and Jenna Margolis, Cary and Lisa Kaplan, Curtis Sliwa, Robert Wolfson, Alan Brachfeld, Randy Gordon, Donna Drake, Lou Vaccarelli, Tim Sabean, and Richard (Big Daddy) Salgado, Love you guys.

There are countless others who have helped me realize my success and potential, that I could never thank all of you. To all the people I was unable to mention, I also give my most sincere and heartfelt thanks.

(Read this Song with a Light Rap Flavor)

The School of Hard Knocks
That's where I earned my degree
Yeah, I majored in life
And got my Ph.D.
So bring on the white collar robots
We'll prove that we can compete
Cause, Harvard can't teach
What you learn from the streets

Yeah, the white-collared robots
The cultural elite
You all look the same and sound
Just like a parakeet
As a well-rounded person
Your grade's an incomplete
Cause, Harvard can't teach
What you learn from the streets

The pavement was my classroom
That where my class would meet
Hey, knowledge lasts forever
When it's written In Concrete
So come on Mr. Robot
Let us prove we can compete
Cause, Harvard can't teach
What you learn from the streets!

by Sam Liebman

CONTENTS

PREFACE

BECOME A REAL ESTATE PROFESSIONAL

WHILE SOME COLLEGES and graduate programs may offer a few courses, none will give you the full circle of knowledge and exposure essential to becoming successful in this industry. Nor will you receive an education from the *School of Hard Knocks*, which is crucial for achieving the status of a real estate professional.

Real estate is quickly changing from a trade to a profession. Larger brokerage and managing companies are gobbling up smaller firms as the industry continues to become more corporate and specialized. I believe this trend will continue, eventually leading the smaller firms into extinction. Large real estate firms are now attracting talented graduates from Ivy League and other top schools who want careers in real estate. Imagine the advantage an individual would have if they could obtain a four-year real estate degree from a prestigious university when applying for employment at one of these larger national firms!

I wrote this book primarily as an answer to the limited opportunities available in the current marketplace to obtain a professional real estate education. This book is written with my personal philosophy and teaching style I've developed over the years. The concepts presented in this book are based upon my many years of both traditional and non-traditional education and experiences. I tried to make it both comprehensive and entertaining to keep the reader continuously motivated.

FOREWORD

IT'S 1962 OR '63, on a beautiful spring afternoon in my hometown of Canarsie, Brooklyn. A bunch of kids are on Remsen Avenue flipping baseball cards. I was the king of flipping and would completely wipe out all the kids. I was collecting my wins when, all of a sudden, a little shrimp around 6 years old challenges me. I politely laugh and turn him down, but the shrimp wouldn't take no for an answer. Then, he starts to mock me.

"What's the matter, you scared?"

He wouldn't stop, so I finally said, "OK, kid."

Well, in less than 10 minutes, the shrimp's small stack of cards is gone.

This shrimp starts punching and trying to kick me, and I'm dodging and making moves to make him miss. I don't want to hurt him. After all, I'm around eight and twice his size. But self-defense *did* enter my mind. His fury continues for a longer period than I would have guessed. The little shrimp is exhausted and retreats to the comfort of the stoop, where he puts his face in his hands and starts crying. I walk over and say, "Hey, kid, here are your baseball cards."

That kid is Sam Liebman, and that day began a friendship that has continued for almost 60 years.

Growing up in Canarsie exposed you to the good, the bad, and the ugly. From Brownsville, the Jews came, many of whom were store owners and businessmen. Their families stressed that education was the way to succeed, but for some of the young men, the lure of the street action was too strong. The Italians were blue-collar and hardened in their ways. Sam was short and had a mouth, but always wanted to be accepted and compete with the big boys. No matter how many times he was rejected or picked on, he came back for a better day. Playing street games was his release—*and* how he won acceptance from his much bigger, older peers.

Setbacks caused him to keep trying harder each and every time an opportunity presented itself. He could have gone in the wrong direction, but his strong self-esteem saved him from an early demise.

Sam channeled his "I'm as good as you" attitude and boundless energy to use his street-smart learning to become a success in the cutthroat real estate business. There were guys along the way who would have tried to use his intelligence and skills to help them in their street hustles. Sam put his hand in the fire, but he didn't get burnt. He didn't crawl into the belly of the beast where many of those we grew up with traveled. As we look back, those friends and associates of our younger days are dead and buried or broken and doing prison time. Sam realized at some point that life did not end in Canarsie. The things we learned the hard way would also push us to achieve, never forget our roots, and give back. We learned to fight for what we knew was right. Never surrender, or retreat in the face of fear.

These are the lessons we learned in the streets, playgrounds, schoolyards, and candy stores of Canarsie. It's what made us who we are today.

—Curtis Sliwa

Curtis Sliwa is known by millions as a radio talk show host, media personality, and the founder and leader of The Guardian Angels anti-crime organization with chapters in 14 countries and over 140 cities throughout the world.

INTRODUCTION

WHEN YOU COMBINE and master the knowledge learned from the streets with a traditional education and extensive work experience, the product is *me*. I have walked the walk and earned the right to talk the talk. I have the track record and credentials to be an asset to you.

The lessons of the street are contained in a specialized curriculum of their own. Only a few insiders with many years of exposure and experience learn under this school's tutelage. The graduate's education has been learned through many painful and expensive real-life experiences in the trenches. You have to be beaten up and fall down a few times to learn what really goes on.

Sometimes I think that I have dealt with every conceivable form of life or lowlife in business. However, each day I discover a new species.

I am a product of the streets of Canarsie, Brooklyn. I attended Canarsie High School, where I learned nothing—which was completely my fault. While in class, I would watch the clock, anxiously waiting for 3:00 to arrive so I could leave and play ball. I didn't drop out in the 10th grade or do drugs, but the odds of my becoming a success were the same as winning the lotto without buying a ticket. Though I was smart, I was a terrible student because I had so many personal problems with my dysfunctional family that I couldn't focus on or absorb what my teachers said. I was also extremely obnoxious and disruptive in class.

My 10th grade math teacher got so angry with me once that he announced to the class, "Everyone, look at Sam Liebman. He'll be driving a truck for the rest of his life." I deserved it, but the irony is that he quit teaching soon after I graduated and bought a Tropicana delivery route. I hope I didn't influence his decision. Somehow, I got into Brooklyn College. I switched my major at least four times before finally settling on accounting.

In College, I Majored in Minors

During my sophomore year in college, I experienced my first epiphany in my ability to retain and process knowledge thanks to the unique teaching style of Professor Robert Minors, my first accounting teacher. I give him part of the credit for changing my academic life.

My first accounting class with Professor Minors was rather memorable. The class was held in a lecture hall with approximately 25 students in the class. On the first day of class Professor Minors stormed in, holding a large piece of cardboard in one hand and a briefcase in the other. He grabbed the microphone and pointed to the large letters on the cardboard sign.

FLUNK NOW, AVOID THE RUSH!

He began to rant. "This is a hard class, people! Anybody got a girlfriend? Raise your hand." He grinned. "Get rid of her; you'll have no time to see her. You're gonna study, study, study! It's my way or the highway. You better be razor-sharp, or it's goodnight, Marie."

With a sneer, he added, "I don't care if you report me. I have tenure."

The man had my full and undivided attention as well as, all, and I mean *all,* the other students in the classroom. Minors didn't just introduce me to accounting that day. He introduced me to a style of teaching and learning which is still embedded in my soul.

Then he got serious. "OK, scholars, write this down."

He then began dictating concepts to us, giving simple examples to help us understand more easily. I walked out of each class with five to ten pages of notes, which ended up replacing the textbook for the course.

Minor's accounting classroom was akin to watching a standup comedy show. His unique teaching style used sarcasm and playful humor, and I couldn't wait for class to start to see what this man would say next.

We knew it was a show. Although the professor did keep his distance from us, I felt like I had a friend watching over me. Someone who actually cared that I learned. No wonder the good old professor was voted Teacher of the Year by CCNY. Professor Minors was my teacher for Accounting 2, Accounting 3, Intermediate Accounting, Business Law, Taxation, and a CPA Review course.

CHAPTER 1

WELCOME TO THE NEW MILLENNIUM, WHERE INSTANT GRATIFICATION TAKES TOO LONG

DO YOU KNOW what the best job in the world is? No, it's not playing center field for the New York Yankees. The best job in the world is managing your own big, fat bank account. Great hours, no pressure, and you can't get fired. How can you get such a job, you ask? The answer is to learn how to build wealth and by receiving a steady stream of what is called passive, residual, or unearned income. As the comedian Chris Rock once said, "Shaq is rich. The man who signs his check is wealthy."

Earned income is typically generated from your job or business. You have to work very hard to receive earned income. Unearned income, also known as passive or residual income, is the opposite. You will continue to receive unearned income, even if you don't work anymore. I generally refer to this type of income as "screw you" money. "Screw you" money is usually generated from owning a large asset base. By owning income-producing real estate, you can build a large asset base that will generate this type of income for your entire lifetime, as well as your children's lifetime. Many of our investors have received back their original investment and continue to receive cash distributions on a monthly basis.

It's been said that more money is made in real estate than in any other industry. Real estate is a great business to be in. It's prestigious, rewarding, and recession-proof. You can make money in both good or bad times. I wish I had a dollar for each time I heard a business owner complain about the rent they were paying. It's usually followed by the comment, "I should have bought the building."

How to *Not* Become Successful

As previously mentioned, there are few, if any, higher education institutions that offer a formal real estate education. What *is* available, however, is a marketplace polluted with worthless motivation preacher-teachers whose focus is on peddling their misleading books, tapes, and seminars.

Does the following sound familiar?

Our course is so *easy* that you can read it *quickly* and *immediately* make money and see *instant* results. *Simply* follow my *step-by-step*, *time-tested*, *proven* methods, programs, and strategies, spending *only a few minutes a day*, and you'll be on your way to becoming a *millionaire* and achieving *financial independence*. No more 9 to 5! Spend more time with your family and live the American dream!

Bullshit!

I mean if you want to talk ridiculous, let's talk ridiculous. What about "Brain surgery made easy! Learn in your spare time!" Can you imagine a college professor telling his students that his course was so easy that anybody can learn the material in two weeks?

What's happened to us? We've become incredibly impatient. Try turning on a three-year-old computer. Remember how fast it was when you first bought it? Now you'll be mumbling to yourself, "Damn it's slow," or "Come on already!" while you wait impatiently for it to finish processing. Imagine how slow a 10-year-old computer would seem if you used it today!

Nowadays, we want success right away with the least effort possible.

Et tu, Harvard?

I recently read a book written by a team of experts about how to become financially independent. These experts included attorneys, CPAs, and graduates from the Harvard Business School, as well as other professionals with decades of financial experience. As I was skimming through the pages, I could not believe what I was reading.

"Cut out the soda at lunch and save about $300 per year, besides water is free."

"Brew your own coffee and save another $300 per year."

"Cancel your magazine subscriptions. Your library card is free."

As I was reading this crap, I was laughing so hard that I probably missed the part that advised the reader to use both sides of the toilet paper to save another $300 per year. What about getting rid of your air-conditioning unit or turning off the pilot lights on the stove to save electricity? If these so-called experts really wanted to give us some good advice, they should have warned the reader not to waste their money buying their silly book (save another $35).

Let's assume you listened to the tapes and read the fancy manuals. Now you're dreaming about the millions you're going to make. Do you really have the audacity to believe that because you finished a two-week indoctrination course that you're ready to go and grab the fortune you believe is yours? Isn't that what they promised you? Sorry, but it doesn't work that way.

If you buy into this ridiculous philosophy, you're displaying a total disrespect for the process of learning real and worthwhile knowledge. Worst of all, you're fooling yourself. Sophisticated and advanced concepts and knowledge take *years* to master: no pain no gain!

Is your goal in life to become an average Joe? Do you want to get into a business that does not separate you from the rest of the pack? Not me! I want skills that are unattainable by the average Joe. Do you really want to conduct business armed with just buzzwords and other phrases and jargon used in the industry?

Learn Street Knowledge

Street knowledge is the kind the successful pros use. The so-called tricks of the trade. Street knowledge is more than common sense, and it can only be learned from personal experience. Develop your street smarts by learning to think outside the box. Be a sponge and absorb knowledge from as many sources as you can. Street knowledge is about what really goes on in the real world, and is just as important as textbook knowledge. You need both to succeed. When I watch the people going to work for corporate America, I see a group of white-collar robots who all look, think, and act the same.

The lessons of the street are a specialized curriculum of their own. Only a few insiders with many years of exposure and experience learn under this school's tutelage. The graduate's education has been learned through many painful and expensive real-life experiences. In order to become successful, you have to be beaten up and spend time in the trenches. This is how you learn what really goes on.

Here is an example of what I refer to as street knowledge:

Have you ever watched a trial on TV? I love the part when one of the lawyers goes on a tirade against the person testifying. Then the other lawyer stands up and yells, "I object!"

The judge yells, "Sustained!" then instructs the jury to "Please disregard those comments." Does the jury forget about the comments they heard? No chance! The damage is done.

Learn to Be a Student of the Game

Often in professional sports, a coach is credited with preparing their team for any situation that may occur. These are the teams that are always successful; the ones that win the championships and are fundamentally sound. Meanwhile, you'll hear the losing team say, "They knew exactly what we were going to do before we did it," or "Nothing worked," or "They were totally prepared for everything we tried." Learn to be a student of the game. Master the core fundamentals systematically, one step at a time.

When you are working for someone else, *you are learning at their expense, not yours*. The employer is paying for your downtime, your continuing education, and most importantly, any mistakes you make. You may get fired, but the employer stands to lose a lot more. They could lose a large account or business contact, have to give concessions to the client for your errors, or have to defend against a lawsuit. When you're in your own business, *you are learning at your own expense,* or if you have investors, at their expense as well. If anything goes wrong, it's you and the investors who have to foot the bill.

The World's Largest Book: The Book of Excuses

Assuming you're normal (if such a thing exists), you will have experienced the fear of change or the unknown. Everybody is afraid. It's human nature.

Will not having answers to the following fears (or are they excuses) motivate you or completely discourage you?

"I wouldn't know what to do if…"

Nobody rents the units, something breaks, the building catches on fire, the tenants don't pay their rent, someone dies in an apartment, a bank won't give me a mortgage, my expenses go up and rents don't.

"I don't want…"

The headaches, tenants calling me at home or at work, to get sued, to lose my money.

"What if…"

Real estate taxes go up, the real estate market goes down, I can't sell the property, interest rates go up?

All of the above concerns can be reclassified into one large category: fear of the unknown. Successful real estate professionals know exactly what to do in all of these instances, without even breaking a sweat. ***This is where you need to be!***

Motivation

In order to be successful in any business, you have to be motivated. Period… end of sentence. It's a given. Motivation is one of the most important building blocks in a healthy learning environment.

However, motivation comes to a complete halt once an element of fear enters the picture. Even the smallest subliminal fear can cause damage to your learning process. If the fear isn't readily apparent, then you must make it surface and address it head-on. You must learn to self-correct: as you experience fear, look it straight in the eye, confront it, and analyze it. Ask yourself questions such as "Why am I feeling this way? What is the cause of this fear?" Once you recognize and identify a problem, you can take steps to reduce or eliminate it. To this day, whenever I experience an element of anger or fear, I self-correct by telling myself not to overreact, which, nine out of ten times, works to reduce any stress or fear I may experience.

Suppose you were learning how to obtain financing to purchase a property, but you were recently turned down for a credit card or auto loan. Fear would begin to enter your mind. You might be asking yourself, "How can I get a loan for a building, when I can't even get an auto loan?" How motivated do you feel now? I bet not very motivated at all.

Congratulations! You gave fear the ability to sabotage your chance for a successful career in real estate.

If you had a fear of banks based upon your prior experiences, wouldn't this preoccupation get in the way while you were trying to learn? You might remember feelings of rejection and embarrassment. You might not be able to absorb what I'm teaching you. To reduce and eliminate these feelings, you must go back to the root of the problem and self-correct it. This is accomplished by slowly building up your confidence and self-esteem by exposing yourself to positive, rather than negative, experiences. Motivation is greatly increased when little or no fear exists and when you build on positive experiences.

The more you change your negative perceptions, the more you will eliminate the stumbling blocks you need to become successful. Retaining knowledge can't be achieved if your mind is cluttered with fear. The more exposure you get, the less fear, and the more your mind will let you learn. If you are fortunate enough to get exposure, it can change your position in life at a much faster rate than another person who doesn't. Providing exposure to real-world situations is one of the main goals of this book.

FEAR! The Number 1 Stumbling Block for Success

If I offered to give you a million dollars to find a great real estate deal for me and promised I'd make you a partner, Would you be motivated to do it? Now, what if instead of giving, I changed the offer and said that I'd *lend* you a million dollars? However, I also added that you must personally guarantee the loan and put up your house as collateral. Could you do it? Would you be motivated to do it? The question is a lot harder to answer.

Notice the difference here. In the first offer, you weren't on the hook for anything. In the industry, this is known as not having any skin in the game. It wasn't your money. Once you put yourself on the line and have skin in the game, you are more prone to risk and fear.

Managing or Eliminating Fear

One way to reduce, manage, or eliminate fear is to be totally prepared for any situation that may occur. In other words, you need to know your stuff! That's where the infomercials and motivational preacher-teachers fail miserably. They expect you to go right to the major leagues without first going through the minors. Their curriculum never thoroughly prepares you with the knowledge, experience, and confidence necessary to actually make the call to the broker, find the listing, or negotiate the contract. All you've done is read or listened to how it is done in the optimum situation; you still haven't done it yourself.

Let's say you want to learn how to drive a car. You can read all the self-help books, listen to 10,000 hours of tapes, and attend thousands of courses on driving. However, if you want to learn how to drive a car, there is only one way: Get behind the wheel of a car with an instructor sitting by your side, providing hands-on guidance. Very few people would have the courage (or stupidity) to start driving after reading a book or listening to tapes on how to drive a car. If you ever find a product on the market advertising "The 24-Hour Driver" or "The Immediate Driver," veer left and drive away because this type of product will no doubt be a *crash course*. The reason books, tapes, and lectures won't help you learn how to drive is because they can't teach you how to overcome the inherent fear of actually getting behind the wheel and starting to drive.

When astronauts train for a trip into space, they focus on many simulated exercises that attempt to duplicate the real-life situations that may occur. Some of the training exercises involve a great deal of risk. However, the training is intended to give the astronauts real-life knowledge and test the skills necessary to succeed.

It's the same with learning real estate. Imagine if you had a similar learning experience.

Fear Is in the Eye of the Beholder

One day, while I was relaxing at our country club pool, I observed a group of very young children as they were about to enter the water. My observation revealed to me the three different types of approaches.

The first type is the kid who dips his foot in the pool and immediately runs away.

The second type is the kid who dips his foot in the pool, waits a minute, then dips the other foot in, and a few minutes later, is fully in the pool.

The third type is the kid who doesn't bother to dip his foot in the pool but rather jumps in headfirst with no hesitation.

I believe these kids are all wired differently. However, we all know that with the right instruction, eventually, they should all be able to swim.

I know many businesspeople who are on the verge of bankruptcy, have IRS liens, and have so many creditors calling the office for money that you can't get a free phone line. Yet they haven't lost one second of sleep. They go about their day like everything is fine. On the other hand, I know other businesspeople who are so afraid of the IRS that a simple letter regarding a small late charge would cause a loss of a night's sleep.

These aren't isolated incidents, either; I would say I have encountered an equal number of both.

What this Book Offers

My hope is that through the eyes, ears, and experiences of someone like me, this book will provide you with the first steps in building a strong foundation in the real estate fundamentals that you can continue to build upon. You will learn how to use street smarts in the most favorable way to get where you want to go, preferably by the shortest route possible.

I want you to become an opportunist equipped with the skills that will allow you to think of alternative solutions in tough situations. I try to apply street-smart techniques that deal with everyday life, not with unattainable situations or principles and techniques that involve large corporations, celebrities, or other entities that don't apply to the average person. You are going to receive the best practical experience you can possibly get from reading a book.

The first parts of the following pages will focus on teaching you some very important fundamentals that you must master. I will focus on simulating real-life situations as much as possible to provide you with as much exposure to what goes on in the real world.

Forget about all the bits of advice you've heard about real estate before. This book will teach you all the concepts, techniques, and tricks of the trade you'll need to build a strong foundation. Forget about cash flow, depreciation, mortgages, down payments, property management, tenant problems, and how rich you will be. Instead, use the knowledge I'm sharing with you to start building up your knowledge of the fundamentals of real estate properties so that by the time you're done reading your knowledge of real estate will increase *exponentially!*

Let's get started!

Street Success Concepts to Remember

1. By owning income-producing real estate, you can build a large asset base which will generate unearned income—what I call "screw you" money—for your entire lifetime, as well as your children's lifetime.

2. A building with a weak foundation will eventually crumble. The same can be said about learning the real estate business. Without mastering the fundamental concepts of this business, your chances for success will be seriously compromised. The foundation of knowledge upon which you will build will become weak, and just like a building, eventually crumble.

3. Learn to think out of the box and obtain street knowledge—the real knowledge the pros use. Street knowledge is what goes on in the real world. Be a sponge and learn from as many sources as you can. Remember, you need to combine street knowledge with a traditional education to become successful.

4. One way to reduce, manage, or eliminate fear is to become totally prepared for any situation that may occur. In other words, you need to know your stuff!

5. Motivation comes to a complete halt once an element of fear enters the picture. Even the smallest subliminal fear can cause damage to your learning process. If the fear isn't readily apparent, then you must make it surface and address it head on. You must learn to self-correct: as you experience fear, look it straight in the eye, confront it, and analyze it.

CHAPTER 2

UNDERSTANDING THE BASIC ARITHMETIC & ANALYTICAL CONCEPTS NEEDED FOR SUCCESS IN THE REAL ESTATE BUSINESS

LET ME INTRODUCE you to some fundamental arithmetic computations and concepts. You must master these to fully understand *how* and *why* a property substantially increases in value. These rather simple tools I am sharing will enable you to have a basic foundation to analyze a deal, but more importantly, they will put you on the right track to becoming successful.

Please make sure that you fully understand these concepts and computations before you read any further chapters.

To simulate real-life situations, I am going to use one of my properties to study: The Ambassador Court Apartments located in East Dallas, Texas. The Ambassador is a garden-style apartment complex consisting of two separate buildings containing a total of 35 units.

Understanding the Rent Roll

⇨ *Increasing the rental income of a property is an area where you have control over your own destiny.*

There are many ways at your disposal to increase a property's rental income, but first you must understand the components that make up the ***rent roll*** of a property. Generally, a rent roll is a listing showing all the unit numbers, types of unit, unit sizes, names of the tenants occupying the units, lease move-in dates, start and termination dates, base monthly rent, and other charges.*

There are a number of factors that affect the rent roll, and sometimes you'll even see two identical units renting for different amounts. One might be more upgraded than another; one might have a long-term tenant who pays lower rent in exchange for repeated leases; one might have a better view/access to parking/etc.

When it comes to upgrading units, there are many ways you can go about this, all of which will yield their own revenue streams. We'll get to that later in this chapter.

⇨ *The real potential for increased property value often lies in the growth _potential_ of the existing rent roll.*

If current rents are ***at or above*** those of nearby comparable properties, then this property will have limitations for increased rent growth and property value. More on this concept later.

⇨ *A property whose rent roll is at or above market rents is known in the industry as being "maxed out," meaning little or no room for growth.*

⇨ *Increases in Base Rent Versus Increases in Operating Expenses*

---

*See Appendix 1: Example of the actual monthly rent roll for Ambassador as of January 1, 2018.

Let's compare increases in base rents versus an increase in operating expenses. The results may surprise you.

⇨ *The base rent of a property is generally defined as the amount of rent a tenant will pay before adding any additional charges for such items as electric, water and sewer, trash, etc.*

Let's assume that the Ambassador's gross base rent at the end of Year 1 is $301,440 and the property's operating expenses are $150,000. Further assume that both base rents and operating expenses will increase by 3% per annum, starting in Year 2. At the end of a five-year period, the cumulative annual base rent has increased by $48,012, while the cumulative annual operating expenses have increased by $23,891.

The net effect is an increase in annual net operating income (NOI) cash flow of **$24,121** ($48,012 - $23,891). This might not seem like a large amount of money to you yet. However, as you will soon learn, if you owned this property in today's market, your gross equity, assuming a 5.5% cap rate, would have increased by approximately **$438,564**. We will discuss the cap rate concept later in the chapter.*

Keep in mind that all we did was hold on to the property for five years and increase the base rents and operating expenses by only 3% per annum. We didn't take into consideration many other opportunities available to increase the rental income and the net cash flow generated from the property during the five-year period.

Are you shocked? Trust me - it's true! And it gets <u>much better,</u> as you will soon see!

---

*See Appendix 2: Example of Increase in NOI in 5 years.

The Effect of Capitalizing and Compounding the Rent Roll

⇨ *Assuming a rising rental market, each time a tenant's rent is increased; the amount of the increase becomes <u>capitalized,</u> meaning it's added to the base amount of the prior rent. The new capitalized amount becomes the new base rent that future increases are based upon. This results in a future compounding of the rents, leading to much higher amounts in the future.*

Capitalization causes a compounding effect on the annual base rent increases each year during the five-year period. This is an extremely important fundamental concept for you to understand. As you will soon see, when you apply cap rate power to the resulting NOI, the results become staggering.*

When you apply a 3% increase in the second year, your income jumps more than it did the first year because that 3% is counting the increase from the first year. Then in year 3, you get an even bigger bump! Your income goes up as a matter of routine, not because of any special circumstances. This might seem like magic or something not quite legal, but it's absolutely above the board and there are no wands or rabbits in hats involved.

Permanent Versus Temporary Increases

Whenever a tenant rent is increased, the increase is often considered to be a ***permanent increase***. Except for downturns in the rental market, chances are rents will continue to increase rather than decrease. This is especially true with low-paying tenants who are subject to various rent controls.

However, some increases or decreases in operating expenses are most likely to be ***temporary*** in nature. In all likelihood, these expenses will return to normal or stabilize in relatively short periods of time. Temporary

---

*See Appendix 3: Example of the economic effects of how capitalization causes a compounding effect on the annual base rent increases each year during the five-year period.

increases are usually caused by volatility in the market due to a wide range of factors. For example, utilities, insurance expenses, etc.

Insurance premiums for our properties located in Dallas, Texas, have increased by approximately 35% for 2020. This is due to the many hailstorms that occurred and the huge number of insurance claims made by owners to recover damages. Even though the increase was large, it still represents a temporary increase, since a reduction in future claims should cause the market to stabilize with decreased premiums.

⇨ *An increase in base rent is generally considered to be a <u>permanent</u> increase. However, some increases or decreases in operating expenses are most likely to be temporary in nature. In all likelihood, these expenses will return to normal or stabilize in relatively short periods of time.*

⇨ *The price you pay for a property is a permanent cost. You can't change the price once you close. On the other hand, a high interest rate on the mortgage obtained at the time of purchase is a temporary cost because the interest rate normally changes over time. As a result, it is generally more advantageous to acquire property in an environment featuring high interest rates and high cap rates because you should have the opportunity to refinance and obtain a lower interest rate in the future.*

Understanding Net Operating Income (NOI)

A very simple, but extremely powerful concept which represents one of the most common methods used in the industry to value a property is called the **net operating income** of a property, also known as the ***NOI.***

For now, we will define the NOI of a property as base rental income **minus** total operating expenses, ***excluding debt service, depreciation, capital reserves, etc.*** (in larger properties of more than 50 units, a provision for capital reserves should be included in operating expenses).

Understanding Cap Rates

Now we're going to focus on another simple but ***extremely powerful*** concept. It's known as the capitalization rate, more commonly referred to as the cap rate, a simple method and one of the most common methods in the industry for estimating the value of a property.

Keep in mind that estimating property value by this method is simply a rule of thumb, nothing more. As you will later learn, there are other methods to estimate property value, but this method will help you understand the fundamental concepts of increasing property value more easily.

⇨ *Understanding cap rates and their effect on property value is ground zero for success in the real estate business.*

Whenever a prospective property is first presented to me, my automatic response is, ***"What cap rate are they asking for the property?"***

Broker: Sam, are you interested in a 20-unit, 5-story residential building located at Avenue B and 8th Street? The seller is asking $1,100,000.

Sam: What is the cap rate the property is selling for?

Notice, I did not ask about the property's physical condition, the neighborhood, the size of the units, or the income and operating expenses yet. *I wanted to know what cap rate they were asking for the property.* It's my litmus test to gauge my initial interest in the property.

At my level of experience, all I need to know is the cap rate the property is selling for (and a few other details), and I can quickly do a simple "back of the envelope" calculation to determine my level of interest. ***This is where you need to be***!

The cap rate can be depicted as a very simple but powerful formula, especially when combined with other concepts.

> ## Cap Rate = Net Operating Income ("NOI")/Selling Price

Or inversely:

> ## Property Value = Net Operating Income ("NOI")/Cap Rate

⇨ *The higher the cap rate, the lower the value of the property. The lower the cap rate, the higher the value of the property.*

Assume the NOI is $150,000.

Keep in mind that the cap rate and the property value work in inverse proportion. If you're not a mathematician (and I'm not), that means that as the cap rate drops, your property value increases.

A **decrease** in the cap rate from 8% to 6% will result in an **increase** in property value of $625,000 ($2,500,000 - $1,875,000). This is what is happening in the current insane real estate market where cap rates are extremely low, known as **cap rate suppression**. Anybody who currently owns real estate has seen the value of their property skyrocket if they acquired the property during a high cap rate environment and are now in an environment where there is cap rate suppression.*

Conversely, an **increase** in the cap rate from 6% to 8%, assuming the same $150,000 NOI, will result in a **decrease** in property value of $625,000. This is what happened during the last downturn in the real estate market.

---

*See Appendix 4: Example of property value increases or decreases as cap rates increase or decrease. Assuming NOI of 150,000.

⇨ *If you can find a way to increase the NOI of the property, you can increase the value of the property significantly.*

A 3% increase in the rent roll should always generate larger numbers than a 3% increase in operating expenses because the rent roll consists of a larger base for increases than operating expenses. Based on this, the net operating income (NOI) of the property should increase over a period of time just by holding on to the property.

⇨ *By its nature, a property's base rent consists of a larger dollar base than the property's operating expenses. Therefore, a 3% increase in in the rents should always be greater than a 3% increase in operating expenses.*

Assuming a cap rate of 6%, an increase in the NOI of $24,120 over a five-year period ($175,560 - $151,440) a fairly small amount, leads to an increase in the value of the property of ***$402,008*** over the 5-year period ($2,926,008 - $2,524,000)! ***This is no typo!****

All we did in this example was to increase rents and operating expenses by only 3% per annum. Remember that we didn't take into consideration any other opportunities available to increase the rental income and the net cash flow generated from the property, which we discuss later in the chapter.

The capitalization and compounding effects of an increasing rent roll combined with a low cap rate environment are the fundamentals of becoming rich through real estate investment.

Understanding the Difference Between Gross and Rentable SF

There are two components of a property's size: gross and rentable square footage.

---

*See Appendix 5: Cumulative Increase in Property Value in 5 Years.

Assume a property consists of an acre of land (43,560 SF), of which 67% (29,185 SF) is used for parking and the other 33% (14,375 SF) is used for the building. Further assume that the building consists of two stories or a total of 28,750 Gross SF (14,375 x 2 floors).

The building's size of 28,750 is known as the **gross square footage** of the building. However, the buildings have walls, stairwells, elevators, basements, etc. that are not actual living space. These areas are known as common areas and should be deducted from the gross square footage in order to compute the **rentable square footage** of the building. The rentable square footage is the number of SF that base rent can be charged. The difference is known as the **loss factor**. Each building has its own unique loss factor, depending upon its unit mix, amenities, and type of construction. Commercial and residential buildings have different methods of determining the rentable square footage base for which rent is charged.

It's important to note that rent is generally charged on the building's rentable square footage (RSF).

Many landlords, including myself, ignore the loss factor and charge tenants for all or a portion of the common areas. Tenants make use of the common areas, and therefore should pay rent on these areas. I have needed to explain the reasoning to tenants who actually measured the square footage in their units and found it contained less square footage than they were being charged for.

Side Note: Assume a property charges base rent on the actual size of the units. If you can add a loss factor to the base rent it will present a good opportunity for increased rent and property value. Tenants need to under-stand that they also use the common areas.

The Effect of Upgrading Units and Increasing the Rent Roll

Many real estate brokers use the term "value-add" while marketing a property for sale. This industry term means that if you upgrade a unit, there is a readily available market to achieve a higher rent. These are the types of properties I try to acquire. My goal is to invest additional capital into the property to increase cash flow, NOI, and property value.

Let's look back at Ambassador's rent roll from the Appendix 1 example. The total rentable SF of the property is 21,131, and there are 35 units. This means that the average unit size is approximately 604 SF. Additionally, the total monthly rent roll is $21,176 or $605 per unit (21,131 SF/35 units).

Assume that Ambassador's average monthly rent can be increased by $100 per unit by making an investment of $3,000 per unit in upgrades, such as upgraded appliance packages, new wood floors, etc.

When it comes to upgrading units, my general rule is that if the payback of my investment is four years or less, make the investment.

Assume you upgrade 18 units to the tune of $3,000 each. You'll of course get to increase the base rent, say by $100, at the beginning of the second year to reflect the improved living conditions. Then you'll apply the previously discussed 3%. In this case, however, you're increasing the rent more thanks to the increased base rent you got from the upgrades. This will quickly pay off, as the rent increases at the end of the first year will be $21,600, leading to a cumulative increase of $62,144 over a five-year span.*

The effect of the awesome power of capitalization and cap rate power will substantially increase NOI and the value of the property. It's a simple way to make money that many property owners miss because they're focused

---

*See Appendix 6: Example demonstrates the cumulative effects on base rent of upgrading 18 units.

on short-term returns and not playing the long game. The long game is the one you want to win, and we'll show you why.

We increased the NOI of our property in five years by the relatively small amount of $38,253. However, assuming a 6% cap rate, this translates into an increase of $637,554 in property value over a five-year period. Remember, we only upgraded 18 units and didn't consider the additional net cash flow that will be generated from the property over the five-year period, as well as other benefits you will be receiving, including tax benefits, amortization, income from additional charges, and other benefits.*

The payback period is two and a half years ($54,000/$21,600). Also notice that after the two-and-a-half-year payback period, the property value should increase by $54,000 because the additional cash flow generated will pay back your investment.

Introducing a Potential Pitfall - The Maxed-Out Rent Roll

Earlier in this chapter, I introduced the following two concepts:

The real potential for increased property value often lies in the potential for growth of the existing rent roll.

A property whose rent roll is at or above market rents is known in the industry as being "maxed out," meaning little or no room for growth.

In the above example, we only upgraded 18 of the 35 units. Obviously, we could have upgraded all the units, and the results would have been even better. Now, what if all the units were upgraded? In that case, all the units should then be rented at market levels.

Now to look at the above two concepts. A maxed-out rent roll could be an area of concern if you wished to sell the property. If the property's

---

*See Appendix 7: Example demonstrates the effects on property value of upgrading 18 units.

location is strong and continues to grow, this is less of an issue. However, if the market softens and rents become stagnant, it could hurt your property value. A potential seller would ask the same questions you should: *Is there room for growth in the rent roll? Will the rents be maxed out? Can the property still be considered as a value-add property?*

Many owners will sell their property after only upgrading 30% - 50% of the units. The belief is that a relatively higher price can be obtained if the property presents additional potential for rent growth to a prospective purchaser. Again, this type of property is known in the industry as a value-add opportunity.

Other Pitfalls of a Maxed-Out Rent Roll to Consider

As we discussed when we talked about upgrading all the units at the Ambassador, all the units were re-rented at market rates after being upgraded. As a result, the property can no longer be classified as a ***value-add property*** unless there are other improvements you can make to increase rents significantly. In fact, the property may now be perceived by a prospective purchaser as a ***maxed-out*** property.

The property may be maxed out, and unless it is in an area projected for high rent growth, you may need to adjust the selling price.

Real-Life Example:

We currently own over 500 garden apartments in a "hot" section of East Dallas, Texas. Our properties were constructed before the 1970s and do not boast the amenities associated with a newly constructed building. We are upgrading the properties so that we can increase monthly rents to $850 for a 700 SF unit ($1.21 per SF). However, the area is "hot," and there are brand new garden apartment complexes being constructed nearby that provide better amenities for their tenants. Because new construction costs are extremely high and because they provide a superior product, they are getting rents of $1,155 for a 700 SF unit ($1.65 per SF). If the area becomes overbuilt, the new projects may experience higher vacancies. In order to survive, the *newer properties* will need to lower their rents to the point where the rent differential between the newer and *older communities* will become smaller, giving prospective tenants a choice of living in a nicer community for a smaller rent differential. This will force the older communities to lower their rents to compete. Our managing team constantly monitors the rents and occupancy rates of our competitors in order to detect warning signs. Just keep this example in the back of your mind.

Understanding the Statement of Net Cash Flow

There are alternate ways to classify the different components and categories comprising the income and expenses generated from the property's operations. Sometimes the distinction is made because of different laws governing each of these categories. We'll review that later. For now, the statement of net cash flow will serve as a useful tool to use to analyze any real estate transaction. It won't matter if the property contains 35 units or 400 units; the basic concepts are the same.*

Understanding Effective Gross Income

We begin by examining gross income, and the most common types of income generated by the operations of this garden apartment complex. Later we will focus our attention on *operating expenses, net operating income, and net cash flow*. We will look at the net cash flow before the debt service category at this time.

We previously defined net operating income as base rental income minus total operating expenses, excluding debt service, depreciation, capital

---

*See Appendix 8: Statement of Net Cash Flow – Ambassador Apartments.

reserves, etc. We will now replace "base rental income" with "effective gross income," and the revised formula will be as follows:

> # Net Operating Income (NOI) =
> ## *Effective Gross Income* Less Total
> ## Operating Expenses

Gross Potential Income:

The ***base rent*** the tenants will be charged if ***100%*** of the property is leased and occupied. In the gross potential income is $301,440 per annum. (Electric and late charges are <u>not</u> included in determining gross potential income.)

Gross potential income refers to the <u>base rent </u>the tenants will be charged if 100% of the property is leased and occupied.

Electric Reimbursements:

The Ambassador bills tenants for their pro-rata share of the total electric bill, less approximately 15% for the common areas of the building.

Vacancy and Collection Loss:

Every property experiences turnover or units that are not leased for various periods of time. Therefore, an allowance should be made for a loss of rent due to these factors. This allowance is commonly known as the ***vacancy factor*** or ***vacancy allowance***.

Market conditions, type of tenancy, physical condition, and other circumstances contribute to how high or low the vacancy factor should be. Most times this can be determined by examining the historical operations of the property. Additionally, no matter how carefully you screen your tenants, there will be tenants who don't pay their rent. The most common reasons are job loss, loss of a roommate, and divorce. Therefore, an allowance for collection losses should also be included. I have assumed a vacancy and collection loss of 5% due to my historical knowledge of this property.

Include Tenant Reimbursements in the Vacancy Allowance.

Many prospective purchasers and brokers neglect to add these items when calculating a vacancy factor for vacancy and collection loss, thus **overstating** effective gross income.

This comes into play when you receive a property setup from an owner or broker who doesn't include a vacancy and collection loss factor for tenant reimbursements in their calculation of effective gross income. Not doing so is to their advantage, since the higher the effective gross income and resulting NOI, the higher the selling price of the property can be. This is an old broker's trick, but many prospective owners and banks are oblivious to it.

If a unit is vacant or if a tenant skips, you will not only lose the base rent but the reimbursement charges as well.

When applying a vacancy and collection loss factor to gross potential income, tenant reimbursements should always be <u>included</u> in the calculation or both income and property value will be overstated.

My mantra is to always be cognizant of the effect that an increase or decrease in NOI has on property value. This starts from the acquisition period and continues through the ongoing operations of the property. For example, whenever employees seek raises, service contracts are negotiated, or repairs are made, I automatically think about how it will affect property value.

From acquisition through the ongoing operations of the property, you must <u>always</u> be cognizant of the effect that an increase or decrease in NOI has on property value.

Rent Concessions:
To attract tenants during slow times, many owners will offer incentives such as rent specials or rent concessions to prospective tenants.

Other Income:

Garden apartment complexes often charge an application fee to cover the cost of a credit report and an administrative fee for the time the staff spends to process a tenant's application. Generally, late fees are charged if rents are not received on time. There are various other charges categorized as other income, including pet fees, damage reimbursements, subletting fees, and vending income.

Understanding Operating Expenses

The most common types of operating expenses are summarized below.

Payroll and Fringes:

Staff salaries, leasing commissions, payroll taxes, health benefits, workers compensation, and unemployment insurance premiums.

Repair and Maintenance:

General repairs and supplies for the interior and exterior areas of the property, e.g. painting, appliances repair, carpentry, supplies, electric, plumbing, fence and gate, locks and keys, pool, and glass mirrors and screens.

Turnover Expense:

Costs incurred to prepare a unit for a new tenant, e.g. carpet cleaning, carpet dyeing and repair, cleaning supplies, contract cleaning, painting, and window covering and repair.

Contract Services:

Service contracts for items such as exterminating, landscaping, trash removal, security, and HVAC.

Administrative:

Telephone and answering service, bookkeeping and accounting, bank charges, computer maintenance and support, office supplies, legal and eviction, postage, freight and delivery, copying and printing, copy machine, education and training, dues and subscriptions, and other expenses.

Advertising and Marketing:
Apartment publications, locator fees, brochures, banners and flags, promotional, hospitality gifts, resident relations, parties, etc.

Utilities:
Electric, gas, water and sewer, cable TV, and other services.

Real Estate Taxes:
The tax assessed on the property by the local tax authorities.

Insurance:
Premiums for property and liability coverage, umbrella policies, etc.

Management Fees:
Costs for an outside property manager. Compensation is usually a monthly fee equal to 3% to 5% of *total cash collections.*

Management fees for smaller properties of four to ten units generally require a larger management fee of 5% to 10% because the resulting fee at 3% wouldn't be cost-effective for prospective property managers.

Capital Reserves:
Generally, a bank requires an owner to deposit funds on a monthly basis into a replacement reserve account to be held by the bank. Qualified expenses are reimbursed by the bank, and generally include the cost for carpeting and wood flooring, appliance costs, HVAC costs, etc. For larger properties, a reserve for capital expenses are included in operating expenses for purposes of determining NOI.

Debt Service:
The mortgage paid to the bank or other financial institution that holds the mortgage on the property. Mortgage payments are composed of two components, interest and principal.

Understanding Cash-On-Cash Return on Investment

I am now going to introduce you to another simple concept called the *cash-on-cash return (the COCR)*. Generally, the COCR is simply the net cash flow (*defined as net operating income, less debt service and capital reserves, but before depreciation or other non-operating expenses*), divided by the capital investment you made. The COCR represents the percentage return you will receive on your cash investment in the property.

> **Cash-on-Cash Return =**
> **Net Cash Flow/Invested Capital**

Please don't be discouraged if you don't fully understand some of the formulas or concepts presented in this chapter. We will be reinforcing them again and again in future chapters.

Street Success Concepts to Remember

Before you continue reading, make sure that you *fully understand* the following concepts.

1. Increasing the rental income of a property is an area where you have control over your own destiny.

2. The real potential for increased property value often lies in the *growth potential* of the existing rent roll.

3. A property whose rent roll is at or above market rents is known in the industry as being *maxed out*, meaning little or no room for growth.

4. The base rent of a property is generally defined as the amount of rent a tenant will pay before adding any additional charges for such items as electric, water and sewer, trash, etc.

5. By its nature, a property's base rent consists of a larger dollar base than the property's operating expenses. Therefore, a 3% increase in rent roll should always be greater than a 3% increase in operating expenses.

6. Assuming a rising rental market, each time a tenant's rent is increased, the amount of the increase becomes capitalized, meaning it's added to the base rent of the prior year. The new capitalized amount becomes the new base rent that future increases are based upon. This results in a future compounding of the rents, leading to much higher amounts in the future.

7. An increase in base rent is generally considered to be a *permanent* increase. However, some increases or decreases in operating expenses are most likely to be *temporary* in nature. In all likelihood, these expenses will return to normal or stabilize in relatively short periods of time.

8. The price you pay for a property is a permanent cost. You can't change the price once you close. On the other hand, a high interest rate on the mortgage obtained at the time of purchase is a temporary cost because the interest rate normally changes over time. As a result, it is generally more advantageous to acquire property in an environment featuring high interest rates and high cap rates because you should have the opportunity to refinance and obtain a lower interest rate in the future.

9. Understanding cap rates and their effect on property value is ground zero for success in the real estate business.

10. Cap Rate = Net Operating Income ("NOI")/Selling Price, or inversely, Property Value = Net Operating Income ("NOI")/Cap Rate

11. The *higher* the cap rate, the *lower* the value of the property. The *lower* the cap rate, the *higher* the value of the property.

12. The capitalization and compounding effects of an increasing rent roll combined with a low cap rate environment are the fundamentals of becoming rich through real estate investment.

13. It's important to note that rent is generally charged on the building's rentable square footage (RSF.) RSF is the building's actual square footage, or gross square footage, less the square footage of the common areas, such as walls, stairwells, elevators, and basements, that are not actual living space.

14. When it comes to upgrading units, my general rule is that if the payback of my investment is four years or less, make the investment.

15. Many owners will sell their property after only upgrading 30% - 50% of the units. The belief is that a relatively higher price can be obtained if the property presents additional potential for rent growth to a prospective purchaser. Again, this type of property is known in the industry as a value-add opportunity.

16. The property may be maxed out, and unless the property is in an area projected for high rent growth, you may need to adjust the selling price.

17. Gross potential income refers to the base rent the tenants will be charged if 100% of the property is leased and occupied.

18. If a unit is vacant or if a tenant skips, you will not only lose the base rent but the reimbursement charges as well.

19. When applying a vacancy and collection loss factor to gross potential income, tenant reimbursements should always be *included* in the calculation or both income and property value will be overstated.

20. From acquisition through the ongoing operations of the property, you must *always* be cognizant of the effect that an increase or decrease in NOI has on property value.

21. Cash-on-Cash Return = Net Cash Flow/Invested Capital

CHAPTER 3

ANALYZING THE OFFERING MEMORANDUM (OM)

IN THE NEXT few chapters, we are going to discuss the various steps you need to take and the related documents and procedures you need to master *before* you close and take title to a property.

The First 4 Steps to Take Before Taken and Mastered Before you Close and Take Title to the Property:

- *Step 1 - Analyzing the Offering Memorandum - Chapter 3*
- *Step 2 - Preparing a Letter of Intent (LOI) - Chapter - 4*
- *Step 3 - Signing a Contract of Sale - N/A*
- *Step 4 - Performing Due Diligence - Chapters 5 and 6*

This chapter focuses on a marketing document known as the offering memorandum (**OM**). The first step to take before purchasing a property is to *receive* or *create* an OM, then evaluate it. The OM is almost always prepared by the licensed real estate brokerage company offering the property for sale. If a broker is not involved, you will need to internally prepare one for yourself, but you first need to know the pertinent information that should be contained in a comprehensive offering memorandum. An OM includes summary information about the following categories, which are presented below in no particular order. Additionally, there are many variations of the OM, but the core information should be the same.

Summary of the Offering Memorandum (OM)

- Property Overview and Highlights
- Location Summary
- Offering Summary
- Site Description
- Building Information
- Construction Information
- Mechanical Information
- Utilities
- Amenities
- Tax Information
- Zoning Information
- School Information
- Unit Mix
- Sale and Rent Comparables
- Financial Analysis
- Floor Plans and Property Photos

Please keep in mind that an OM is only a snapshot or guide to the property, nothing more. Use it to gauge your initial interest and determine if you go forward with a further in-depth investigation for the purposes of step two, submitting a letter of intent (LOI) to purchase the property.

⇨ *The OM should be viewed as a snapshot or guide to the property, nothing more. Use it to gauge your initial interest to determine if you wish to go forward.*

⇨ *Evaluating the OM is performed before you (i) submit an LOI, (ii) negotiate a contract of sale, and (iii) start to perform your due diligence.*

The majority of OMs are very detailed, but some lack the necessary information you will need to properly evaluate the investment. This is especially true when dealing with unsophisticated owners and brokers. On some occasions, I have spent a great deal of time and money on due diligence only to find out that the information presented in the OM was inaccurate or false.

Real Estate Brokers

The listing broker usually has signed an exclusive agreement with the seller to market the property. As a result, the broker is contractually obligated to represent the seller, **not** the buyer. To obtain the listing, the broker most likely had a prior relationship with the seller and wants to remain in the seller's good graces so that they will continue to give him additional properties to sell. Real estate brokers are a necessary evil because they have the most knowledge available to determine market value and the largest audience to market the property to prospective purchasers.

⇨ *When analyzing an OM, always remember that the broker is not your friend and doesn't have your best interests at heart. They represent the seller, not the buyer.*

That said, there are good, bad, and really bad brokers. It is my experience that, due to greed and extreme competition to obtain listings, brokers hide behind a disclaimer, and often their OMs do not present accurate information about the property. Every OM that is prepared by a real estate broker will have a disclaimer that basically states that even though they have prepared the information contained in the OM, they do so without providing any assurance that you can rely on. Below is a good example of the typical disclaimer that brokers include in their OMs.

> *This Offering Memorandum (OM) has been prepared to provide summary, unverified information to prospective purchasers, and to establish only a preliminary level of interest in the subject property. The information contained herein is not a substitute for a thorough due diligence investigation. We have not made any investigation, and make no warranty or representation, with respect to the income or expenses for the subject property, the future projected financial performance of the property, the size and square footage of the property and improvements, the presence or absence of contaminating substances, PCB's or asbestos, the compliance with State and Federal regulations, the physical condition of the improvements thereon, or the financial condition or business prospects of any tenant, or any tenant's plans or intentions to continue its occupancy of the subject property. The information contained in this OM has been obtained from sources we believe to be reliable; however, we have not verified, and will not verify, any of the information contained herein, nor have we conducted any investigation regarding these matters and make no warranty or representation whatsoever regarding the accuracy or completeness of the information provided. All potential buyers must take appropriate measures to verify all of the information set forth herein.*

⇨ *You must conduct your own independent investigation and due diligence (Step 4) to verify all information contained in the OM.*

Side Note: In the current super-competitive market for properties, an owner would be foolish not to use an outside real estate broker to market the property for sale. The key to obtaining the highest price for a property is by marketing it to as many prospective purchasers as possible, even if a broker fee must be paid. If you're lucky, there will be a bidding war.

A good broker should work to obtain the highest possible price for the property from prospective purchasers who have the best ability to close. However, there are times when the ideal situation for purchasing a property is to purchase the property "off-market." This doesn't necessarily mean without paying a broker fee, but it means without the property being mass-marketed. If you buy the property without the benefit of direct competition, it should allow you to purchase it at a better price and stop any bidding war.

⇨ *An owner would be foolish not to use a real estate broker to sell their property. A key to obtaining the highest price for a property is to market it to as many prospective purchasers as possible even if a broker fee must be paid. On the other hand, when purchasing a property, the ideal situation is to purchase the property "off-market" because it provides you the opportunity to avoid direct competition and a possible bidding war.*

For the purposes of studying the OM, in this chapter, we will be focusing on evaluating garden apartment communities located in Texas.*

A garden apartment community is characterized by a group of low-rise buildings, two to five stories high, on a common parcel of land. They often consist of multiple buildings with their own addresses. They feature open landscaping, catwalks, and various pathways that are considered common areas for the residents. Amenities include, but are not limited to, outdoor pools, clubhouses, playgrounds, laundry rooms, and barbecue areas. Parking is located throughout the complex, usually offering a mix of covered and non-covered parking spaces.

To examine in detail the specific information that should be included in an OM you may receive, refer to Appendix 1. Please note that if the OM is lacking any of this information, you need to request that the broker or owner obtain it, or you need to obtain the information yourself. Any missing information hinders your efforts to properly evaluate the investment. That being said, some of the pertinent information you will need to review will not be provided until a contract of sale (Step 3) between you and the seller is executed and the due diligence period begins. However, the idea is to have as much information at your disposal to see if you want to further pursue the opportunity.

Appendix 1 shows a Comprehensive Pro-forma OM for a *fictional* garden apartment community for you to study. I have arbitrarily named the subject property the ***Dallas Arms Apartments***. A comprehensive OM like this is not typical, but by studying and mastering this illustration, you will be able to determine what information is missing from any OM you may receive.*

Property Overview and Highlights

The OM usually starts with a narrative, referred to as a property overview or executive summary, that describes the property's positives and why it's such a great opportunity for prospective purchases. They want to paint a picture of the property, highlighting any recent renovations that might increase its value or appeal to prospective renters. Discuss the surrounding market and the in-house tenant base. They try to sell the financial windfall a buyer will get by purchasing the property and make it look like the best investment on the market.

Propaganda Contained in the OM:

- **Turnkey Property** with attractive unit mix and historically high occupancy
- **Outstanding Location** along the path of development of the Fort Worth Area
- **Rents Approximately 20 Percent Below Market,** significant upside by implementing interior upgrade program

---

*See Appendix 1 - Comprehensive Pro-forma OM for a *fictional* garden apartment community.

- **Outstanding Opportunity for Expense Reduction** through water conservation program
- **Additional Income Stream Possible** through offering reserved parking

I previously noted that because the stakes are so high, almost every owner knows what their property is worth. This is because brokers have educated not only owners but themselves on how the value of a property can change by making improvements. Historically, this was not the case. For example, many owners and brokers were unaware of the savings achieved by installing low-flow showerheads or by replacing power-draining incandescent light bulbs with energy-efficient LED light bulbs. This is also true of the broker's other recommendations. Often, these potentially expense-saving factors are already factored into the brokers' projections and selling price of the property.

Offering Summary

Sales Price ($3,800,000)

The listed sales price is the seller's *initial* asking price. Once a property goes to market, the demand for the property will ultimately determine the final purchase price. The initial asking price generally will not be the final purchase price. In this crazy market, I have seen the initial asking price bid up by 25% to 50%. My point is that the seller's asking price changes depending on market conditions and is not written in stone.

➡ *The seller's initial asking price is subject to change depending on market conditions and is not written in stone.*

Apartment Community Name (the Dallas Arms Apartments)

Usually, a garden apartment community has a name that identifies it in the marketplace. For the purposes of this illustration, we have named the property the Dallas Arms Apartments.

Street Address

Every OM should state the address of the property and the managing agent's address or mailing address, telephone number, and email address. You need this information when performing your due diligence. Additionally, if the property has more than one building, you will need to obtain the address of each of the individual buildings, especially for insurance purposes.

Price per Unit (a.k.a Per Door) ($63,333)

In many areas, a rule of thumb to determine property value is by comparing the price per unit a.k.a price per door of *similar* properties in an area. For example, we currently own an 85-unit garden apartment complex that we purchased for $4,500,000. We spent approximately $1,500,000 completely renovating the property. As a result, our investment in the property is $6,000,000, or $70,588 per unit. There is a similar property across the street that was only partially upgraded. It has a pool and a few more amenities than our property and was recently purchased for $95,000 per unit. It would seem on the surface that our property is worth more than $70,588 per unit since our property was completely renovated and upgraded, but this may not be the case. In a later chapter, we will see that every property has a separate and unique personality. No two properties are the same: every property is different, with different potentials, different tax assessments, different physical conditions, and different amenities, etc. As you learned in Chapter 2, the cap rate method of determining property value is a much more accurate method for determining property value than the price per unit method. Unsophisticated investors will sometimes purchase property based on the price per unit, only later realizing they made a bad deal.

➡ *No two properties are the same; every property is different with different potentials, different tax assessments, different physical conditions, and different amenities, etc. Determining property value by the price per unit (a.k.a. price per door) method is not a prudent way of determining property value.*

Offered Free and Clear (Yes)

This means there are no mortgages on the property that need to be assumed by the purchaser. The new purchaser is free to obtain new financing, which is usually beneficial for the purchaser. Sometimes, however, the seller's mortgage may have a few years remaining on its term and repayment would result in the seller incurring a large prepayment penalty. In these cases, the seller does not want to pay a large prepayment penalty, and the deal may be subject to the purchaser being forced to assume the existing mortgage. Additionally, the purchaser is often charged a 1% fee to assume the existing mortgage.

If the seller's mortgage has a remaining term of four or more years with a below-market interest rate, it may be advantageous for the purchaser to assume the mortgage, even if a point must be paid to the bank.

Site Description

Lot (Parcel) Size (2.29 Acres)

One acre is equal to 43,560 SF. Therefore, the lot of the Dallas Arms Apartments contains a total of 99,752 SF. Lot size usually comes into play when the property is viewed more as a development site than as an operating apartment complex. Determining factors are usually linked to the property's allowable zoning regulations. Many times, I see an old, dilapidated apartment building located in an upcoming area for sale. Does it make more sense to renovate the building or demolish it and construct a new higher-end building? There's a saying in the industry: *How much is the dirt worth?*

Assume, given the permissible zoning, the dirt that Dallas Arms Apartments is on is worth $45 per SF. That means the property, as a development site, would be worth $4,488,840 and would be more valuable as a development site than as the existing operating building. One of the criteria a professional appraiser uses to value a property is called the "Highest and Best Use" method. In this example, the value of the dirt ($4,488,940) rather than the value as the existing operating apartment complex ($3,800,000) would represent the highest and best use of the property.

Building Size (62,500 SF)

Building size refers to the gross size of the building, including hallways, living space, catwalks, etc. The building size can also include terraces and balconies. In most cases, the building size and the *net rentable amount* of SF will be different. For example, the building size of Dallas Arms is 62,500 SF, but the amount of rentable SF is only 57,066 SF.

Total Parking Spaces (86)/ Tenant Parking Ratio (1.40 Spaces per Unit)

The Dallas Arms Apartments has 86 parking spaces, two of which are reserved for handicapped parking. Therefore, the net number of spaces available for resident parking is 84 spaces. Since there are 60 units, the *tenant* parking ratio is 1.40 spaces per unit (84 spaces/60 units). For garden apartment communities, I like a tenant parking ratio of 1.25 to 1.50 or higher. Of course, this will depend upon the unit mix, unit size, number of occupant drivers, and the available street parking, etc.

Handicapped Spaces (2): Most OM's do not disclose how many spaces are reserved for handicapped parking, and, as a result, the parking ratio depicted would be incorrect.

⇨ *It is imperative that the parking ratio is adequate to service the existing tenancy and for you to know if there is a parking problem in the area.*

Covered Parking (No)

Covered parking is a valued amenity, especially in Texas where hailstorms that can potentially cause damage to the tenants' cars are commonplace. Most tenants will pay extra for a covered parking space. Installing covered parking is usually cost-prohibitive, so it's a big plus if it exists. The property in our example shows no covered parking available.

Attractive Landscaping (Yes)

This is another amenity that helps property value. Properties with beautifully landscaped courtyards surrounded by large trees create a special ambiance, but it's very expensive to maintain such extensive landscaping. You must know what the market demands.

Building Information

Building Type

The real estate industry developed various property classifications to make it easier to communicate about investment properties and areas. The classifications to describe the different types of property are either A, B, C, or D. These letter classifications are determined in part by age, level of construction, tenant income levels, growth and appreciation potential, amenities, etc.

Class A: Garden apartments built within the past 10 years and generally considered luxury units. They feature high-quality construction, high-end exterior and interior amenities, well-maintained landscaping and courtyards, pools and an attractive rental office and/or clubhouse. These buildings are often located in desirable areas where they offer the most amenities, have low vacancies, and typically demand the highest rents. These buildings demand the lowest cap rates and highest per-unit prices.

Class B: Garden apartments built within the past 10 to 20 years. They are usually well-maintained and have a middle-class tenancy. Exterior and interior amenities are usually dated and below those offered by Class A properties. They offer quality construction with little deferred maintenance required. Average rents are lower than those of Class A properties. Class B properties are typically valued at slightly higher cap rates than Class A properties and generally offer decent cash flow on acquisition.

Class C: Garden apartments built within the past 30 to 40 years. The tenancy usually consists of transient blue-collar and low- to moderate-income tenants with rents at below-market levels. Class C properties generally feature dated and/or limited exterior and interior amenity packages, catwalks, and original appliances. The property needs extensive deferred maintenance. Rents are substantially lower than in Class B properties and offer an affordable option to tenants in the submarket. These buildings usually provide higher cash flow and cap rates than Class A and B properties but are much more management intensive.

⇨ *During the past 10 years, great success has been achieved by purchasing Class C garden apartment communities located in Class A and B areas and repositioning them to Class B properties.*

Class D: Garden apartments built over 30 years ago, worn or dilapidated properties, transient tenancy, limited or no amenity packages, and low-quality construction in poor condition. Generally, these properties have many Section 8 (government-subsidized) tenants. Class D properties are generally located in lower socioeconomic high-crime areas and attract low rents, coupled with high turnover, large vacancy, and bad debt. These properties require intense management with limited appreciation and can be purchased at high cap rates. Class D properties are the most challenging and are definitely not for novices. These types of properties might seem to be cash cows on paper; however, the cash flow is often greatly diminished by the number of repairs needed and the lack of payment by tenants.

Area Type

Areas have different classifications, too. When describing different areas, the classifications are very similar with the same A, B, C, and D designations, as follows:

Class A: newer growth, low-crime areas

Class B: older, stable, low-crime areas

Class C: older, declining, stable areas, moderate crime

Class D: older, rapidly declining, high-crime areas

Many times, the trend in a Class C or D area is a revitalization of that area. This is where the best investments are.

The Dallas Arms Apartments represent a Class C property in a Class A location.

Number of Floors (2) and Number of Units (60)

Garden apartment buildings normally don't have elevators. If the building or buildings comprising the community have or more floors, the units on higher floors will command less rent than those on the lower floors. No one wants to walk up three to four floors carrying groceries or other packages. Additionally, apartment views are not expected and are less important for Class C properties. Tenants living on the lower floors may experience noise from tenants walking on the upper floors. This is especially true in Class C and D properties where the subfloors are in disrepair.

⇨ *Generally, garden apartment units located on the second or higher floors may be a little harder to rent and thus may demand lower rents than those units on the first floor. This is because of the convenience factor. Carrying packages up three or four flights of stairs, especially with an older tenancy, isn't desirable. This factor should be taken into consideration when projecting rental income.*

With regard to the number of units, I want to mention that this information is needed to calculate average unit size, average unit rent, rent per SF, etc. as further described below. It is important when determining if the existing zoning will allow additional units to be constructed on the property.

Average Unit Size (951 SF)

Knowing the average unit size and how many baths a unit has is important, as smaller units command a higher dollar rent per SF than larger units command. For Class C properties, the following unit sizes are optimum.

Studios: 400 to 450 SF

One bedroom, one bath: 575 to 675 SF

Two bedrooms, one or two baths: 900 to 1,000 SF

Three bedrooms, two baths: 1,150 to 1,500 SF

Two-bedroom, one-bath units are the most undesirable since most tenants do not like to share a bathroom.

Sometimes a unit is too large for the market it's located in. For example, a one-bedroom, one-bath unit consisting of 800 SF may be too expensive for one person to occupy, but it may prove to be adequate if the prospective tenant has a roommate. It also will be more expensive for the owner to renovate or upgrade the unit with carpet or wood flooring and to paint. Additionally, the tenant's cost for utilities will be higher, especially when the tenant is rebilled based on the SF of the unit. The excess space may not be needed by the tenant. Units with excess space will often cause over-occupancy and illegal subletting, which translates to increased utility costs and higher wear and tear on the unit.

I like larger unit sizes when the property is located near good schools since a larger unit should attract more families who want to take advantage of a good school system which leads to lower turnover and less operating costs.

⇨ *The larger the unit, the <u>lower</u> rent per SF you will obtain and the <u>more</u> it will cost to upgrade the unit with carpeting and/or wood flooring. Additionally, units with excess space will often cause over-occupancy and illegal subletting which translates to increased utility costs and higher wear and tear on the unit.*

Average Current Rent per Unit ($937)

This is important to know so you can compare the base rents of comparable communities in the area. You must take into consideration any additional costs tenants are required to pay. For example, if the tenant pays rent on an All Bills Paid (ABP) basis, then the rents will be higher than those properties' base rents that are not based on ABP.

ABP means that the tenant only pays a fixed rental amount and all utilities are included in this fixed amount. Non-ABP properties mean that the tenants are charged for utilities and other costs which can mean paying an additional $80 - $100 per month. ABP will be further discussed later in this chapter.

Year Built (1962)

The Dallas Arms Apartments were built in 1962, almost 60 years ago. As a result, the buildings' infrastructure may be compromised unless the property has been well-maintained and/or renovated. I can almost guarantee you that if the buildings were not well-maintained, there *will* be infrastructure problems currently or in the near future. This is often the reason the owner decided to sell the property.

I want you to realize that the repair/replacement of any of these systems can be extremely expensive. It's a big plus if the property has been well-maintained and/or renovated, especially when you are just beginning to purchase property and lack the necessary construction experience.

⇨ *The infrastructure of an older building and its systems may be compromised unless the property has been well-maintained and/or renovated. The repair or replacement of any of these systems can be extremely expensive; therefore, if the property has been well-maintained and/or renovated it's a big plus.*

Current Physical Occupancy Percentage (95%) and Current Leasing Percentage (98%)

Physical occupancy percentage represents the percentage of units that are physically occupied by tenants at any given time. Many OM's will also show the leased percentage which is, the percentage of signed leases for units not yet occupied. The leased percentage may be higher or lower than the physical occupancy percentage.

⇨ *Physical occupancy percentage represents the percentage of units that are physically occupied by tenants at any given point in time. Leased percentage represents the number of signed leases at a given point in time. The leased percentage may be higher or lower than the physical occupancy percentage.*

For example, assume for June, the leased percentage is 98% and the physical occupancy percentage is 95%. What does this mean? It could mean that two new leases were signed during the week of June 25 to June 30, but the tenant won't be moving in and paying rent until July 1. This means that the two new leases are included in the leased percentage, but are not included in the physical occupancy percentage until they move in. At that time, the tenant will start paying rent.

What if two tenants give notice that they're vacating their units at the end of the month? For June, these two units are still included in the physical occupancy percentage, even though they are soon vacating. You can see how leasing and physical occupancy percentages can be misleading.

Current Area Occupancy (95%)

Learning about the current occupancy percentage of similar properties located in the immediate area is very important. For example, if the area's occupancy percentage is below 90%, it may prove difficult to secure attractive financing. Keeping the units rented and increasing rents in future years may turn out to be problematic. If the property you're considering has an occupancy percentage less than 85% - 90% but is located in an area with an above 90% area occupancy percentage, it may represent an opportunity. A determination of why the occupancy is low may reveal poor management, a property in need of deferred maintenance, and/or dated interiors. You can work to address these issues.

You will want to consider areas with either *high or low barriers to entry*. My general rule is to purchase properties that have a high barrier of entry. This means there are few new construction opportunities due to little remaining land or strict zoning regulations that make it extremely hard to build. A high barrier to entry limits competition, which should translate to a more stable occupancy and higher rent growth. Historically, I have avoided areas, including parts of Florida, that I categorize as having low barriers of entry that offer vast opportunities to build new apartment communities. I refer to low barriers of entry areas as *water, money, and build areas*.

⇨ *Areas where vacant land is scarce and/or strict zoning laws make it very difficult to allow new multi-family apartment communities to be constructed are known in the industry as having a "high barrier of entry." High barriers of entry areas limit competition, which stabilizes occupancy rates and leads to higher rent growth and will demand lower cap rates.*

Net Rentable SF (56,066 SF)

As discussed in Chapter 2, base rent is generally charged on the building's net rentable square footage, which is the building's total square footage or gross square footage, less the square footage of the common areas, including walls, stairwells, elevators, basements, and anything else that is not actual living space. The difference between the gross building size and the net rentable SF is known as the loss factor and is usually attributable to common areas for which rent is not charged. The determination of net rentable SF is usually made by the owner or the managing agent for the property and is either actually measured or arbitrarily made. On occasion, a tenant will physically measure the unit and find it is only 600 SF, but they're being charged for 650 SF because they're paying for portions of the loss factor.

⇨ *The difference between the gross building size and the net rentable SF is known in the industry as the loss factor and is usually attributable to common areas, such as hallways, walls, etc., for which rent is not charged.*

Cap Rate (6.32%) and NOI ($240,080)

As discussed in Chapter 2: Cap Rate = Net Operating Income ("NOI")/ Selling Price

NOI = Effective or net gross income minus total operating expenses, excluding debt service, depreciation, etc. However, for larger buildings Capital Reserves are included in operating expenses.

Renovated (Yes)/ Last Date Renovated (2012 - 2015)

When analyzing an OM, I want to know what capital improvements were made to the property during the past five years. Many times, an OM will highlight improvements that have been made. If improvements aren't mentioned in the OM, it should indicate the potential for current and/ or future problems. For example, a roof's useful life is generally 10 – 15 years depending on climate and the beating it's taken, so if the roof was recently replaced it's a plus. If the roof is older, then the building may experience leaks, or the entire roof may soon need to be replaced, which is extremely expensive.

Average Rent per SF ($.95 per SF)

The average rent per SF lets you compare the property's rent to the area's similar communities. You must take into consideration any additional costs the tenants are required to pay, including utilities which can equate to paying an additional $80 to $100 per month.

Construction Information

Roofs (Pitched, Shingles)

Garden apartment buildings tend to have either a flat roof or a pitched roof. A pitched roof has shingles and at least two slopes that meet at a peak, while a flat roof is usually rubberized tar paper. To enable rainwater to drain from the roof, a flat roof is slightly pitched by a couple of degrees.

Pitched roofs last longer than flat roofs but are more difficult to clean, inspect, and maintain. Sometimes they afford plenty of usable space in the loft area, either for storage or additional living space, such as a study or playroom. In a climate like Texas with severe hail or thunderstorms common, it is important to have a roof that is able to handle large amounts of rain, and pitched roofs offer increased drainage capacity which limits leaks and costly repairs. Pitched roofs often have intricate designs and are aesthetically more attractive than flat roofs.

It's important to know the beating the roof has taken. If the roof has taken a beating, it might not last the estimated useful life of 10 years, and the property will certainly experience leaks as the roof ages.

Flat roofs are significantly cheaper, easier to walk on for maintenance and inspections, offer more stability, and can save on energy costs. Flat roofs require more maintenance to prevent leaks and costly repairs. They also cost more than pitched roofs to repair. The drainage capacity of flat roofs is not as effective as pitched roofs, meaning drains off the roof can become clogged, leading to more damage and leaks. Another disadvantage of flat roofs is their ability to bear weight, making them more likely to collapse as a result of a severe storm. Because flat roofs are less stable in holding weight, watch out for properties that have mounted HVAC units on a flat roof. Flat roofs do sometimes offer the potential for additional income opportunities, such as leasing portions of the roof for signage or telecommunication equipment.

Mechanical Information

HVAC

HVAC stands for heating, ventilation, and air conditioning. Garden apartment complexes generally have the following two types of HVAC systems.

Chiller System

A chiller is usually one large compressor unit that sits outside the building and supplies HVAC to all the units through air handlers located in each individual unit, usually in the ceiling of a closet. Hot or cold water runs through a pipe into each individual air handler that has a fan that blows either the hot or cold air into the unit, producing either heat or air conditioning. The water's temperature is regulated by the chiller to produce either hot or cold water. Each tenant can only control the fan, which limits the amount of heat or air conditioning into the unit. There is a master meter for the entire building. Chillers are extremely expensive (avg. $25,000 to $75,000 each), and if the property has many buildings, multiple chillers may be required.

Chillers must be regularly cleaned and maintained, or their useful life is shortened. An outside contractor will be needed unless your managing agent has the staff and expertise to perform these services in house. If a chiller goes down on a hot or cold day, your telephone will ring off the hook with complaints. Therefore, when purchasing a property that contains a chiller system, you must have an outside consultant examine the condition of the property's chillers. Another way to find out the chiller's condition is to review any active service contract and the procedures of the managing agent for regular maintenance.

Individual HVAC System

With this system, instead of one chiller that services the entire building, each apartment has an individual HVAC unit with the blower portion in the apartment and the compressor in the back of the building or mounted on the roof. The cost of the electricity will be included as part of the apartment's electricity service. The tenant needs to call the utility company and open a separate account in their name. The tenant then becomes responsible for the bill for their unit, and the owner is not responsible unless the owner elects to open the account in their name and pay the bills directly. A property that has individual HVAC units is a big plus. Unlike with chiller systems, tenants can better control their unit's temperature and the owner isn't responsible for non-payment of the bill. If individual HVAC units are roof-mounted on a flat roof, their weight can be a potential problem.

Electrical (Individually Metered)

Garden apartment complexes generally have the following two types of electric metering:

Master Meter:

In this system, the building has one master meter for the common area (i.e., hallways, stairwells, etc.) and one meter for all of the individual units. The meter is in the name of the owner, who is fully responsible for the utility cost.

Individual Unit Meters:

In this system, there are meters for the common areas of the building in the owner's name and individual meters in each unit in the tenant's name. The tenant opens a separate account in their name with the utility company. The tenant is responsible for the bill, and the owner will not be responsible unless the owner elects to open the account in his name, pay the bills directly, and then rebill the tenants. It's a big plus when a property already has individual electric meters, as the system is extremely expensive to install.

Hot Water (One Gas Boiler)

Garden apartment complexes generally have the following two types of systems to produce hot water:

Boilers and Storage Tanks:

Boilers and storage tanks produce hot water for the entire building. In garden apartment complexes, it's common for the owner to pay for hot water.

Individual Water Heaters:

Each unit has its own water heater run by electric or gas and is usually located in a vented closet within the unit.

Fire Protection (Smoke Alarms and Fire Extinguishers)

Garden apartment complexes normally have hardwired or battery-operated smoke detectors in each unit. Class C buildings generally have battery-operated smoke alarms, which require batteries to be periodically replaced. Class C buildings also have one or two individual fire extinguishers on each floor. Hardwired smoke alarms are more expensive to install but are safer and more reliable, plus then you don't have to worry about checking and replacing batteries.

Electrical Wiring (Aluminum)

In Texas, older buildings often have aluminum wiring rather than copper wiring. Aluminum wiring has been determined to be a fire hazard.

Until recently "pig-tailing" was an accepted method for remediation. Pig-tailing is very expensive and involves splicing a short length of copper to the original aluminum wire using a special wire nut containing an anti-sparking gel. Pig-tailing is no longer an acceptable method of remediation. In lieu of rewiring the entire building, special aluminum contact electrical outlets and switches may be used in conjunction with the existing aluminum wiring. Copper wiring was more expensive at the time but is the best wiring to have, so if the property has copper wiring it's a big advantage.

⇨ *Aluminum wiring in the units is a fire hazard. In lieu of rewiring the entire building, special aluminum contact electrical outlets and switches may be used in conjunction with the existing aluminum wire. Copper wiring is very expensive, but is the best wiring to have, so if the property has copper wiring, it's a big advantage.*

Utilities

The obligation for utility costs for Class C properties is determined on either an ABP basis, a RUBS basis, or a combination of the two.

All Bills Paid (ABP)

The owner pays 100% of the cost for electric, gas, water and sewer, and trash, regardless of the type of meter or HVAC system The tenant's only responsibility is paying their base rent, which is usually higher than properties with a RUBS system, as described below. ABP properties are usually found in Class C buildings in weaker markets consisting of blue-collar and low- to moderate-income tenants. Many tenants are more comfortable knowing what their fixed monthly obligations are and may prefer an all bills paid property.

Ratio Utility Billing System (RUBS)

The cost for either electric, gas, water and sewer, and trash, or any combination of these, are billed back to the tenants based upon an allocation using a formula that takes into consideration the number of occupants and square footage of each unit. RUBS has proven to promote decreased usage of utilities by the building as a whole. Generally, the OM will highlight that there is a value-add opportunity to increase income by implementing a RUBS program. The market in the immediate area dictates the viability of such a program. I have seen some properties that bill back more than 100% of the total utility costs to their tenants.

The OM states that each unit in Dallas Arms is separately metered for electricity and HVAC. In our properties, we require tenants to open their own account with the utility company. This way the owner is not responsible for non-payment by the tenant. Many communities have a master meter, so the owner pays the electric bill and then re-bills each tenant for their pro-rata share of the cost. If the tenant doesn't pay their reimbursement, the owner will absorb the cost because it's ultimately the owner's responsibility to pay the utility bill.

The cost for telephone and cable service is almost always paid by the tenant in Class C properties. Additionally, Class C properties are generally not wired for direct internet and cable TV service. Tenants usually open an account with the cable company or other providers and pay for these services separately. Water and sewer charges for Class B and C properties are generally paid for by the owner or, in some cases, paid by the owner and charged back to the tenants.

⇨ *Always try and have the tenant open their own separate account with the utility company. If the tenant doesn't pay their reimbursement, the owner will be absorbing the tenant's utility cost because it is ultimately the owner's responsibility to pay the utility bill.*

Amenities

Laundry Room (Yes)

Having a separate laundry room is a necessity rather than an amenity. Using a card system for the laundry equipment helps to limit theft. Since many laundry rooms have old equipment that breaks down, resulting in tenant complaints, laundry rooms that contain new state-of-the-art equipment are a great amenity and selling point.

Washer and Dryer in Units (No)

Washer and dryer connections in the units are a plus, especially if the building has a laundry room that is small or not nearby. However, the question becomes who supplies the equipment, the tenant or the owner, and is the unit large enough?

Leasing/Management Office (Yes)

It's good to have a central office as a base for leasing and managing the property's operations, especially in larger complexes of 50 or more units. The property needs a leasing associate onsite to show vacant units, attend to tenant needs, and monitor tenant behavior. Properties that have onsite employees and a central management office are more desirable than those that don't.

Controlled Access Gates (No)

Gates are a big plus if they presently exist on the property. Gates provide tenants with more security by limiting access to the property, thus limiting crimes, including car theft, damage, and robberies. It is extremely expensive to install these gates around the property if they don't already exist.

Pool (No)

On the face of it, you'd think that having a pool is a big plus. I don't agree, at least when it comes to smaller Class C properties. A pool can become a real nuisance and it increases your liability, especially if children are living at the property. Maintaining a pool in good working order is also expensive. We have filled in most of our pools and replaced them with barbecue grills and picnic-style seating areas. However, due to the type of tenancy, pools are a must for luxury-type Class A and B properties and larger Class C properties.

Other (No)

Pet stations, playground areas, barbecue grills, Wi-Fi at the pool area and other common areas, resident business center, fitness center, fireplaces, and other extra amenities lead to higher rents and the property becoming more desirable.

Tax Information

Assessed Value, Tax Rate, Current Taxes

We will discuss the various components for determining real estate taxes in subsequent chapters.

Zoning Information

I am going to introduce you to a few general zoning terms. Zoning is the division of land into districts that have uniform zoning regulations, including, but not limited to, those on land use, handicapped rules, parking requirements, height, setbacks, lot size, density, and floor area ratio (FAR). In other words, every area has strict rules so you can't just build anything you want.

You must have the appropriate zoning before you can build on the land. However, sometimes the zoning changes after the building is constructed, and the building(s) previously constructed may either be over or underbuilt and/or non-conforming according to current zoning regulations. If the buildings are overbuilt, there may be the potential for problems that may need to be corrected if discovered by the local authorities. For example, unless you are grandfathered, you may need to create additional parking spaces or build a handicapped ramp to conform to current zoning ordinances. These changes can be very expensive.

Lot Size (2.29 Acres)

One acre is equal to 43,560 square feet. Therefore, Dallas Arms contains a total of 99,752 square feet.

Density (27.39 Units per Acre)

The maximum number of units that can be built on the site.

- Since the Dallas Arms Apartments contains 2.29 acres, a maximum of 63 units (2.29 acres x 27.39 allowable units per acre) can be built on the site according to existing zoning ordinances.

- Dallas Arms already has 60 units on the site, the property is basically "fully built," except that three additional units would be allowed.

- Many sites may allow more units than currently exist on the site due to the permitted zoning ordinance. In this case, the site is deemed to be "underbuilt," and there is the potential for additional construction and subsequently more net operating income and property value.

Zoning (MF-2(A))

This represents a specific classification for allowing construction in the zoning district the property is located in. For example, in Dallas, the MF-2(A) classification means Residential Multifamily - Low Density. Permitted construction in this zoning area would be subject to the rules and regulations contained in the zoning laws and regulations under the category of MF-2(A).

Height Restriction (30 FT)

This refers to how high and therefore how many floors or stories are permitted to be built on the site. Sometimes additional density is allowed, but it's irrelevant because the height restriction won't allow additional floors to be constructed. A general rule of thumb is that a residential building will require approximately 11 feet per floor. This would equate to the following number of stories that can be built:

22 FT = 2 stories

33 FT = 3 stories

44 FT = 4 stories

55 FT = 5 stories

66 FT = 6 stories

Dallas Arms has a height restriction of 30 feet, and the building is two stories, in accordance with existing zoning regulations. Ceiling height, mechanical room housing, and other such factors must also be considered to determine the number of stories that can be built on the site. I want you to be aware that if the zoning for this site allows for both higher height and density, it could potentially accommodate a five- to six-story building so the site would be deemed to be underbuilt since the potential for additional construction exists.

To determine the correct zoning for a property lot size, density, zoning class, and height restrictions must all be considered in determining the potential for additional construction on the site.

School Information

Schools

When looking at a property, I find out if it has a school system that is highly rated and conveniently located nearby. Good school systems are tremendous draws to a community and lead to much less resident turnover. Residents are leery of taking their kids out of school and relocating. A key to operating a successful property is to reduce turnover, especially in garden apartment communities. Remember each time a tenant vacates, you need to hire a cleaning company, repair and/or replace the carpet, pay rental agent fee, offer rent specials, and suffer rent loss until a new tenant takes occupancy. This is not the case when a tenant renews their lease.

⇨ *A key to operating any successful property is to reduce turnover. Remember each time a tenant vacates you will need to hire a cleaning company, repair and/or replace the carpet, pay rental agent fees, offer rent specials, and suffer rent loss until a new tenant takes occupancy. This is not the case when a tenant renews their lease.*

Another factor to consider is the distance from the schools and if public transportation is available nearby. If a bus stop is less than a block or two away, it's a big plus, but watch out for poorly rated school systems that are not easy to get to. You should obtain information on elementary schools, middle schools, and high schools in the area.

Good school systems that are nearby or near public transportation that are readily available are tremendous draws to a community and lead to much less resident turnover. Low resident turnover is one key to lowering operating costs and a higher NOI which translates to higher property value.

Unit Mix

Unit Mix Schedule

The OM should contain a unit mix schedule. The unit mix schedule should, but does not always, contain the following information:
- Unit Type
- Number of Unit Types, i.e. the number of one-bedroom, one-bath units

- Average SF of Each Unit Type
- Average SF Subtotal, the total average SF for each unit type
- Percent of Units, the concentration percentage for each unit type, i.e.: average numbers of 1-bedroom, 1-bath units.
- Current Monthly Rent and Current Monthly Rent Per SF
- Current Total Monthly Income
- Proforma Monthly Rent, this is usually projected by the broker
- Proforma Rent Per SF
- Proforma Total Monthly Rent

Side Note: Brokers will generally look at the past five to 10 units that have been leased, then use the average as the pro forma rent for all the units. They will then apply a cap rate to this inflated pro forma rent to calculate the projected property value. This is very deceiving and unrealistic.

I want to see a unit mix schedule that includes the current monthly rent, current monthly rent per SF amount, and total actual monthly rent, *next to* the broker's pro forma monthly rents which I will consider, but not rely on, until I can verify the information.

The current actual monthly rent is $49,820 or $.87 per SF. The pro forma monthly rent is $54,320 or $.95 per SF. This represents a difference of $4,500 or $54,000 per annum. Please be advised that on many occasions the unit mix schedule will only show the pro forma rent information and not the actual rent information. I can't stress enough how important it is to focus on the current actual monthly rents the property is receiving and not the pro forma monthly rents that the broker has projected.

⇨ *Your focus should be on the actual monthly rents the property is receiving and not the Pro-forma rents that the broker often presents. The broker's Pro-forma monthly rent should be considered but not relied on until the amounts can be verified.*

Rent Comparables

An OM should include a detailed schedule of rents for comparable properties within a three- to four-mile radius from the property. I have found that most of the information in rent comparables is inaccurate. It may not be intentional, but the broker does not always have access to accurate information. Many rent comparable schedules do not factor in who pays the utilities, whether the individual units being compared have been upgraded or renovated, rent specials and concessions, or the amenities offered by the comparable property. Furthermore, advertisements from competing properties usually only highlight the asking rents, rent specials, and concessions and avoid disclosing other charges the tenant will be required to pay, such as utilities.

Additionally, almost all brokers subscribe to a service that tracks the asking rents of apartment complexes. The asking rents are often different from the actual rents. Many factors, such as current occupancy percentage, oversupply of units in the area, and other factors contribute to the actual rent that an owner charges.*

Sales Comparables

An OM should include a detailed schedule of sales for comparable properties sold during the past two years that are located within a three- to four-mile radius from the property. I have found that most of the information presented in these comparables is inaccurate because, as before, access to accurate information is often unavailable, especially in a non-disclosure state like Texas. Texas is a non-disclosure state so there are no published documents that show the actual sales price for a property. Large real estate brokerage companies often either share the information with each other or have the information because they were the broker or co-broker involved in the transaction. In many states, the sales price is public knowledge and can easily be found. Even with the information being readily available, many of the sale comparables

---

*See Appendix 2 – Rent Comparable Schedule.

don't take into consideration the physical condition of the property and various other factors. Additionally, often the comparisons are made based on the price per unit or per door method of valuation, which you have learned is not a prudent way of determining property value. Remember, no two properties are the same! Each and every property is unique, with different potentials, different tax assessments, different physical conditions, amenities, etc.

Floor Plans and Property Photos

An OM should also include photos of both the interior and exterior sections of the property. Many, but not all, OMs also include copies of the various units' floor plans.

Financial Information

An OM should contain the current income and expenses for the *actual* trailing 12-month period, which is usually a fiscal year. Additionally, the OM usually includes a 5-year cash flow projection prepared by the broker based upon the broker's pro forma income and operating expenses. These amounts may not be based on the actual revenues or the property's historic operating expenses, but rather upon an industry-determined fixed dollar amount per unit.

Below is an example of a broker's assumptions and adjustments that supported their financial projections of income and operating expenses presented in the OM.

Income

Pro forma rents were raised by $175 per month on all floors to reflect rental comps in the area.

Expenses

- Payroll expense was decreased to $1,200 per unit to reflect market averages.

- Administrative expenses were set at $200 per unit in order to reflect market averages.

- Repair and maintenance expenses were reduced to $400 per unit.

- Turnover expenses were increased to $175 per unit in order to reflect a stabilized property.

Please be aware that these assumptions may not reflect the reality of the property's operations. As mentioned above, no two properties are the same!

Street Success Concepts to Remember

1. The following four steps should be taken and mastered in the following order before you close and take title to a property.

   Step 1 - Analyzing the Offering Memorandum - Chapter 3

   Step 2 - Preparing a Letter of Intent (LOI) - Chapter 4

   Step 3 - Signing a Contract of Sale - N/A

   Step 4 - Performing Due Diligence - Chapters 5 and 6

2. The OM should be viewed as a snapshot or guide to the property, nothing more. Use it to gauge your initial interest to determine if you wish to go forward.

3. Evaluating the OM is performed before you (i) submit an LOI, (ii) negotiate a contract of sale, and (iii) start to perform your due diligence.

4. When analyzing an OM, always remember that the broker is not your friend and doesn't have your best interests at heart. They represent the seller, not the buyer.

5. You must conduct your own independent investigation and due diligence (Step 4) to verify all information contained in the OM.

6. An owner would be foolish not to use a real estate broker to sell their property. A key to obtaining the highest price for a property is to market it to as many prospective purchasers as possible, even if a broker fee must be paid. On the other hand, when purchasing a property, the ideal situation is to purchase the property "off-market" because it provides you the opportunity to avoid direct competition and a possible bidding war.

7. The seller's initial asking price is subject to change depending on market conditions and is not written in stone.

8. No two properties are the same; every property is different with different potentials, different tax assessments, different physical conditions, and different amenities etc. Determining property value by the price per unit method is not a prudent way of determining property value.

9. One acre = 43,600 SF.

10. It is imperative that the parking ratio is adequate to service the existing tenancy and for you to know if there is a parking problem in the area.

11. During the past 10 years, great success has been achieved by purchasing Class C garden apartment communities located in Class A and B areas and repositioning them to Class B properties. This is what we will be focusing on in this book.

12. Generally, garden apartment units located on higher floors may be a little harder to rent and thus may demand lower rents than those units on the first floor. This is because of the convenience factor. Carrying packages up three or four flights of stairs, especially with an older tenancy, isn't desirable. This factor should be taken in consideration when projecting rental income.

13. The larger the unit, the lower rent per SF you will obtain, and the more it will cost to upgrade the unit with carpeting and/or wood flooring.

Additionally, units with excess space will often cause over-occupancy and illegal subletting, which translates to increased utility costs and higher wear and tear on the unit.

14. The infrastructure of an older building and its systems may be compromised unless the property has been well-maintained and/or renovated. The repair or replacement of any of these systems can be extremely expensive; therefore, if the property has been well-maintained and/or renovated it's a big plus.

15. Physical occupancy percentage represents the percentage of units that are physically occupied by tenants at any given point in time. Leased percentage represents the number of signed leases at a given point in time. The leased percentage may be higher or lower than the physical occupancy percentage.

16. Areas where vacant land is scarce and/or strict zoning laws make it very difficult to allow new multi-family apartment communities to be constructed are known in the industry as having a "high barrier of entry." High barriers of entry areas limit competition, which stabilizes occupancy rates and leads to higher rent growth and will demand lower cap rates.

17. The difference between the gross building size and the net rentable SF is known in the industry as the loss factor and is usually attributable to common areas, such as hallways, walls, etc., for which rent is not charged.

18. It's important to know the beating the roof has taken. For example, in Texas hailstorms are a common event, so if the roof has taken a beating it might not last the estimated useful life of 10-15 years and the property will certainly experience leaks as the roof ages.

19. Aluminum wiring in the units is a fire hazard. In lieu of rewiring the entire building, special aluminum contact electrical outlets and switches

may be used in conjunction with the existing aluminum wire. Copper wiring is very expensive but is the best wiring to have, so if the property has copper wiring, it's a big advantage.

20. Always try to have the tenant open their own separate account with the utility company. If the tenant doesn't pay their reimbursement, the owner will be absorbing the tenant's utility cost because it is ultimately the owner's responsibility to pay the utility bill.

21. To determine the correct zoning for a property lot size, density, zoning class and height restrictions must all be considered in determining the potential for additional construction on the site.

22. A key to operating any successful property is to reduce turnover. Remember each time a tenant vacates you will need to hire a cleaning company, repair and/or replace the carpet, pay rental agent fees, offer rent specials, and suffer rent loss until a new tenant takes occupancy. This is not the case when a tenant renews their lease.

23. Good school systems that are nearby or near public transportation that are readily available are tremendous draws to a community and lead to much less resident turnover. Low resident turnover is one key to lowering operating costs and a higher NOI which translates to higher property value.

24. Your focus should be on the actual monthly rents the property is receiving and not the pro forma rents that the broker often presents. The broker's pro forma monthly rent should be considered but not relied on until the amounts can be verified.

CHAPTER 4

THE LETTER OF INTENT (LOI)

THIS CHAPTER WILL provide you with an introduction to the Letter of Intent ("LOI") and the information it should contain. Remember, you must master the basic real estate fundamentals before you start purchasing property.

Chapter 3 - Analyzing the Offering Memorandum - simply taught you what information should be included in a comprehensive OM that should serve as a snapshot or guide to the property and nothing more.

Remember, the OM is a marketing document prepared by the broker who represents the seller, not the buyer.

You also learned to perform some pre-due diligence procedures to determine if you wish to go forward with submitting an *offer* to the seller to purchase the property. The offer made to the seller is called a Letter of Intent (LOI).

The LOI is a non-binding document that simply expresses your intent to purchase the property and serves to set forth the basic terms and conditions upon which the buyer and seller will enter into a much more definitive document known as the contract of sale ("Contract").

The LOI is subject to subsequent verification of a litany of information until you are satisfied with its accuracy. Verification procedures are performed both during LOI negotiations and after the contract is executed.

At the time you submit the LOI, you must be cognizant of the fact that you haven't yet verified the information contained in the OM and should not rely on such information until verified by performing comprehensive due diligence on the materials.

The LOI is usually submitted on the buyer's stationery and is sent to either the broker or seller by email and/or registered mail.

I write my own LOIs, but you can always consult with the broker or an attorney. Make the LOI look as professional as possible, as your submission will be viewed as a reflection of your experience and professionalism.

The next step after you have obtained a fully executed LOI is to negotiate the contract. From my many years of experience, I have learned what specific issues, though important to me, will trigger the most resistance from the seller. I use the LOI to draw attention to those issues and try to resolve them before I spend time and money on further negotiating the contract. Substantial time and money are expended by both the buyer and seller from the start of negotiating the LOI to obtaining an executed contract. Both the buyer and seller are taking risks and gambling that the transaction will ultimately close. Generally, neither party has any idea about how ethical or how difficult either of them may be with regard to the negotiations.

Remember that the next step after you have obtained a fully executed LOI is going forward and negotiating the contract. Try to identify what specific issues, though important to you, may trigger the most resistance from the seller. Then use the LOI to draw attention to those issues and try to resolve them before you spend time and money on further negotiating the contract.

Be careful not to scare the seller off with unreasonable demands. However, some fundamental issues should be discussed and agreed to and subsequently included in the contract. The most common of these points include, but are not limited to, the following:

- Purchase price
- Amount of the earnest deposit a.k.a contract deposit required, that it's refundable, and/or when it will "go hard" (become non-refundable)
- Who chooses the title company?
- Time allowed for the due diligence period
- Time allowed for the closing
- Records that will be provided by the seller
- Mortgage contingency and time constraints
- Who is responsible for the broker's commission?

A seller is not going to go through the trouble and expense of having his attorney prepare a contract before the basic economic terms and conditions are previously negotiated and agreed upon.

I have included an LOI example in the appendix using a 2010 purchase of a large garden complex located in Dallas The LOI above was prepared in 2010, which was a strong buyers' market. I requested many documents and records after the execution of the LOI but before the execution of a contract and the beginning of the due diligence period. As a result, I was able to negotiate very favorable terms that I don't believe would be possible in the current strong seller's market. This gave me a jump start on performing my due diligence, but in the current strong seller's market, most sellers will not provide this information until the execution of the contract and the start of the due diligence period. It is recommended that you review the LOI example in the appendix before continuing.*

Following is specific information that should be included in any LOI you submit. The example in the appendix is fairly comprehensive and provides a good example to learn from. However, if you're purchasing a smaller property, your LOI doesn't need to be as comprehensive and some of the provisions may not need such detail.

Introductory Paragraph

*This Letter of Intent (the "**Letter of Intent**") will outline the terms and conditions under which **Rolling Cash Realty, Inc. 1430 Broadway - 14th Floor New York, NY 10018** (the "**Purchaser**") is interested in negotiating for a definitive written agreement (the "**Contract**") to purchase from **XXXXXX LLC** (the "**Seller**") the fee simple title to the land and the improvements thereon and the appurtenances thereto, and all personal property owned by Seller and used or useful in connection with the operation and maintenance of the improvements, referred to as **XXXX XXXX Ave. Dallas, TX 75214 a.k.a, XXXXX Apartments** (the "**Property**"). Based upon information previously made available to Purchaser and our preliminary evaluations, and subject to the satisfaction of conditions precedent set forth herein, the Purchaser is prepared to negotiate for a definitive transaction with respect to the Property and to proceed to consider this transaction on the following terms.*

The introductory paragraph includes and identifies the following:

- Name and address of the *Purchaser*
- Name and address of the *Seller*
- Name and address of the *Property*

---

*See Appendix 1- Example of a comprehensive LOI.

- A disclaimer that the LOI will serve only as a basis for determining whether to go forward and prepare a definitive agreement known as the *contract of sale.*

Even though I didn't do so in my introductory paragraph above, it's a good idea to include the following information in your LOI in order to avoid any future misinterpretation:

- Number of units
- Type of property, i.e.: garden apartments, student housing, etc.
- Address of each individual building and the name of the community, if applicable
- Number of buildings and number of stories
- Number of acres
- The year, or range of years, built
- Number of rentable SF

Example:

Property Description: A 450-unit, garden apartment complex, known as 5200 5201, 5202 & 5203 Gaston Ave. Dallas, TX 75214 a.k.a, the Apex Apartments, sitting on 6 acres of land and consisting of four (4), six (6) story buildings built in 1980 with approximately 330,000 rentable square feet.

If your offer includes other assets to be included in your purchase besides the property, always remember to specifically include them in the LOI. For example, an income-producing sign on the top of the building, a small tract of land across the street from the property, certain equipment, etc.

Purchase Price

The purchase price for the Property shall be $12,000,000 (the "Purchase Price"). Purchaser shall acquire the Property free and clear of any mortgage or *other indebtedness or liens. The Purchase Price, plus or minus prorations, shall be paid by wire transfer on the Closing Date (as hereinafter defined).*

The above paragraph means that you're purchasing the property without assuming the seller's existing mortgage or requesting that the seller provide you with financing. Another industry-wide way of saying this is that you're purchasing the property for $12,000,000, **all cash**.

Example:

Purchase Price: The purchase price for the Property shall be $12,000,000, payable all cash at closing.

The term *all cash* doesn't mean that the buyer is paying the seller with a suitcase full of currency. Unless the transaction involves a 1031 tax-free exchange or a large buyer flush with cash, the net proceeds from a mortgage will usually be used by the buyer, along with a cash down payment, to pay the purchase price. The term all cash generally means that the buyer will not be required to assume the seller's mortgage, nor will the seller provide the buyer with a mortgage.

In the real estate industry, the term all cash generally means that the buyer will not be required to assume the seller's mortgage, nor will the seller provide the buyer with a mortgage.

Purchase Money Mortgage

A mortgage that's given to the buyer by the seller at closing is known as a purchase money mortgage. If the seller is giving the buyer a purchase money mortgage, that should be included in the LOI in *both* the introductory and the purchase price paragraphs. In that case, there is no need for a mortgage contingency paragraph (discussed below) because there will not be any contingency about obtaining a mortgage.

Example:

Purchase Price: The purchase price for the property shall be $12,000,000, subject to the seller providing the buyer with a purchase money mortgage equal to 75% of the purchase price. Said purchase money mortgage shall have a term of 5 years and is payable with interest at 5% per annum along with amortization based upon a 25-year payout.

Contingencies

Many times, a contingency will present itself whereby the purchase price needs to be adjusted up or down, depending upon an event taking place or not. In that case, you will need to insert additional language into the LOI.

Example:

Purchase Price: The purchase price will be $8,000,000 or $7,600,000, depending upon whether income from the two rooftop antennas is excluded from the transaction because the seller was not able to obtain the necessary easements. Purchaser will notify the seller of its intentions within 20 days after execution of this letter.

Closing Date

The date which is thirty (30) days after the expiration of the Due Diligence Period (or such earlier date as both parties may mutually agree) (the "Closing Date"), provided that if such date is not a business day in Dallas, Texas, the Closing shall be held on the next business day thereafter. Buyer may extend the Closing Date for one (1) additional period of thirty (30) days, by written notice to Seller on or before the originally scheduled Closing Date and the deposit of Additional Earnest Money of $50,000 with the Escrow Agent.

Like the due diligence period, the seller will usually try to limit the time period for the closing. In this crazy seller's market, I have seen sellers demand closing periods of 30 days with due diligence periods of 10 – 15 days or no due diligence period at all. Please keep in mind that you need as much time as possible to close. Situations may arise that are beyond your control. Examples are bank delays, delays in receiving third-party reports, title problems, etc. If you don't have enough time to close, you'll be at the seller's mercy and under tremendous pressure because your earnest deposit a.k.a. contract deposit will be at risk, not to mention the legal and other expenses you have already incurred.

Keep in mind that you will need as much time as possible to close. Many times, situations arise which are beyond your control. If you don't have enough time to close, you could lose your earnest deposit and still be liable for the expenses you've incurred to date. Always try to negotiate for an option to extend the closing date by an extra 15 to 30 days in return for increasing the earnest deposit and agreeing for it to go hard (become non-refundable) after the expiration of the due diligence period.

The most common scenario I see in the industry is a 30-day due diligence period and closing 30 days later. However, I always try to negotiate for an option to extend the closing date by an extra 15 to 30 days in return for increasing the earnest deposit and agreeing for it to go hard (become non-refundable) after the expiration of the due diligence period.

Example:

Buyer may extend the Closing for one (1) additional 30-day period by depositing $75,000.00 additional Earnest Money with the Title Company ("Additional Earnest Deposit"). The Additional Earnest Deposit shall be non-refundable except for Seller's default and other applicable provisions of the Contract. The Additional Earnest Deposit shall be applied to the Purchase Price at Closing.

Real Estate Commissions

Seller shall be responsible for all commissions that may be payable to brokers and shall indemnify, defend, and hold harmless Purchaser therefrom.

Always include in your LOI whether the buyer or seller will be responsible for any broker commissions that may be due. If there is no broker, then the LOI should state that there is no broker. The LOI should also state that the parties should mutually indemnify each other against any broker's claim that may arise as a result of the transaction.

Customarily the seller is responsible for the broker's commission. However, buyer's brokers may represent the purchaser directly. In these cases, it is the purchaser's responsibility to pay the broker commission. On various occasions, I have seen the seller negotiate to have the purchaser pay the commission, even though the broker is representing the seller.

Potential Problem

When properties contain an office or store tenant, there may be a contingent broker commission due in the future. Many broker commission agreements contain a provision that entitles the broker to receive a commission if the tenant renews their lease and/or exercises any remaining options available to them. It is possible that three to five years after you close, the tenant will exercise their option, and you will receive an invoice from the broker for a commission.

Keep this in mind when you perform your due diligence. This may be another negotiating point.

Earnest Deposit

The earnest deposit is also known as in the industry as earnest money or more commonly, the contract deposit.

For purposes of this LOI discussion, we will use the term earnest deposit.

Earnest Deposit *$150,000 shall be deposited in a segregated interest bearing escrow account (together with earnings thereon, the "Earnest Deposit") with xxxxxx Title Company, or any other title company as determined by Purchaser, ("Title*

Company"), within 3 business days after acceptance of the Contract. The Earnest Deposit shall be held by the Title Company and applied toward the Purchase Price at closing, or remitted to either Seller or Purchaser prior to closing, as specified in the Contract. The Earnest Deposit shall be fully refundable prior to the expiration of the Due Diligence Period (as hereinafter defined). After the Due Diligence Period, any refund of the Earnest Deposit shall be determined pursuant to the Contract.

The Amount of the Earnest Deposit

The amount of the earnest deposit can range from 1% to 10% of the purchase price and depends upon such factors as customary percentages in the area, purchase price, type of property, demand for properties, etc. However, it's always open to negotiation.

Customary Percentages

In Texas, the customary earnest deposit percentages are much lower than those of New York (especially Manhattan), independent of purchase price, type of property, demand for properties, etc. A property selling for $5,000,000 in Manhattan might command a percentage of 10% of the purchase price. A property in Texas for the same price might only command a percentage of 2% to 3% of the purchase price. Generally, the earnest deposit percentage will decrease as the purchase price increases.

Type of Property

This is also a factor in determining the percentage of earnest deposit required. For example, shopping centers may require a percentage of 5% to 10% of the purchase price, while multi-family properties require lower percentages. No rhyme or reason for this. It's just the way it is.

➡ *In the current seller's market (evidenced by extremely high demand for properties) sellers are able to command higher earnest deposit percentages than those in a buyer's market.*

⇨ *The amount of earnest deposit is always negotiable, ranging from 1%
to 10%. of the purchase price and depends upon such factors as customary
percentages in the area, purchase price, type of property, demand for properties, etc.*

In the LOI example above, the earnest deposit was only $150,000
(1.25%) for a property with a purchase price of $12,000,000. This was the
result of 2010 being a strong buyer's market. I couldn't get away with such
a low percentage in the current seller's market.

Real-Life Example:

Last year I was negotiating with a seller to purchase a 250-unit garden
apartment complex that required an earnest deposit of 4% of the
purchase price ($480,000). Not only was that high, but the owner
wanted it to be non-refundable day one. This meant that if I didn't
ultimately purchase the property, regardless of what negative information I learned while performing due diligence, I would lose my entire
earnest deposit of $480,000. I told the seller that his demand was
ridiculous, and I passed on the opportunity. I subsequently learned
that another prospective purchaser: a hedge fund, gave the owner the
non-refundable earnest deposit of $480,000 and ultimately didn't
purchase the property. They simply wrote off the loss as a cost of
doing business.

Sellers want a large earnest deposit to make sure the buyer is serious about
purchasing the property according to the provisions contained in the executed LOI and subsequent contract. The seller does not want the buyer to
tie up the property while looking to flip it for a profit. The seller wants the
buyer to have some money at risk (*skin in the game*) while incurring the
cost of preparing a contract, assembling all the documents for the buyer's
due diligence, etc.

Always make sure to include in the LOI that the earnest deposit shall
be refundable in the event you don't purchase the property, subject to

meeting certain negotiated time periods, such as the expiration of the due diligence period.

Earnest Deposit Going Hard

When the earnest deposit, or portions of it, becomes non-refundable, it is known in the industry as *going hard*. Look out for the time periods when your money is at risk of going hard. I want to stress that I always try to negotiate for as much time as possible for due diligence, mortgage contingency, and closing periods.

Always make sure to be aware of the time periods when your money is at risk of becoming hard (non-refundable) and always try to negotiate for the most time possible during the due diligence, closing, and mortgage contingency periods.

When is the Earnest Deposit Due?

Generally, within three *business* days after you receive a fully executed contract. Make sure that the LOI and contract state the number of *business days,* not simply the number of days. For example, if you don't state the number of business days and you receive an executed contract on a Friday, you will need to have the title company receive the earnest deposit by Monday. If you state three business days, then the funds won't be due until Wednesday of the following week.

Always make sure that the LOI and contract state the number of business days until the earnest deposit is due.

Interest Bearing Account

The time between sending the earnest deposit to the title company and the time you close can be two to three months or even more. Always request that your earnest deposit be held by the title company in an FDIC-insured interest-bearing account. Why not earn interest? In a high interest rate environment, the interest on a large earnest deposit may not be so nominal.

Always request that your earnest deposit be held by the title company in an FDIC-insured interest-bearing account.

Closing Costs

Seller shall be responsible for all basic title charges of Purchaser's owner's policy of title insurance, updating of existing survey expenses, transfer fees, documentary stamp taxes, recording fees, transfer taxes, escrow fees, costs incurred to repay any liens and all other expenses due or incurred in connection with the transaction. Purchaser and Seller shall each pay the fees and expenses of their respective legal counsel incurred in connection with the transaction. Any interest, taxes, rents, service contracts, operating expenses, etc. will be prorated as of the date of the closing as is customary for commercial real estate transactions in Dallas, TX.

Always include in the LOI that the buyer and seller shall each pay their respective legal fees incurred in connection with the transaction, as well as any prepaid interest, taxes, rents, service contracts, operating expenses, etc., that will be prorated as of the date of the closing.

Title costs are discussed in detail later in the chapter. With regard to survey costs, the seller usually provides the buyer with their existing survey, and the buyer, at their cost, usually pays for it to be updated.

Prorate Prepaid Expenses

The following example shows the importance of prorating prepaid expenses. Real estate taxes are one of the largest operating expenses of a property. Many states require real estate taxes to be prepaid on a quarterly, semi-annual, or annual basis. The title company prorates these expenses and itemizes them on the settlement statement at the closing.

Real-Life Example:

Assume that real estate taxes are $100,000 per year and are ***prepaid*** on a semi-annual basis on Jan 1, 2020, and July 1, 2020. Further assume that you closed on December 10, 2020. This would mean that the July 1, 2020, installment of $50,000, which was paid by the seller, would be prepaid for the period of July 1, 2020 to December 31, 2020. Because you closed on December 10, 2020, by prorating this expense the ***seller*** would be due a credit at closing for the taxes due during the buyer's ownership period of 21 days, computed as follows:

> Real Estate Taxes paid ($50,000) for the period of 7/1/20 to 12/31/20 = 183 days.
>
> Per Diem amount = $50,000/183 days = $273.22 per day.
>
> Seller Credit Due = 10 days x $273.22 = $2,732.20.

The numbers can be much larger depending upon when you close. For example, if you closed on August 10, 2020, the seller would have prepaid the taxes during the buyer's period of ownership of August 11, 2020 to December 31, 2020, or 142 days and the ***seller*** would be due a credit of $38,797.24, computed as follows:

> Seller Credit Due = 142 days x $273.22 = $38,797.24.

Another example would be if the property received a $10,000 oil delivery on December 1, 2020, and you closed on December 20, 2020. This expense should also be prorated, and the seller would be entitled to a credit of approximately $6,452 ($10,000/31 days x 20 Days). Keep in mind that the prorated credit could go the other way, and the buyer could receive the credit. It depends on what period the expense is for and the date you actually close.

Other items that are usually prorated are prepaid rents, service contracts, utility bills, etc. The title company usually performs the proration calculations, but you must be cognizant of what items should be prorated.

Inspection of the Property

After the acceptance of this Letter of Intent and through the Closing Date, the Purchaser and its agents and consultants shall have access to the Property and the books and records relating to the ownership and operation of the Property and shall be permitted to make, at Purchaser's sole cost, such inspections, studies, reports, tests, copies and verifications as they shall deem necessary or appropriate to determine, in Purchaser's sole and absolute discretion, whether the Property is satisfactory. The Purchaser agrees to indemnify and hold Seller harmless from and against any claims or damages arising by reason of such inspections, provided that such indemnity and hold harmless obligations shall not extend to (a) the mere discovery of any condition at the Property (e.g., existing environmental conditions), or (b) any claim or damage arising from any act or omission of Seller.

It is important to let the seller know ahead of time what type of testing procedures you are planning, especially if the testing will be invasive, such as boring and soil testing, inspection of buried oil tanks, etc. If the seller agrees, he will probably insert language requiring the buyer to restore the premises to the condition before the testing.

Due Diligence Period

The due diligence period is also known in the industry as the feasibility inspection period, the review period, and the feasibility period.

For purposes of this LOI discussion, we use the term "Due Diligence Period."

The Purchaser shall undertake a due diligence review with respect to the Property. To facilitate such review, Seller shall, within ten (10) business days from the date hereof, provide to Purchaser the information listed on Exhibit A hereto. As a condition precedent to closing the Contract, Purchaser shall have approved, among other things:

a. The condition of title to the Property. <u>Your attorney should take care of this.</u>

b. The form of title insurance policy and the company issuing the same; the policy shall contain, to the extent available, such endorsements and affirmative coverage's as may be required by Purchaser or its lender. The Title Company shall also deliver to Purchaser or its counsel copies of all recorded documents affecting or relating to the title to the Property. <u>Your attorney should take care of this.</u>

c. The survey of the Property, which shall be a current TLTA survey or ALTA survey. <u>Your attorney should take care of this.</u>

d. Leases, service contracts, warranties, licenses, permits and all other agreements relating to the Property.

e. "As-built" plans and specifications for the Property.

f. The condition of the improvements and the machinery, equipment and other personal property owned by Seller and used in connection with the ownership and maintenance of the Property.

The Purchaser shall notify Seller in writing of its approval or disapproval of the results of its due diligence review of the Property within forty five (45) days after execution of the Contract (said 45-day period is called the "<u>Due Diligence Period</u>") provided that if such date is not a business day in Dallas, Texas, the Due Diligence Period shall be on the next business day thereafter. The obligation of the Purchaser to complete its due diligence review within the Due Diligence Period shall be contingent on the Purchaser's timely receipt of all required information. The Due Diligence Period shall be extended for an additional thirty (30) days to the extent a material issue has been identified by Purchaser during the initial [forty five (45)] day period. If Purchaser does not elect in writing to move forward with the transaction on or prior to the last day of the Due Diligence Period, then

Purchaser shall be deemed to have elected to terminate the Contract and receive a refund of the Earnest Deposit.

I want to highlight the following:

- Make sure that the due diligence period states the number of *business days*, not just the number of days in the LOI and contract.
- In the first paragraph of this section of the LOI above, it states that *"Seller shall, within ten (10) business days from the date hereof, provide to Purchaser the information listed on Exhibit A hereto."* This means that the due diligence period (45 days in this instance) doesn't start until you receive all the information you requested in your LOI.
- The above paragraph of the LOI also states that, *"The obligation of the Purchaser to complete its due diligence review within the Due Diligence Period shall be contingent on the Purchaser's timely receipt of all required information."*

Remember that the LOI and the contract should state that the due diligence period does not start until the seller provides the purchaser with all the information requested in the LOI and subsequently, the contract.

Exhibit A:

- Three full years of the most recent financial statements, along with a year-to-date financial statement.
- The most recent capital and operating budgets.
- Copies of all leases now in effect, with current amendments and modifications and all related correspondence.
- All agreements, easements, permits, licenses, contracts (including service), ground leases, or agreements governing parking.
- All environmental studies.
- All engineering studies, including but not limited to, all structural, plumbing, electrical, and mechanical studies.

- A schedule of personal property.
- As-built plans.
- Any zoning ordinances related to the site.
- The most recent survey along with any soil tests, topographical maps, etc.
- A current accounts receivable schedule.
- The most recent appraisal, if any.
- Any other information reasonably requested by the purchaser.

Often the seller will not have all of the requested information. It is your duty to request the information and ascertain if the subsequent information from the seller will enable you to satisfy your due diligence requirements. By requesting the information in the LOI, you may receive an early warning signal of some existing or potential pitfalls you may need to overcome before you incur additional expenses once the contract is executed.

It is during the due diligence period that the buyer performs various due diligence procedures to verify information of the property's books, records, reports, physical condition, etc. to determine the property's acceptability for investment.

Key Points to Remember

- The seller will usually try to limit the time period of the due diligence period. In this crazy seller's market, I have seen sellers demand due diligence periods of only five to 10 days or no due diligence period at all. Unfortunately, buyers desperate to find properties often prostitute themselves and ignore the traditional methods of purchasing property, so they try to acquire property at any cost.
- The most common due diligence period I have seen is 30 days, but remember that the 30-day countdown commences the first business day following execution of the contract by both purchaser and seller

and receipt of all due diligence materials. The required materials should be stated in the LOI and the contract.

- If, for any reason, the buyer in its sole discretion desires to terminate the contract prior to the end of the due diligence period, the buyer should be able to receive their earnest deposit back, including any interest earned.

The due diligence period commences the first business day following execution of the contract by both purchaser and seller and receipt of all due diligence materials (as described in the contract). Additionally, the buyer in its sole discretion and at any time before the end of the due diligence period can ask for their earnest deposit back along with any interest.

- At the end of the due diligence period, if the buyer determines, at its sole discretion, to continue with the purchase of the property, all of the earnest money will now go hard (become non-refundable), except for a breach by the seller of the contract.

Title Insurance and the Title Company

The LOI example above mentions in the introduction that the purchaser *"is interested in negotiating for a definitive written agreement (the "Contract") to purchase from XXXXXXX LLC (the "Seller") the fee simple title to the land and the improvements thereon and the appurtenances thereto, and all personal property owned by Seller."*

Fee Simple Title

It is your attorney's job to make sure you receive fee simple title. Fee simple title is the most common way real estate is owned and represents the most complete ownership interest you can have in real property. Fee simple title is absolute title to land, free of any conditions, limitations, restrictions, or other claims against title.

Whenever a property is acquired, the buyer must always obtain title insurance for <u>both the fee (the property) and any mortgage on the property.</u> A bank or any other lending institution will always require that a title policy is obtained ensuring the legitimacy of the property's title. The title company will issue a report known as the title policy which provides title insurance that protects the lender and buyer against lawsuits regarding the title.

The responsibility for the cost for title charges is negotiable, but in Texas, it is customary for the seller to pay the cost for basic charges of the purchaser's owner's policy of title insurance, The buyer would be responsible for any special endorsements required by their lender and also for the costs of any escrow fees, recording costs, etc.

Title Costs

These are statutory in most states and can be very expensive. In Texas, the rates for title insurance are issued by the state insurance commission. Below is an example of the title insurance cost for both the property (fee) and the mortgage.

Title Insurance Example:

Assume you purchase a property at a cost of $3,000,000 and obtain a mortgage of $2,250,000. The cost for title insurance, as determined by a premium schedule from the Texas insurance commission, would be as follows:

Owners Policy (Fee)	$14,981
Mortgage Cost	200
Total	**$15,181**

In most states, if you purchase title insurance simultaneously for both the owner's policy and the mortgage, you receive a discount on the cost for the mortgage coverage. However, if you don't purchase title insurance simultaneously for both, then the title insurance cost for the mortgage will be computed at a significantly higher rate.

Real-Life Example:

Assume you purchase a property for $3,000,000, all cash. A month later you obtain a mortgage in the amount of $2,250,000. In this case, instead of $200 for the mortgage premium you will pay an additional 50% of the owner's policy premium or $7,491 ($14,981 x 50%). The total title costs will be $22,472 instead of $15,181.

Your attorney is responsible for dealing with the requirement of obtaining title insurance for you, as well as raising any concerns or objections with the seller's existing title policy. For example, the title policy may list exceptions that aren't covered. Examples are certain easements, matters of survey, encroachments, etc. If the title company has any exceptions that won't be covered under the policy, then the purchaser will need to ascertain the risks associated with the exception. These exceptions will potentially "cloud title" to the property, and even though you elect to take the risk of closing, it doesn't mean that another potential purchaser would. This can affect the property's marketability.

The Function of the Title Company

To ensure clear title, the title company does a complete examination of the property records, known as a title search. The title company looks to ensure that the seller who is claiming to own the property actually does in fact own the property. The title company searches for outstanding liens, mortgages, judgments, or unpaid taxes that may be attached to the property. The title company also looks for easements, restrictions, or leases that may impact the legal ownership of the property.

Besides issuing title insurance, the title company acts as the intermediary and takes charge of the closing process. It gathers and aggregates all the necessary documents from the lender, attorneys, buyer, and seller. Once a closing date is selected, all funds and documentation for the closing are sent to the title company for processing. The title company provides other services as well including, but not limited to, the following:

- Reviewing the sales contract for accuracy and completeness.
- Maintaining the earnest deposit and other escrow accounts, which contain the funds required to finalize the purchase and ensuring that such escrow is only utilized for closing costs.
- Examining the associated title and clearing any claims or liens against the property to ensure that the buyer receives a legitimate and clear property.
- Preparing a settlement statement at closing showing the waterfall of receipts and disbursements to the seller and buyer.
- Preparing the closing, the title company provides the necessary documents, explaining the stipulations to both the buyer and seller, verifying tax payments, and distributing any associated funds to the rightful party during the closing.
- Receiving the required funds from the lender and buyer, paying the necessary expenses contained in the settlement statement, and disbursing the funds required for the purchase price to the seller.

Choosing the Title Company

Sometimes the title company is referred to as the *abstract company*, but there is a difference between them. An abstract company researches a property and does the title report. The title company is the underwriter and actually provides the insurance. They can be one and the same or separate companies.

Generally, the *buyer* pays for the title insurance policy and chooses the title company for the transaction, but on other occasions, the seller and/or attorneys try to encourage or force their title company onto the buyer, and it becomes a negotiation point. There are various legitimate reasons for this including, but not limited to, the following:

- A strong relationship with a title company makes it easier to work through potential problems that may arise.
- Some title companies are more familiar and sophisticated with the type of property being purchased.
- Local title companies may be more familiar with the local authorities which may be needed to rectify potential problems.
- The seller may feel more confident knowing their title company is holding the earnest money and is in control of its final destination.
- Certain escrows may require a strong relationship, which may limit the amount of the escrow required by the title company in certain situations.

Title insurance is an extremely competitive business. Because title fees are statutory, the most popular way title companies get business is to wine and dine their customers. Title companies may provide the best tickets to events, send clients on free vacations, and provide other gifts and incentives to obtain and retain business. As a result, a seller or attorney will often try and push for their title company.

Since title insurance fees are state-regulated, you should always fight for the largest and most reputable title company. Forget about the free tickets.

There is a federal law (Section 9 of the Real Estate Settlement Procedures Act, "RESPA") that prohibits a seller from requiring a buyer to purchase title insurance from any particular title company if the buyer is paying for the title insurance.

Never use a title company based in a different state than where the property is located for the transaction. Many times, a local title company will have better contacts and familiarity with the laws and authorities of that state.

Real-Life Example:

The owner of a New York-based title company presented an off-market deal to purchase a property located in Texas. The title company was also acting as the broker for the property and informed us that the seller lived in another country. After agreeing on the purchase price and various other terms and conditions, we prepared an LOI and sent it to the owner for signature. He immediately replied that because the sellers didn't reside in the country, his company must be used as the title company. My spider-sense told me that something wasn't kosher, and I told him that unless we chose the title company, we wouldn't do the deal. He complained to my partners that I was going to ruin this potentially great deal because I was being unreasonable. I finally blamed it on the lender and got a letter from them stating that they wanted a Texas-based title company. He relented, and we used a large national title company that subsequently issued the title policy. Some complicated issues came up, but eventually, we closed. Six months later, I received a lawsuit claiming that the seller didn't have the authority to sell the property. Apparently, some documents had been forged, but it wasn't my problem because I had obtained title insurance. The title company that issued the policy had to defend against the lawsuit.

Financing Condition

The financing condition period is also known in the industry as the mortgage contingency period.

For purposes of this LOI discussion, we will use the term "Mortgage Contingency Period."

The obligation of Purchaser to close the acquisition of the Property is conditioned upon Purchaser receiving third-party financing for no less than 75% of the Purchase Price on terms and conditions satisfactory to Purchaser. In the event Purchaser fails to receive third-party financing satisfactory to Purchaser at or prior to the closing (hereinafter defined), Purchaser may, in Purchaser's sole discretion, terminate the Contract by written notice to Seller delivered at or prior to the Closing.

Mortgage Contingency Percentage

Except for 1031 Tax Free Exchanges and large hedge funds and other investment companies flush with cash, most buyers will probably need to obtain a mortgage to acquire the property. It is extremely important that your LOI contains a mortgage contingency, which means that if you fail to obtain a *satisfactory mortgage,* you can cancel the contract and receive your earnest money back. The negotiation usually involves the amount of the mortgage, as it relates to the purchase price and the length of time for the contingency period. The seller will fight for a lower mortgage percentage, a higher down payment, and a shorter period. The purchaser will fight for a higher mortgage percentage, a lower down payment, and a longer period.

In today's seller's market, I have seen sellers limiting the mortgage contingency to only 60% to 70% of the purchase price or less. The seller may not feel confident that the purchaser can obtain a highly leveraged mortgage, and this may result in the seller being concerned about their ability to close.

Part Two to the Mortgage Contingency

The financing condition paragraph in the LOI above states the following: *"The obligation of Purchaser to close the acquisition of the Property is conditioned upon Purchaser receiving third party financing for no less than 75% of the Purchase Price <u>on terms and conditions satisfactory to Purchaser.</u>"*

"On terms and conditions satisfactory to <u>Purchaser</u>" means that not only is the mortgage contingency percentage an issue, but the other terms of the mortgage will also be an issue for the purchaser. For example, assume you obtain a mortgage for 75% of the purchase price, but the interest rate

and bank fees are extremely high, much more than you anticipated, and are unsatisfactory. This clause protects you from these contingencies and allows you to receive your earnest deposit back.

Banks currently require higher cash down payments and lower mortgage percentages. During the past 10 years, it was common for banks to lend 75% to 80% of the purchase price. It appears those days are gone for the foreseeable future. In fact, banks are requiring that the acceptable loan to value ratio be equal to the lesser of the purchase price or a percentage of the appraised value of the property, based upon a lender-approved third-party Member of the Appraisal Institute (MAI) appraisal as well as a pre-determined yield. MAI (Member of the Appraisal Institute) is a trade organization that monitors appraisers and holds them to a higher standard than appraisers who are simply licensed and not members of any monitoring organization. The industry acknowledges an appraiser with an MAI designation as being the most reputable.

Example:

Loan Amount: the lesser of: (1) $27,500,000, (2) 64.99% of the appraised value of the Property, based upon Lender approved, third-party MAI appraisal, and (3) the amount that would produce a Lender determined Pro-forma Year 1 debt yield of 7.55%.

Side Note: The loan to value ratio is known in the industry as leverage and will directly affect your cash on cash return on investment.

Mortgage Contingency Period

Another factor is the amount of time the seller will allow for the mortgage contingency period. Because of intense competition for properties in the current marketplace, sellers are demanding shorter mortgage contingency periods. However, sellers need to be reasonable and should be somewhat flexible since you can't control the pace at which lenders issue a commitment. All my LOI's contain a mortgage contingency, and I have, in the past, required a 75% loan to value percentage and a 30-day period to obtain a written commitment from the bank. Currently, I might need to be more flexible on the percentage, but I won't budge on not having a mortgage contingency clause in the contract with a reasonable time frame, and neither should you.

Always include a mortgage contingency clause in your LOI and contract. This clause should include (i) the mortgage percentage, (ii) the time allowed obtaining a written commitment from the lender, and (iii) that the contingency is subject to terms and conditions satisfactory to the purchaser.

The Contract

In addition to the items set forth above, the Contract shall provide, among other things, the following conditions precedent to the Purchaser's and Seller's obligation to consummate the transaction:

a. There shall be no material adverse change in any of the items approved by the Purchaser during the Due Diligence Period.

b. Seller shall deliver to Purchaser a current estoppel letter, satisfactory to Purchaser, from all tenants. Each tenant listed on the rent roll will be in occupancy of the Property and in full compliance with the terms and conditions of its lease.

c. On the Closing Date, unless otherwise required by Purchaser, all management and leasing agreements with respect to the Property shall be terminated and Seller shall be solely responsible for any termination fees, if any, due to the manager, all leasing commissions owing, and any accounts payable.

After the execution of the Contract, Seller or its agents shall not amend or modify any lease or other material contract and shall not enter into any new lease, material contract or obligate the Property for any capital commitment, without the Purchaser's prior written approval, which approval shall not be unreasonably withheld if Purchaser receives the written request therefore during the Due Diligence Period, and which approval otherwise may be withheld in Purchaser's sole discretion. Further, after the expiration of the Due Diligence Period, Seller shall not modify or enter into any service contracts or maintenance agreements or other licenses without the prior written consent of Purchaser (which consent may be withheld in Purchaser's sole discretion).

The above excerpt from the LOI above is self-explanatory. You want to ensure there are no material adverse change in any leases or contracts that existed or which you agreed to during the due diligence period. Examples are fictitious tenant leases, below-market leasing of units to related parties, renegotiated laundry contracts, etc.

Although not included in the above LOI, many times I will include in the due diligence section of the LOI a clause stating that the purchaser will have the right to review and approve all new leases, contracts, and any other agreements purchaser deems necessary to review during the due diligence period. Seller agrees to notify purchaser upon becoming aware of any potential or actual vacancies that occur during the due diligence period.

Try to put in the LOI the right to review and approve all new leases, contracts, and any other agreements during the due diligence period. For example, you don't want the seller leasing a unit at what you consider a below-market rent. Additionally, you wouldn't want the seller to enter into a new 10-year laundry contract without your input.

Termination of Service Contracts

In general, the seller will ask the buyer if they wish to assume or cancel various service contracts in force for the property. Sometimes the service contract will need to be assumed, but it is often the buyer's option to assume or cancel.

The following is an example of a provision you might want to include in your LOI:

Unless otherwise required by Purchaser, all management and leasing agreements with respect to the property shall be terminated and seller shall be solely responsible for any termination fees, if any, due to the manager, all leasing commissions owing, and any accounts payable.

Additionally, unless you agree, you want the right to cancel any existing management agreements, laundry contracts, etc. and for the seller to be solely responsible for any termination fees, if any. For example, you want the right to switch managing agents after you close.

Sometimes a contract has language that permits the contract to remain in effect after the closing. This is often seen with contracts for the laundry room, cable and internet company, signage companies, etc. These companies initially invested a large amount of capital which they wouldn't have a chance to recoup if their contract was terminated before expiration.

Estoppel Letter

If the property contains retail or other commercial tenants, the bank will require the borrower to obtain a certified letter from a tenant verifying the terms and conditions of the lease, stating that its current status is true and correct. This simple document is known as an estoppel letter. Retail and other commercial leases often contain a provision stating they are required to provide the owner with an estoppel letter upon request. Owners will often balk at this request because they may be hiding information that they don't want the buyer to know. Examples include, but are not limited to, fictitious leases at above-market rates, incorrect terms, unapproved assignments of the lease, etc. The best excuse you can use is to advise the owner that it will be a bank requirement for closing. estoppel letters are not normally required for residential tenants. Estoppel letters are usually prepared by the seller's attorney and sent to the tenants for completion and execution.

An estoppel letter is a certified letter from a tenant that verifies that the terms and conditions of the lease and its current status are true and correct.

If the property contains a retail or commercial tenant, always include an estoppel letter provision in your LOI.

The estoppel letter will generally require the tenant to confirm the following information:

- The start and end date of the lease
- Terms for renewals and/or extensions of the lease, including relevant dates
- The amount of base and additional rent due
- The amount of rent and additional rent that is in arrears
- Verification that the lease is unmodified and in full force and effect
- The amounts of any security deposits
- If the tenant is subletting any portion of the property

Withdrawal of Property from Market

During the term of this Letter of Intent and thereafter while the Contract remains in effect, Seller agrees not to market or show the Property for sale or enter into any agreement with respect to the sale of the Property.

I always try to require the seller to take the property off the market while we are in the process of negotiating the LOI and the contract. One reason is that I don't want the seller to get additional opportunities to receive higher price offers. This may cause the owner to be less cooperative while we are in negotiations or even give the owner motivation to try to break the contract after execution. Some owners will balk at this request because they want to ensure they have back-up buyers in case a contract is not executed.

Assignment

Purchaser shall have the right on or before the Closing Date to assign its rights and obligations hereunder and under the Contract to an affiliate of Purchaser.

This clause refers to the introductory paragraph where the name of the purchaser is provided. If I'm the seller, I don't want to give the buyer the opportunity to assign the contract, then flip it for a profit. If the buyer flips the contract, the seller will have to deal with a stranger who could give him more trouble than the original buyer. If I'm the buyer, I want the opportunity to flip the property and will fight for the right to assign the contract. The seller generally will permit an assignment to an entity that the buyer has at least a 51% controlling interest in.

If you are a flipper, the amount of time the seller will give you to close is very important. The LOI example above stated the following in the introductory paragraph:

*This Letter of Intent (the "**Letter of Intent**") will outline the terms and conditions under which **Rolling Cash Realty, Inc. 1430 Broadway - 14th Floor New York, NY 10018** (the "**Purchaser**") is interested in negotiating for a definitive written agreement (the "**Contract**") to purchase…*

A better clause would be the following:

*This Letter of Intent (the "**Letter of Intent**") will outline the terms and conditions under which **Rolling Cash Realty, Inc. or an entity to be formed for the benefit of the transaction**, 1430 Broadway - 14th Floor New York, NY 10018 (the "**Purchaser**") is interested in negotiating for a definitive written agreement (the "**Contract**") to purchase…*

I usually use a shell company as the purchaser for LOI purposes. This company serves as a nominee entity, which is a company that will operate temporarily on behalf of the eventual owner. The final owning entity will be formed after I receive an executed contract. I don't want to incur the expense and paperwork of forming a new entity that won't be used if a contract isn't executed and I don't purchase the property.

Depending upon your experience, you probably won't know the actual type of entity you will use until you consult with your accountant and attorney. The actual entity might be a limited liability company (LLC), partnership, trust, etc.

Single Purpose Entity (SPE)

Many banks require you to take title to the property in a single purpose entity (SPE). A single purpose entity is an entity that holds itself out as being a legal entity that is separate and apart from any other individual or entity. The SPE (i) maintains its own books, records, and accounts separate and apart from the books, records, and accounts of any other individual or entity, (ii) conducts business in its own name and uses separate stationery, invoices, checks, etc., (iii) does not guarantee or assume the debts or obligations of any other individual or entity and will not commingle its assets or funds with any other individual or entity.

A single purpose entity (SPE) is an entity that holds itself out as being a legal entity that is separate and apart from any other individual or entity. The SPE will maintain its own books, records, and accounts separate and apart from the books, records, and accounts of any other individual or entity.

It is best to always form and use a separate or single purpose entity for each acquisition you make. That's the accountant in me speaking. Additionally, open a separate bank account for each property's operations and keep separate books and records for each entity. If an owner keeps purchasing properties and lumps them in the same entity and uses one bank account for all the properties, it almost always results in disaster.

As a general rule, always form and use a separate entity for each acquisition you make. Do not keep purchasing properties in the same entity. Additionally, open a separate bank account for each property's operations and keep separate books and records for each entity.

Holding multiple properties in the same entity has many disadvantages including, but not limited to, the following:

- It is more difficult to determine the income, loss, and cash flow generated by each of the properties.

- It complicates and limits your ability to obtain the most advantageous financing.

- When a bank wants to see the operations of the property you are financing, along with a balance sheet and income statement, having one bank account for multiple properties may make it difficult to provide this information to the bank.

- If you're not able to identify the assets, liabilities, and capital accounts for each individual property, it's extremely difficult to determine the correct tax basis in the event you sell or refinance one of the properties. This can affect the gain or loss on the sale of the property and the amount of your tax liability.

- Generally, purchasing multiple properties in the same entity may require you to obtain one mortgage for all of the buildings. If that happens, the bank may require cross-collateralization of all of the properties in the entity. When you want to sell one of the properties before the loan matures, you would need permission and a release from the bank to sell the property. This is not easy, and the transaction would be both complicated and costly.

- A potential liability, such as an environmental problem with one property, may affect the value, equity, and financing ability of the other entity's assets. *This will not be a problem if you use a separate entity aka single purpose entity for each property you acquire.*

Real Life Example:

I have a friend who purchased a property in the name of SOHO Property Associates. The property had a bad environmental problem, and the property was subsequently sold. Unfortunately, my friend was penny wise and dollar foolish. Soon after, he purchased another property, and instead of liquidating the old entity and forming a new one, he stupidly used SOHO Property Associates as the entity for the new property he acquired. The problem was that the old liabilities from the previous property continued to haunt him for years. There were several lawsuits he needed to defend due to the past environmental problems, which cost him hundreds of thousands of dollars. This would not have been a problem if my friend would have used a newly formed separate entity a.k.a. single purpose entity for his new acquisition.

Non-Binding Agreement

This Letter of Intent is only intended to set forth general understandings and agreements of the parties and to provide the basis for negotiating the Contract. This Letter of Intent is not a binding commitment or agreement between the parties to purchase or sell the Property until the Contract, which must be in form and content satisfactory to each party and its counsel, has been executed by the parties. This Letter of Intent does not obligate either party to proceed to the completion of an agreement. Further, this Letter of Intent does not obligate the parties hereto to negotiate, in good faith or otherwise, toward the execution and delivery of the Contract. If the parties fail to enter into the Contract on or before twenty (20) business days from acceptance of this Letter of Intent, this Letter of Intent shall be of no further force or effect.

Note the last sentence of the above paragraph; "If the parties fail to enter into the Contract on or before twenty (20) days from acceptance of this Letter of Intent, this Letter of Intent shall be of no further force or effect."

Always include in your LOI the fact that it is non-binding on the parties, and state the number of business days it will terminate if the parties fail to enter into a contract from the date of acceptance of the LOI.

Confidentiality

Buyer and Seller shall at all times keep this LOI and the negotiations and subsequent agreements relating to the Property confidential, except (i) to the extent necessary to comply with applicable laws and regulations, and (ii) for consultation with either party's legal counsel or accountants. Any such disclosure to third parties shall indicate that the information is confidential and should be so treated by the third party. No press release or other public disclosure may be made by either party or any of its agents concerning this letter or the negotiations and subsequent agreements regarding the Property without the prior written consent of the other party.

I usually include a confidentiality clause in my LOIs, even though I don't know how enforceable it is. It's important to provide comfort to the seller and let him know you respect the confidential nature of the information you receive.

For example, rental brokers are extremely interested in the actual rents of competing properties in the area. Getting their hands on a competitor's rent roll would be very valuable but could potentially hurt the seller.

Street Success Concepts to Remember

1. Remember, the OM is a marketing document prepared by the broker who represents the seller, not the buyer.

2. The LOI is a non-binding document that simply expresses your intent to purchase the property and serves to set forth the basic terms and conditions upon which the buyer and seller will enter into a much more definitive document known as the contract of sale ("contract").

3. At the time you submit the LOI, you must be cognizant of the fact that you haven't yet verified the information contained in the OM

and should not rely on such information until verified by performing comprehensive due diligence on the materials.

4. The LOI is usually submitted on the buyer's stationery and is sent to either the broker or seller by email and/or registered mail.

5. Remember, that the next step after you have obtained a fully executed LOI is going forward and negotiating the contract. Try to identify what specific issues, though important to you, may trigger the most resistance from the seller. Then use the LOI to draw attention to those issues and try to resolve them before you spend time and money on further negotiating the contract.

6. If your offer includes other assets to be included in your purchase beside the property, always remember to specifically include them in the LOI, for example an income-producing sign on the top of the building, a small tract of land across the street from the property, certain equipment, etc.

7. In the real estate industry, the term "all cash" generally means that the buyer will not be required to assume the seller's mortgage, nor will the seller provide the buyer with a mortgage.

8. Keep in mind that you will need as much time as possible to close. Many times, situations arise which are beyond your control. If you don't have enough time to close you could lose your earnest deposit and still be liable for the expenses you've incurred to date. Always try to negotiate for an option to extend the closing date by an extra 15 to 30 days in return for increasing the earnest deposit and agreeing for it to go hard (become non-refundable) after the expiration of the due diligence period.

9. Always include in your LOI whether the buyer or seller will be responsible for any broker commissions that may be due. If there is no broker,

then the LOI should state that there is no broker. The LOI should also state that the parties should mutually indemnify each other against any broker's claim that may arise as a result of the transaction.

10. The earnest deposit is also known as in the industry as earnest money or more commonly, the contract deposit.

11. The amount of earnest deposit is always negotiable, ranging from 1% to 10%. of the purchase price and depends upon such factors, as customary percentages in the area, purchase price, type of property, demand for properties, etc.

12. Always make sure to include in the LOI that the earnest deposit shall be refundable in the event you don't purchase the property, subject to meeting certain negotiated time periods, such as the expiration of the due diligence period.

13. Always make sure to be aware of the time periods when your money is at risk of becoming hard (non-refundable) and always try to negotiate for the most time possible during the due diligence, closing, and mortgage contingency periods.

14. Always make sure that the LOI and contract state the number of business days until the earnest deposit is due.

15. Always request that your earnest deposit should be held by the title company in an FDIC-insured interest-bearing account.

16. Always include in the LOI that the buyer and seller shall each pay their respective legal fees incurred in connection with the transaction, as well as, any prepaid interest, taxes, rents, service contracts, operating expenses, etc., that will be prorated as of the date of the closing.

17. The due diligence period is also known in the industry as the feasibility inspection period, the review period and the feasibility period.

18. Remember that the LOI and the contract should state that the due diligence period does not start until the seller provides the purchaser with all the information requested in the LOI and subsequently, the contract.

19. The due diligence period commences the first business day following execution of the contract by both purchaser and seller and receipt of all due diligence materials (as described in the contract). Additionally, the buyer in its sole discretion and at any time before the end of the due diligence period can ask for their earnest deposit back along with any interest.

20. Whenever a property is acquired, the buyer must always obtain title insurance for both the fee (the property) and any mortgage on the property. A bank or any other lending institution will always require that a title policy is obtained ensuring the legitimacy of the property's title. The title company will issue a report known as the title policy that provides title insurance which protects the lender and buyer against lawsuits regarding the title.

21. To ensure clear title, the title company does a complete examination of the property records, known as a title search. The title company looks to ensure that the seller who is claiming to own the property actually does in fact own the property. The title company searches for outstanding liens, mortgages, judgements, or unpaid taxes that may be attached to the property. The title company also looks for easements, restrictions, or leases that may impact the legal ownership of the property.

22. Since title insurance fees are state regulated, you should always fight for the largest and most reputable title company.

23. Never use a title company based in a different state than where the property is located for the transaction. Many times, a local title company

will have better contacts and familiarity with the laws and authorities of that state.

24. The financing condition period is also known in the industry as the mortgage contingency period.

25. Always include a mortgage contingency clause in your LOI and contract. This clause should include (i) the mortgage percentage, (ii) the time allowed obtaining a written commitment from the lender, and (iii) that the contingency is subject to terms and conditions satisfactory to the purchaser.

26. Try to put in the LOI the right to review and approve all new leases, contracts, and any other agreements during the due diligence period. For example, you don't want the seller leasing a unit at what you would consider to be a below market rent. Additionally, you wouldn't want the seller to enter into a new 10-year laundry contract without your input.

27. An estoppel letter is a certified letter from a tenant which verifies that the terms and conditions of the lease and its current status are true and correct. If the property contains a retail or commercial tenant, always include an estoppel letter provision in your LOI.

28. Depending upon your experience, you probably won't know the actual type of entity you will use until you consult with your accountant and attorney. The actual entity might be a limited liability company (LLC), partnership, trust, etc.

29. A single purpose entity (SPE) is an entity that holds itself out as being a legal entity that is separate and apart from any other individual or entity. The SPE will maintain its own books, records, and accounts separate and apart from the books, records, and accounts of any other individual or entity.

30. As a general rule, always form and use a separate entity for each acquisition you make. Do not keep purchasing properties in the same entity. Additionally, open a separate bank account for each property's operations and keep separate books and records for each entity.

31. Always include in your LOI the fact that it is non-binding on the parties, and state the number of business days it will terminate if the parties fail to enter into a contract from the date of acceptance of the LOI.

CHAPTER 5

PERFORMING PSYCHOLOGICAL DUE DILIGENCE

YOU'VE ALREADY LEARNED about the first three steps that should be taken and mastered before you close on a property: analyzing the offering memorandum, preparing a letter of intent (LOI), and signing a contract of sale (not discussed in this book). Now you're ready to begin Step 4, performing due diligence. This is the final and most important step you must take before you close and take title to the property.

➡ *Remember that once you close, there is no turning back. The property is now yours, along with any warts you didn't uncover after completing your due diligence.*

Too many times, I have heard sellers, brokers, and others say, "*There's no time to perform such detailed due diligence. You'll lose the deal.*" I say, "*So I'll lose the deal!*" It's a giant mistake to believe that you must have a hair trigger or you'll lose a deal.

To succeed, you must understand that there are two different types of due diligence to be performed.

Psychological Due Diligence

Generally, this refers to performing an in-depth investigation of not just the *property*, but the *property owner* as well. Finding out what makes the owner tick is a key place to uncover both *hidden value* and *existing and potential problems* overlooked by others.

⇨ *Learn to use psychology while performing your diligence in order to find out what makes the owner tick.*

Analytical Due Diligence

Generally, this involves analytical due diligence procedures such as examining the seller's books and records, leases, operating expenses, financial projections, etc. *The scope of this book will not include an in-depth discussion on performing analytical due diligence.* The actual procedures for performing analytical due diligence are very comprehensive; an entire book can be devoted to the topic.

This chapter is devoted to psychological due diligence. Our due diligence discussion in this chapter will focus on learning how to think out of the box and become skilled in uncovering hidden value and existing and potential problems.

The common belief among unsophisticated purchasers is that due diligence simply involves verifying all the information in the OM and performing a thorough investigation of the property's financial records, such as rent rolls, service contracts, operating expenses, building systems, etc. That's just the beginning. In my world, due diligence involves becoming a detective and uncovering the "Inside Story" of the property as well as the property owner. Every property has not one, but two, separate and distinct personalities; one for the property and one for its owner.

⇨ *Always remember that every property has an inside story. Equally important to remember is that every property owner has an inside story, too.*

I cannot stress enough the importance of performing extensive due diligence on both the *property* and the *property owner*. It's not only common sense, but it's your duty to yourself, your partners, and your investors.

⇨ *Performing due diligence involves much more than simply verifying the property's financial records, building systems, and related documents. It should also emphasize taking steps to uncover both hidden value and potential problems.*

The primary goals of performing due diligence are to:

- Verify the information contained in the OM by a thorough investigation of the property's books and records.
- Uncover the inside story of both the property and the property owner to uncover both hidden value and potential problems.
- Gain as much leverage as possible to be in the best negotiating position to purchase the property.
- Fully understand whether the prospective investment fits your personal economic objectives and risk tolerance requirements.

There Are No Lifeguards in Real Estate

When purchasing a car, there are various consumer reports available, as well as countless ratings and statistical information that are *specific* to the car you are buying. There are also lemon laws that protect the consumer, if the car they purchased is a dud. In other words, you have some recourse. Chances are you can give the car back and get a new one or your money back.

In real estate, there is generally little if any information available that is *specific* to the property you seek to purchase. For example, there are no consumer reports or ratings and statistical information available to you that are specific to say, the ownership of 152 East 54th Street, or 31 Lexington

Avenue. Additionally, in real estate, there are no lemon laws to protect you. Once you close on a property, you can't simply return it because it doesn't work. The property's problems are now your problems. Furthermore, there is very little recourse available to you except for a good old-fashioned lawsuit or a match and some lighter fluid. (Don't do that.)

Understanding Human Nature

To illustrate the importance of understanding human nature, let's look at dealing with brokers. Many purchasers make the mistake of believing the real estate broker is looking out for their best interests. Purchasers fail to recognize that generally, the broker works for the seller who is responsible for paying their commission. *Human nature* reveals to me that the broker's focus is to sell the property and earn a commission. Never believe the broker is going to alert a prospective purchaser to any negative information that would jeopardize their ability to earn a commission.

⇨ *Always be aware of the human nature factor. For example, never believe the broker is going to alert a prospective purchaser of any negative information that would jeopardize their ability to sell the property and earn a commission.*

I know from personal experience that sellers and brokers are not eager to volunteer information that will ruin their chances to sell a property. On many occasions, I scolded a broker for not volunteering certain insider information about the property. They told me to do my own due diligence. Almost all broker OMs have a disclaimer attached, warning prospective purchasers to perform their own due diligence and not rely on the information in their OM. As one developer once told me, his mantra was *"trust nobody."* My mantra is *"trust nobody and verify."*

At other times, brokers insist you physically visit the building with them before they will give you any additional information. I always refuse because I know it is just a dog and pony show to make the owner believe the property is being marketed to many prospective purchasers. When that happens, I tell the broker, *"I buy on the numbers first."* If the broker won't provide the numbers, I tell the broker I'll pass. Most of the time, I get the numbers.

Below are some examples of human nature at work when dealing with brokers.

- *Try not to deal with brokers who are also active purchasers of property.* If a good deal comes along, there's a good chance they'll try to purchase it themselves.

- *It's important to know when you're last on a list.* Every broker has a list of their most important clients. If a good deal comes in, they send it to a limited number of their best clients first. If the clients pass, it will then go on the market. Sometimes I receive OMs from brokers who I have no relationship with. This doesn't mean it's a bad deal; it just means that I didn't get a first look at the opportunity.

- *Never tell a broker that you plan to hold on to the property long-term and you're generally not a seller.* If you say this to a broker, they'll hear, *"I will never make another commission since the property won't be sold again in the short term."* Brokers love purchasers who constantly buy and sell property and will steer good deals toward these types of purchasers. Not very ethical, but another case of human nature.

Do you see how the above concepts deal with understanding the psychological nature of brokers? Brokers aren't the only ones. You must also learn to understand the psychological nature of the seller, contractors, banks, and with professionals and any other person you encounter. Always try to consider what you would be thinking if you were in their shoes.

<u>Real-Life Example:</u>

A few years back, I met with a banker in charge of liquidating a portion of the bank's foreclosed property. Effectively, she was the seller. She indicated the bank was very interested in liquidating the portfolio and getting the property off their books. As she requested, I submitted a detailed package about my organization. I even obtained a list of the bank's foreclosed property from her. After a series of emails and phone calls that went unanswered, I contacted the attorney who introduced us. He informed me that the banker wanted her bosses to see that she was marketing the property to many people. However, the banker was afraid that after she disposed of the property she'd be out of a job. Therefore, the delays, because it wasn't in her best interest to liquidate the portfolio. Not very ethical but another case of human nature.

⇨ *With respect to dealing with brokers, (i) try not to deal with brokers who are also active purchasers of property, (ii) know when you're last on the list, and (iii) never tell a broker that generally, you are not a seller but hold property long term.*

A Game of Hide and Seek

It's safe to say that every seller is aware of something negative about their property they do not want you, the purchaser, to uncover until after the sale - ***then it's your problem***. The negative information may be the reason the property is for sale. Examples include tenancy problems, deferred maintenance, recent adverse events in the neighborhood, latent structural problems, proposed zoning changes, etc.

⇨ *Every seller is aware of some negative information about their property that they do not want you, the purchaser to uncover until after the sale is completed. Additionally, the negative information might be the reason the property is for sale.*

Is that architectural masterpiece with beautiful curb appeal that you're drooling over a disaster waiting to happen? When would you prefer to uncover the fact that this "jewel" of a property has a toxic waste problem or that tenants have been overcharged for rent and are entitled to treble damages or your largest tenant is about to file bankruptcy - before or after you close? Because prospective purchasers are often too busy looking for more properties or just plain uninterested, the seller gets to hide everything and play hide and seek by himself.

⇨ *Real estate is a game of hide and seek. Here's how you play: The seller hides the property's problems, and the purchaser seeks to find them. Unfortunately, it takes much more effort to find a problem than to hide one.*

Always remember, the owner, not the purchaser, possesses the insider information about the property. Human nature dictates owners will hide any negative information about the property. Their feelings of guilt will be quickly erased by self-rationalizations, such as needing to look out for number one, or that the purchaser should have performed their own due diligence. Imagine being a fly on the wall at the moment the owner discovers a frightful problem with their property. I bet you their next response is, *"Let's get rid of this building. Call the broker!"* Don't be the schmuck who buys it. *Never shortcut performing your due diligence.*

Feeling the Pulse of the Neighborhood

Learn to feel the pulse of the neighborhood to figure out what's really going on around the property's location. Read the local newspapers, watch the local news, speak with the locals, and look on the city or town's website. Try to keep your ear to the pavement.

Real-Life Example:

Some years back, my partner and I were on our way to our attorney's office to sign a contract for the purchase of 20 acres of raw land located in the Manorville section of Long Island. We arrived early and decided to take one last look at the property. While driving around the neighborhood, we observed a construction crew working on a new residential development site less than a mile away from the land we were purchasing. We pulled over and started a conversation with the men. I asked how many houses they were building and what the purchase prices were. When I asked why the prices were so high, (in fact, they were much higher than the sales prices I projected), the man replied,

"Because this is the last half-acre development site the town will approve since the recent up-zoning to one-acre lots."

Wow! The new zoning regulations for the land we wanted to purchase would only permit us to build 20 houses on the site, half the number of houses we anticipated building. The results would have been disastrous.

The new zoning information should have been part of our due diligence to uncover the inside story. Obviously, we did not close on the property. In fact, the seller denied any knowledge of the recent re-zoning and refused to reduce the purchase price of the land. We later learned that both the seller and his attorney had seats on the town board. They had insider information, and we didn't uncover it. We almost lost that round of hide and seek.

It amazes me that prospective purchasers will spend countless hours researching the best financing alternatives available but are not willing to give equal time and effort toward uncovering the inside story of the property they are purchasing.

Uncover the Inside Story of the Property

The current real estate marketplace is characterized by intense competition for properties. This is great news for those who own properties but a tremendous obstacle for prospective purchasers. Frankly, for every worthwhile property available, there is a waiting list of prospective purchasers ready and willing to take on more risk for less reward than ever before. Now more than ever, you must find a way to separate yourself from the pack.

⇨ *The potential for finding value centers upon one's ability to identify and acquire properties overlooked by other purchasers lacking the experience or foresight to develop, renovate, or manage them successfully.*

What is Insider Information?

In the stock market, illegal insider trading is the buying or selling of a security by insiders who possess information or knowledge that is not yet public, i.e., the CEO of a company sells a stock after discovering that the company will be losing a big government contract next month, and that information is not disclosed to the public. The fact that the CEO profited by having superior information that was not available to others gave the CEO an unfair advantage.

On the other hand, it is perfectly legal for an owner (the property's CEO) to sell his property after learning that a large tenant will not renew its lease or intends to file bankruptcy. Does this information give the property owner an unfair advantage? Do they possess superior information that was not available to others? Yes! Yet in real estate, unlike the stock market, it's not illegal, even if it is unethical.

It is important to note that in real estate, as opposed to the stock market, you would be considered negligent if you did not seek out insider information. *While obtaining insider information in the stock market can send you to the big house, not obtaining insider information in the real estate business can send you directly to the poor house.* You have no excuse for not doing your homework and uncovering insider information. You must become a master of the game of hide and seek.

⇨ *Obtaining insider information in the stock market is illegal, yet in real estate, it is perfectly legal, and the purchaser would be considered negligent if they did not seek out insider information.*

Please understand the big difference between performing traditionally accepted due diligence procedures and uncovering insider information.

Performing due diligence generally refers to verifying various information specific to the property, i.e. verifying rent rolls, operating expenses, service contracts, maintenance reports, building systems, etc. Due diligence also includes other procedures, such as determining market conditions, location and neighborhood information, etc. However, uncovering insider information is very different.

Insider information would be considered *guarded, restricted, secret, hidden, underground, hush-hush, or off the record.*

Football coaches and players constantly study game films of their opponents to uncover tendencies and patterns that they can use to their advantage. A marginal player may be traded to a team because he knows the signs, plays, or other *inside information* about a chief rival.

➡ *Uncovering insider information includes using any* <u>legal</u> *means possible to detect and expose facts and other data that they do not want you to know about. The "they" are the folks who have a vested interest in selling you the property, i.e.: sellers, brokers, etc.*

It's Detective Work

You must have the mindset of an undercover detective when you search for insider information. The first thing an undercover detective does is to pull the file of potential suspects. They examine the suspect's rap sheet, prior arrest record, and psychological information in an attempt to create a profile of the suspect. What are the suspect's tendencies and behavior patterns? Where might they strike next? The detective goes out and performs fieldwork. They interview neighbors, storekeepers, and anyone else they can find, asking questions: Did you see anything? Where were you on the night of Tuesday, June 1? In real estate, your suspect is the seller.

Learning to feel the pulse of the neighborhood takes work. I will often sit in a neighborhood diner, talk to building residents, people on the street, police officers, and even the town drunk. It is unbelievable how much I learn by doing this. Many times, the results I uncover will affect my purchasing decision.

<u>Real-Life Example:</u>

Early in 1999, I was in contract to purchase a building located in the East Village section of Manhattan. As I walked around the neighborhood, I saw an elderly man sitting on a milk crate across the street from the property. Even though the elderly man was mumbling to himself, I started up a conversation with him. The man told me that he lived in the neighborhood for over 30 years and wanted to share his many stories about the recent changes in the neighborhood. When I told him I was purchasing the building across, the street he suddenly roared,

"I'll never forget that fire. Man, I can still see the flames shooting out of the windows like it was yesterday. I don't know how the hell that building is still standing."

Just what I wanted to hear. Based on the information provided by the old man, we arranged for our engineer to reexamine the property. It wasn't that the engineer had done a bad job. It was because the fire occurred 18 years ago, and the building was gut renovated. A typical engineering report would not uncover such an event.

However, we had insider information. After a more extensive examination, the engineer uncovered charred wooden rafters just below the roof of the building. Additionally, black smoke was embedded in the basement shafts that was not visible to the naked eye. If I purchased the property, I might encounter structural problems or even potential liability in the future. Yet the building was fully insured, had a certificate of occupancy by the City of New York, and no one associated with the property claimed any knowledge of the fire. Not the owner, the tenants, the superintendent, or the broker.

We immediately brought this insider information to the attention of our attorney and the seller. Even though my engineer assured me that there was no need for worry, we successfully negotiated a significantly lower price (almost $200,000 lower) for the property. Thanks, old man.

This is an example of how you can use due diligence to gain leverage and be in the best negotiating position to purchase the property.

Ask! Answer! And Analyze!

Performing due diligence should be viewed as the three (3) step process of ask, answer, and analyze. Think of this process as taking an X-ray and MRI of the property while performing other diagnostic tests and then giving the property your diagnosis.

➡ *Performing due diligence should be viewed as the three-step process of ask! answer! and analyze!*

Step 1: Ask!

Don't be afraid to ask questions. My wife says that I don't have the embarrassment gene. Shyness can cost you a lot of money. Interview neighborhood residents, tenants, etc. and snoop around. Examples of questions you need to ask will be discussed later.

Step 2: Answer!

Obtain answers to all questions in as much detail as possible. At this stage, your job is to be an aggregator or gatherer of information. If a question cannot be answered, it may indicate a potential problem.

Real-Life Example:

We made an offer to purchase a property consisting of 20 residential apartments and a store. As part of our due diligence, we examined a copy of the store lease the broker had given us, which indicated a rent that was above the current market rate. Additionally, the lease was unexecuted by the tenant. At the contract closing, I asked the owner for a copy of the executed store lease. He replied that this was the only copy he could find. I then asked him to provide me with an estoppel letter (discussed in Chapter 4) . The owner refused and then became nasty. I explained that a bank would require this letter, or they wouldn't finance the property. He still refused and got mad, shouting, "*Do you want to purchase the property or not?*" I shouted, "***Not!***" and left with my attorney.

Obviously, the lease was a sham. A fictitious lease at an above-market rent probably with family members, friends, or acquaintances in an attempt to falsely increase the value of the property. I later learned that someone purchased the property and accepted the unsigned lease. Good luck to them. As I mentioned, this highly competitive market convinces some purchasers to take on more risk for less reward than ever before. Not me! And not you, either!

Step 3: Analyze!

After all the questions are asked and answered, the next step is to analyze the information and determine if the investment fits your personal economic goals and risk tolerance requirements.

Every Property Has Two Personalities

Every property has not one, but two separate and distinct personalities: the property itself and the property owner. Every property has an inside story, and every property owner has an inside story, too. Beyond the obvious due diligence procedures such as analyzing rent rolls, operating expenses, etc., there is often more valuable but subtle information available that is completely overlooked. Such information is often hidden or buried and not available to the naked or untrained eye, but it can lead to tremendous profits or tremendous problems and headaches. Your goal should be to uncover not only *existing value,* but *potential value* as well. Conversely, you must uncover not only *existing problems,* but *potential problems* as well.

The Property Owner?

Nine out of ten purchasers are guilty of gross negligence and incompetence because they fail to perform an in-depth investigation of the property owner. Big mistake! If you neglect to learn what makes an owner tick, you will never uncover the owner's reasons for selling. There is no better way, absent a shot of truth serum, to achieve this goal than by creating and analyzing a comprehensive profile of the property owner. Mastering this skill will give you a tremendous advantage in the acquisition process of purchasing real estate. Creating a profile of the owner is the tool that will enable you to uncover untapped potential and expose existing and potential problems overlooked by others.

The owner profile will reveal a treasure trove of information, if it's performed correctly. The owner profile should overflow with insider information about the owner. A property's operations are often a mirror image of its owner.

As discussed below, the owner profile should include detailed questions about the owners: *Personal Situation,* (ii) *Financial Situation,* and (iii) *Professional Reputation.*

⇨ *Remember to ask, answer, and analyze questions about the owner's (i) Personal Situation, (ii) Financial Situation, and (iii) Professional Reputation.*

Real-Life Example:

In the early 1990s we purchased many properties that were in a state of foreclosure. I discovered that many property owners attempted to convince their bank that the property wasn't even worth the principal amount of the mortgage. To achieve this deception, the property owner would enter into fictitious leases at below-market rents with family members, friends, and acquaintances. While negotiating with the bank to restructure the debt on more favorable terms, the property owner would submit to the bank a very low rent roll to support their claim that the net operating income generated by the property could not possibly support the existing debt service. Rather than foreclose, the bank would often cut a deal with the property owner for both a lower interest rate and forgiveness of part of the debt. As soon as the ink was dry on the restructured documents, the property owner would have his buddies vacate their apartments and re-rent them at the much higher market rents. I once asked a property owner how his office building was doing, for which he replied, with a laugh, "*The first or second time around?*"

Many banks played hardball, refusing to negotiate with the property owners, and commenced foreclosure action. Since we were aware of the game the property owners were playing and who they were, we gained a tremendous advantage while negotiating with the bank to purchase certain properties. *We* had the insider information, not the bank. As soon as we closed, we immediately started eviction proceedings, successfully evicting over 50 illegal tenants, dramatically increasing the cash flow and the market value of the property. We were able to purchase about 15 properties for a fraction of their market value. In fact, we increased the property's value by millions of dollars while we were in contract before closing on the property.

Our success was directly attributable to obtaining insider information about the property owners that were notorious for installing fictitious tenants in their buildings and matching them to the properties in foreclosure.

The property owner is always my opponent in the game of hide and seek. The first things I need to learn are who the property owners are and what makes them tick. Then I look for more detailed information: Why is the property for sale? Is the owner in financial trouble? How flexible were they in past dealings? Was the seller a pro? Do they drain all the potential out of the building before they sell? Remember, you want to uncover insider information, which can lead you to uncover the hidden value and potential problems.

Creating an Owner Profile

As mentioned above, the owner profile should include detailed questions about the owner's (i) *Personal Situation,* (ii) *Financial Situation,* and (iii) *Professional Reputation.*

A tool that I developed to give me the best chance of uncovering insider information about the owner is the use of comprehensive questionnaires that are specific to the type of seller I will be dealing with. These questionnaires are essentially checklists in the form of questions that need to be *asked, answered, and analyzed* as part of my due diligence. I also have a standard questionnaire for residential buildings, office buildings, shopping centers, etc.

Below we are going to discuss just a few of the non-traditional think-outside-the-box questions that should be *asked, answered, and analyzed* to gather information about the owner's personal, financial, and professional situation. This is just a sample; many other questions should be asked, answered, and analyzed, but there are too many to discuss in this book. I just want to introduce you to the importance of creating these profiles and learning how to think outside the box.

Question: Why is the Property for Sale?

The most common question every prospective purchaser should ask is, "Why is the property for sale?" After all, if real estate is such a great investment, why would the owner want to sell the property?

There are many reasons a property is for sale. Sometimes the owner simply wants to cash out and retire. Sometimes the partners are fighting, or the owner is tired of managing the property. However, other times the owner wants to get rid of a major headache or an accident waiting to happen. Below are some of the more common reasons an owner will choose to sell his property.

Owner Wants to Cash Out:

The owner may simply decide that it's time to sell the property, pay the taxes, and put the money in the bank. There's nothing wrong with that; every owner has a different comfort level.

Property Value is "Maxed-Out":

The pros realize there is a time where there are no further opportunities for growth. The current market price for the property is high, the rents are at market, the neighborhood is stable, and the building systems are at the turning point when things will start needing to be replaced.

The Market for the Property will Decrease:

There is an old saying on Wall Street: bears and bulls make money, pigs get slaughtered. Many owners are terrified that the current real estate bubble will burst, and they will lose a substantial amount of their equity. The question is, do I sell my over-inflated property for $3,000,000 and preserve my net equity before taxes of $750,000? After all, only two years ago, the market value of the property was only $2,000,000.

Upgrade to a Higher Class of Property:

Many times an owner will want to trade up in terms of the type of property owned. For example, an owner may own five small properties and want to upgrade to one larger property that is less management-intensive.

Tired of Managing:

Management is a headache. I manage most of my properties because an outside management company with no vested interest is never going to do what it takes to add value to the property.

The Ownership Structure:

Often, the structure of the ownership may require that the property be sold at a particular time in order to maximize the internal rate of return on investment. This is often the case when the property is owned by a hedge fund or other institutions that are short-term investors. Another scenario is when the property is owned by an estate whereby estate taxes must be paid within nine months after the date of death. Since real estate is not a liquid asset, the property must be sold to provide cash to pay the estate taxes.

Problem Property:
Just as no two people are the same, no two properties are the same. Simply put, some properties may be similar in nature, but one may have more problems than another. In one building, the tenants pay their rent on time, and there are rarely leaks, break-ins, or police activity. In the other building, it could be completely the opposite.

The Partners are Fighting:
Different personalities, needs, and desires can cause fights between partners. Remember, 10 partners means 10 different human beings, 10 different personalities, 10 different opinions, and 10 different financial positions. Many times, the only solution is to sell the property and go separate ways. That way they avoid a lawsuit, which helps no one except the lawyers. Another situation that often arises is that one owner is getting a divorce.

Anticipating Large Expenses:
Anticipated large increase in the property's tax assessment, imminent infrastructure problems, etc.

Anticipating Large Vacancies:
For example, if the owner anticipates that recent or future overbuilding in the market will cause his property to soon experience higher vacancy losses, they might be inclined to sell the property.

No More Depreciation:
Another reason for a sale of the property is that the owner cannot take any more depreciation deductions to lower taxes. This usually occurs with long-term ownership where the useful life of the asset has ended and it is fully depreciated. If the owner sells the property and purchases a more expensive one, the clock starts anew with regard to the useful life of the property, and they may have the opportunity to start taking even larger depreciation deductions than before.

As discussed above, by *asking, answering, and analyzing* the above-mentioned questions, you can uncover untapped potential and/or expose existing and potential problems.

Question: Who Owns the Property?

Many times, I find that when a property is owned by a large institution there is strong potential to reduce the property's operating expenses, creating increased value immediately.

For example, large institutions often pay the expenses of multiple properties, then arbitrarily allocate the cost based upon the number of units, asset cost, etc. They may have a master insurance policy that covers all their properties. They then allocate the premium cost to various properties, based upon a predetermined basis which often doesn't necessarily reflect what the actual independent cost would be. Large institutions also may overcompensate by overpaying their operating expenses to avoid potential liabilities, such as overstaffing, over-insuring, etc.

Real-Life Example:

Some years back, we purchased a 450-unit garden apartment complex that was owned by a large institution post-foreclosure. We were able to reduce the operating expenses by over $150,000 per annum, which, with cap rate power, can translate to an increase in property value of $2,500,000 to $3,000,000.

Question: How Easily Can the Owner Make a Decision to Sell the Property?

Real-Life Example:

Recently we found a potentially great off-market deal in Dallas, TX. The property was owned for years by a very prominent family, and it was being managed by the granddaughter. She handed us an appraisal and agreed to sell us the property for $14,000,000. I was literally drooling over what I could transform this property into. I agreed to the price and immediately requested a contract be prepared. The granddaughter said she first needed to get it approved by her 95-year-old grandmother, but she didn't foresee a problem. At this point, I knew there would be problems. I was right. The first delay was, "*My grandmother never sold any property, so it takes time for her to make a decision.*" Then an aunt's approval was also needed. But first, they needed to determine how much all the heirs were getting. Making a long story short, it was six months later and nothing had changed, except the value of the property which had increased. The problem was that no single person had the authority to sell the property without approval from their other partners, some of which were estates and trusts.

Learning the actual name on the title to the property gives you insight into the structure of the ownership. You can then determine the level of difficulty the owner will face in obtaining authorization to sell the property. I have wasted a considerable amount of time and money pursuing a property, only to uncover that the owner's partners didn't want to sell.

The type of entity that owns a property usually dictates how difficult it will be to obtain an executed contract. Uncovering this potential problem upfront factors into my decision of whether or not to continue pursuing the opportunity. The two-part question to be *asked, answered, and analyzed* is as follows:

- In what entity is the property owned?
- Who can authorize the sale?

⇨ *The difficulty of obtaining an executed contract is a function of both the entity the property is owned in and how easily a sale can be authorized.*

Please be advised that the information presented below is presented for intro-
ductory discussion purposes only. Please consult your own tax advisor with respect
to the tax aspects for each of these entities as they may be related to your particular
circumstances and tax situation.

The Property is Owned by a C-Corporation:
Good Luck! Many businesses use the most popular form of corporation, known as the C-Corporation. However, in the real estate business, a property owned by a C-Corporation is akin to a death sentence.

When I find out that a property is owned by a C-Corporation, my response is "*next property please.*" I know from experience that there are adverse tax consequences for the owner if they sell a property that is owned by a C-Corporation. This often involves double taxation of the gain, first at the corporate level, then again at the individual level. The owner may not realize this problem until he consults with his attorney or accountant. At that point, a prospective purchaser has expended thousands of dollars in legal and other costs while negotiating a contract. Nine out of ten times, the property owner will decide not to sell the property or will ask you to pay more for the property because of his tax problem. If I uncover that a property is owned by a C-Corporation, I will immediately ask the owner if he discussed this matter with his accountant. Hopefully, he will answer yes.

Generally, real estate owned in a C-Corporation was purchased by owners before the late 1960s to the 1970s. This is also common in businesses that own the property they operate in. Years ago, there weren't any better entity alternatives available, such as limited liability companies or even Subchapter S-Corporations. Owners were more concerned with liability protection than income taxes.

Side Note: A general rule is to never purchase the owner's corporation that holds title to the real estate. Instead, make sure you purchase the fee interest to the real estate and not the stock of the corporation. If you purchase the owner's corporate entity, the corporation's prior, current, and future liabilities become your liabilities. For example, if the owner didn't pay the required payroll taxes, you as the new owner of the corporation could become *personally liable* for the unpaid taxes, in addition to owing any interest and penalties that may be assessed. This general rule also applies to any business you may purchase.

The Property is Owned by a Subchapter S-Corporation:
Normally, an S-Corporation offers corporation protection, but it is taxed as a partnership; therefore, it does not pay any income taxes. Instead, the corporation's income or losses are divided among and passed through to its shareholders. The shareholders must then report the income or loss on their own individual income tax returns. Property owned by an S-Corporation is not necessarily a death sentence, but it is not an ideal tax situation to be in. The problem with this form of ownership is the possibility of "built-in gains" that can present the same problems as a C-Corporation, but it can also include severe basis limitations which can potentially cause a large tax liability if the property is sold. Additionally, many states do not recognize S-Corporation status which would cause a regular corporate rate structure for state purposes.

The Property is Owned by a General Partnership:
The problem with this type of ownership is that, absent an agreement to the contrary, the *unanimous consent* of all the general partners is required to authorize a sale. If the property has 10 general partners, all 10 general partners must vote yes to selling or the property cannot be sold. Sometimes, this can be an impossible feat to achieve, especially if the partners are fighting. Remember that when dealing with 10 different human beings, you are also dealing with 10 different personalities with 10 different opinions in 10 different financial positions.

<u>Real-Life Example:</u>

In Manhattan, there is a group of over 10 office buildings that can never be sold or refinanced. It started in the mid-1930s when the properties were purchased, and a general partnership was formed. The partnership grew to over 100 different partners. Additionally, some of these partners have changed into estates, trusts, and other partnerships. The attorneys have repeatedly tried to unravel the chain of title to these properties, but to no avail. The properties have no debt, and the partners share in the net cash flow generated from the properties' operations. However, the properties have an aggregate market value of over 500 million dollars that can never be realized because no title company will ever issue a title insurance policy for the properties. The problem is no one person or group has the authority to approve a sale.

The Property is Owned by a Religious Organization:
Beware of the "Pope Clause."

Real-Life Example:

A friend of mine was constructing a new 12-story condominium building and wanted to purchase the excess air rights from a property adjacent to his property and add the extra SF to his building. The extra SF represented almost double the profit he could make from his property without the extra air rights. The Roman Catholic Church owned the property, and the contract of sale contained the following provision entitled "Ecclesiastical Approvals." This is an excerpt from the paragraph:

"Notwithstanding the foregoing, in the event Pope John Paul II ceases to be the Chief of State of the Holy See (State of the Vatican City) the sixty (60) day time period contained in this Article 20 shall not expire prior to the installation of a new Pope and the subsequent passage of sixty (days)."

Yep! The contract had a "Pope Clause." My friend had applied for a building permit, which can take some time to obtain even in the best-case scenario. Unfortunately, the pope died, and my friend's project was put on hold for almost six months. If he had uncovered this potential problem earlier in the process, he would have started the approval process earlier. Imagine what the consequences would be if the current real estate bubble burst and my friend missed the market. My spider-sense would have started tingling as soon as I learned that the property was owned by a religious organization. The owner profile would have alerted me of this potential problem. My question would have been how easy the seller can make a decision to sell the property.

The Property is Owned by an Estate or Trust:
This can be difficult because there are usually multiple individuals involved in the authorization process. Difficult, but not impossible.

The Property is Owned by an Individual:
This type of ownership provides the easiest path to obtaining an executed contract.

The Property is Owned as Tenants in Common:
Tenants in Common (TIC) is a way for two or more individuals to hold title to a property. You can't be a tenant in common by yourself, but a property held by a TIC can be owned by two owners or over a hundred owners. In a TIC, each owner can own different percentages of the property.

Under a TIC, each owner can sell his portion of the property whenever he wants, and to whoever he wants, without the approval of the other co-owners. However, if one co-owner wants to sell the entire property and the others disapprove, there are generally only two options available: (i) request that the other partners purchase their share, or (ii) go to court and file a partition lawsuit. If the lawsuit is successful, the court will order that the property be sold, and the other co-owners, even if unwilling, will have to forfeit ownership and receive a portion of the sale proceeds.

If a property you wish to purchase is owned as TIC, make sure you understand where they stand in the approval process.

The Property is Owned by a Limited Liability Company (LLC):
Starting in the mid-1990s, a new entity alternative to a corporation was becoming popular. This new entity, known as an LLC, is a hybrid between a partnership and a corporation. An LLC offers many of the same benefits of

a corporation, along with offering partnership treatment for reporting gains and losses. Absent an agreement to the contrary, voting privileges generally correspond directly to each member's interest in the company's profits. LLCs commonly contain a provision that designates how a sale can be authorized, which creates a much easier path to obtaining an executed contract.

Question: What Is the Age, Religion, Nationality and Health of the Owner?

Knowing this information can often provide insight into the owner's intentions. If the owner is 65 years old and has an illness, chances are that managing the property may be too difficult for him. Selling the property may relieve them of this responsibility. Additionally, they may need the cash to pay medical bills. Often, an owner will ponder their own mortality and decide to slow down and start spending more time with the family. If we assume a property has development potential, the owner may realize that they cannot physically pull it off, so they will sell the property or maybe agree to a joint venture.

Cultural Differences:
There are cultural differences that you should be aware of. I have found that it's common and an accepted practice in some cultures to start negotiating *after* they sign the contract. Some ethnicities, such as the Chinese, may be uncomfortable with certain numbers because they represent either good or bad luck. Sometimes they won't be able to close on a certain date, or they may pass on a property because of a certain number in the property's address. Additionally, something you may say or do with innocent intentions may be interpreted as an insult in another culture. I hate to say it, but hondling (haggling) and re-trading are a common part of many cultures.

Generational Characteristics:
When the phrase "generation gap" is mentioned, baby boomers come to mind. However, many other generations have been named after the baby boomers, each with their own separate and unique characteristics and views

regarding family values, honesty and integrity, politics, work ethic and balance, cultural issues, and familiarity with communications, media, and digital technologies. The different generations are commonly grouped as (i) *old school,* (ii) *baby boomers,* (iii) *generation X,* and (iv) *millennials* often referred to as Generation Y.

You should be aware that these different generations do exist and may describe the property owner you encounter. Understanding the owner's generational characteristics may prove beneficial in negotiations. Each owner will have their own set of values, goals, etc., which are in great part influenced by their upbringing. Being familiar with each generation of owners can help you speak the same language. I have used this technique on many occasions. It's to your advantage to make an owner feel comfortable with you and, conversely, you also need to feel comfortable so that you can trust the information that they present to you. A great book that explains these different generations and their unique characteristics is Liquid Leadership, a best-selling book written by Brad Szollose.

⇨ *Remember to be aware of and consider cultural and generational differences of owners when negotiating to purchase a property.*

Question: How Long Has the Seller Owned the Property?

Sometimes the property is a part of the owner's life; the owner may become attached to the property. Knowing this helps me understand the owner's feelings for the property. For example, if the owner always wanted to develop the property, they might be more inclined to sell to someone who will develop it rather than keep the status quo.

If the property has only been owned for a short period of time and is now for sale, you need to figure out why. Are there management headaches? Structural problems? Something else?

Long-term ownership can present an opportunity if the owner was never aggressive in increasing the rents or monitoring the operating expenses, especially if the owner had a small mortgage and was afraid of jeopardizing the cash flow. A potential problem with long-term ownership is the possibility of an under assessment for real estate taxes in the event of a sale, which will be discussed in subsequent chapters.

Question: Is Real Estate the Owner's Primary Profession?

Doctors, attorneys, and other professionals who have lots of money often purchase real estate for investment, even if the property is in another state. If they have no experience, problems may arise that seem insurmountable. Often, the problems will require additional capital. As the problems and aggravation pile up, so will the rush to sell the property as soon as possible, even if they lose part of their investment.

Question: How much did the Owner pay for the Property and what is the Remaining Mortgage Balance?

This information is important because it gives insight into how much negotiating room the owner has before they start to lose profit and/or capital. Many websites allow you to see an owner's purchase price and information about their mortgage. Attorneys can usually obtain this information for you; however, sometimes the property is located in a non-disclosure state, such as Texas, where the selling price of the property is not required to be disclosed by the title company, owner, etc. In that case, I can usually find out through my network of brokers in the area.

Question: What are the Terms of the Owner's Mortgage (Expiration Date, Prepayment Penalty, Interest Rate, etc.)?

Real-Life Example:

In October 2008, we negotiated to purchase a large garden apartment complex in Texas for a price of $12,000,000. While we performed our due diligence, mortgage rates suddenly jumped over a point to almost 6% with the possibility of additional increases before we could lock in an interest rate. This caused us to contemplate asking for our deposit back and passing on the deal. Then we uncovered some inside information in terms of the owner's mortgage. The owner had waited too long to sell the property because they had hoped to avoid an extremely large prepayment penalty. Now they were faced with a dilemma. If we didn't close, the owner wouldn't have the time to obtain a new mortgage before the old one expired. Since we hadn't planned on the large increase in the interest rate, we informed the owner that, due to the increased interest rate, the market cap rate for the property had effectively increased, causing the property to be worth substantially less than the purchase price we had previously agreed to. The owner was backed into a corner, and we received a discount of almost $1,000,000.

Side Note: The change in interest rate is a *temporary change,* but the reduction in the purchase price is *a permanent change.* As a result of the change in the interest rate, our final purchase price was $11,200,000, and our interest rate was 5.95%. The property is currently worth $21,000,000 and we subsequently refinanced the mortgage a few years ago at an interest rate of 3.86%.

Question: Is the Property Owned by an Out-of-Towner?

My experience is that out-of-town owners tend to be unfamiliar with the local market and often rely on outside consultants, such as managing and leasing agents and contractors, to look out for their interests unsupervised. Human nature has proved time and time again that these owners get taken advantage of, and they will experience over-budgeted costs, additional fees, and the need to loan or invest additional capital. Once again, as the problems and aggravation start piling up, so does the rush to sell the property as soon as possible, even if they lose part of their investment.

Question: Who is the Managing Agent for the Property?

How good or bad the property's managing agent is generally affects how successful or unsuccessful the property will become. I have experienced both scenarios. Properties managed by *good* managing agents should be well-maintained with market rents, low vacancy, etc. Properties managed by *bad* managing agents generally have an opposite situation. In addition, properties with bad managing agents often have existing or future structural and building system problems, which will be very expensive to repair and/or replace, and such costs are normally not reflected in the purchase price.

Question: What is the Owner's Reputation as a Landlord and Property Operator?

Is the owner a seasoned pro? Do they have a reputation of being a good operator who maintains their buildings and aggressively increases rents? If yes, then I ask myself what I can do differently to increase the value of the property. Sometimes the answer is nothing. If the owner has a reputation as a bad operator who doesn't maintain his properties and thus has large vacancies, unhappy tenants, etc. then I may smell an opportunity to reverse the situation and potentially increase the value of the property significantly.

Real-Life Example:

Because of rent control in New York City, the name of the game, until recently, was vacating low-paying tenants, renovating the units, and then re-renting them at much higher rents. This is often achieved by approaching each tenant and offering them money to vacate their unit. If the property owner is known for draining all the potential out of the building before they sell, then you need to ask yourself if they were unsuccessful vacating the remaining units in the building, why would you be successful? Surely the tenants were constantly approached with offers to vacate and chose to decline.

If, on the other hand, the owner was passive in his operational approach, but the property was still well-maintained, then this scenario represents a good opportunity for the new owner to increase property value.

Question: What is the Owner's Reputation as a Negotiator?

Is the owner known as being greedy and difficult or as being reasonable and honorable? How flexible was the owner in past dealings? Does the owner love to litigate? Answering these questions will give you some insight into who you're dealing with and help you plan your approach with the owner.

Real-Life Example:

A few weeks after closing on a small apartment building, I called the prior owner and asked them for some additional documents that we needed. Most sellers would give us the information as a courtesy. This obnoxious owner asked for money. In fact, one time they picked up the phone and said, *"Every time you call, I hear the cash register ring."*

I often reach out to my network of attorneys, brokers, vendors, banks, etc. and inquire about their experiences with the owner of the property I am trying to purchase.

Question: What is the Owner's Personal Financial Situation?

Is the owner in financial trouble or are they financially stable with deep pockets? These questions tell me if I have some leverage available to me during negotiations.

⇨ *A great way to learn about the owner is to establish a network of professionals (such as attorneys, accountants, appraisers, brokers, vendors, banks, etc.,) that you can call on for information about the owner.*

Street Success Concepts to Remember

1. Remember that once you close, there is no turning back. The property is now yours along with any warts you didn't uncover after completing your due diligence.

2. Learn to use psychology while performing your diligence in order to find out what makes the owner tick.

3. Always remember that every property has an inside story. Equally important to remember is that every property owner has an inside story, too.

4. Performing due diligence involves much more than simply verifying the property's financial records, building systems, and related documents. It should also place an emphasis on taking steps to uncover both hidden value and potential problems.

5. Always be aware of the human nature factor. For example, never believe the broker is going to alert a prospective purchaser of any negative information that would jeopardize their ability to sell the property and earn a commission.

6. With respect to dealing with brokers, (i) try not to deal with brokers who are also active purchasers of property, (ii) know when you're last on the list, and (iii) never tell a broker that generally, you are not a seller but a hold property long term.

7. Every seller is aware of some negative information about their property that they do not want you, the purchaser, to uncover until after the sale is completed. Additionally, the negative information might be the reason the property is for sale.

8. Real estate is a game of hide and seek. Here's how you play: the seller hides the properties problems, and the purchaser seeks to find them.

Unfortunately, it takes much more effort to find a problem than to hide one.

9. The potential for finding value centers upon one's ability to identify and acquire properties overlooked by other purchasers lacking the experience or foresight to develop, renovate, or manage them successfully.

10. Obtaining insider information in the stock market is illegal, yet in real estate it is perfectly legal, and the purchaser would be considered negligent if they did not seek out insider information.

11. Uncovering insider information includes using any legal means possible to detect and expose facts and other data that they do not want you to know about. The "they" are the folks who have a vested interest in selling you the property, i.e.: sellers, brokers, etc.

12. Performing due diligence should be viewed as the three-step process of ask! answer! and analyze!

13. Remember to ask, answer, and analyze questions about the owner's (i) Personal Situation, (ii) Financial Situation, and (iii) Professional Reputation.

14. The difficulty of obtaining an executed contract is a function of both the entity the property is owned in and how easily a sale can be authorized.

15. Remember to be aware of and consider cultural and generational differences of owners when negotiating to purchase a property.

16. A great way to learn about the owner is to establish a network of professionals (such as attorneys, accountants, appraisers, brokers, vendors, banks, etc.) that you can call on for information about the owner.

CHAPTER 6

THE PROPERTY PROFILE

What is it? What was it? What can it be?

Similar to performing psychological due diligence on the *owner profile*, the same mindset should be utilized when analyzing the *property profile*. Once again, you must emphasize *uncovering the inside story* of the *property* to uncover *hidden value* and both *existing and potential problems* overlooked by others. This involves much more than simply verifying the property's physical attributes and financial records.

In Chapter 3, we discussed the various components that should be included in a comprehensive offering memorandum or OM. There is an example of a comprehensive OM in the appendix which uses a fictional garden apartment community we named *the Dallas Arms Apartments*, a 60-unit Class C Garden Apartment Community located in Richardson, Texas.

It is important to ensure that whenever you receive an OM from the broker or need to create one yourself, that it's comprehensive and as far-reaching as possible so that it can serve as the property profile for further analysis.

By mastering the information contained in Chapter 3, you should now be aware of the pertinent information that should be contained in a comprehensive OM aka *property profile*.

An OM is in affect a *Property Profile*. From this point on, we will refer to the OM as the property profile.

Your mindset should be that each and every time you perform due diligence on a property to ask, answer, and analyze for yourself, the following three questions:

1. ***What is it?***
2. ***What was it?***
3. ***What can it be?***

My goal for this book is to teach you to open your eyes and expose you to the skill of learning to think outside the box to uncover both *hidden value and existing and potential problems* overlooked by others.

Each and every time you look at a property, ask, answer, and analyze the following 3 questions; (i) What is it? (ii) What was it? (iii) What can it be?

What Is It?

At the end of the day, "***What is it?***" that you're actually purchasing? Is it a potentially sound investment with a substantial upside? Or an accident waiting to happen?

"What is it" has to do with the actual physical condition of the property and its components at the time you plan to purchase it.

To answer the question "***What is it?***" you will need to probe beyond what the property looks like to the untrained eye. Always remember that every property has a distinct personality of its own; no two properties are exactly the same.

If you were the acquisition manager for a real estate company, would you tell your boss that you believe a certain property is a good investment because it's in a great location, looks like it's in great shape, rents are at below-market rates, and it's selling for only $50,000 per unit? If the answer is yes, you won't last very long at that job.

To properly answer the question "*What is it?*" you must do extensive research, have diagnostic tests performed by third-party experts, and perform other investigative procedures.

In Chapter 3, the property profile for *the Dallas Arms Apartments* was organized into categories, then broken down further into subcategories. Below is a brief description of some of the subcategories contained within the categories.

Location:
The property profile says it's a great place to raise kids. It's a well-established area near grocery stores, great schools, retail, theatres, and restaurants. It provides great transportation and is near a large employment base. *Is it really a great location or is it just an average one?*

For each of the following, you must learn to uncover the advantages, disadvantages, limitations, and most importantly, existing and potential problems concealed in the following categories and subcategories.

Site Description:
Building and lot size, parking surface and parking, landscaping information. spaces, etc.

Building Information:
Building type, building class, area class, number of buildings, number of floors, unit information, average monthly rent, year built, occupancy percentage, net rentable SF, NOI, etc.

Construction Information:
Building style, foundation, framing exterior, roof information.

Mechanical Information:
HVAC, electrical, plumbing, fire protection systems.

Utilities:

Providers of the various utilities servicing the property, responsibilities for paying the cost. Utilities including electric, water and sewer, gas, telephone, cable, internet, etc.

Amenities:

Laundry facilities, washer and dryers in units, leasing/management office, pool, tennis courts, controlled access gates, etc.

Tax Information:

Current assessed value, taxing district, current tax rate, current taxes, etc.

School Information:

School district, name of elementary, middle, and high schools, transportation information, distance from the property.

Unit Mix Sale and Rent Comparables Financial Analysis

Shows the unit floor plans with sizes, SF, and the different types of units comprising the property.

I suspect that many of you may be experiencing some trepidation at this point. You might be thinking, *"If I can't change a lightbulb, how can I determine if the various building systems are in good working order?"* The good news is you don't have to know. That's what the experts are for. There are exterminating companies you could hire to determine if there are any infestations of termites or other vermin. There are companies just waiting for your call to perform a physical condition report on the property you anticipate purchasing. Yes, you will have to spend money to engage these professionals, but you may need to since the lender will almost always require you to get these reports as a condition for obtaining a mortgage.

The information contained in the above-mentioned categories and sub-categories is the core of "*What is it?*" that you're purchasing. Are you purchasing a good or bad location; crumbling or well-maintained infrastructure;

a good or bad building type, building class, area class, etc.? Each of these subcategories contains critical information that will enable you to uncover both *hidden value* and *existing and potential problems* overlooked by others.

Third-Party Reports

Generally, when you purchase a multifamily property, the lender will require that the following reports be prepared by independent third-party consultants of *their choice* and at the *purchaser's sole cost and expense:*

- Property Condition Report.
- Phase I Environmental Assessment Report ("ESA")
- Termite Inspection Report
- Property Appraisal Report
- Updated Survey

As a requirement of obtaining a mortgage, the lender will require that the following reports are obtained from independent third-party consultants of their choice at the purchaser's sole cost and expense: (i) Property Condition Report, (ii) Phase I Environmental Assessment Report, (iii) Termite Inspection Report, (iv) Property Appraisal Report, (v) Updated Survey.

Those reports are normally prepared for the benefit of the lender, but they can prove to be very valuable to you both currently and in the future. The various reports will provide you with intimate details of the physical structure of the property and its history and help you uncover the property's family tree.

Use your network of contacts to try and obtain copies of third-party reports from other deals. Good sources are the internet, the third-party consultants themselves, and other real estate professionals. By simply reviewing these reports, you will receive great insight into their purpose and conclusions.

Side Note: The physical structure of a property is often referred to in the industry as the property's "*bones.*"

The findings and recommendations in these reports will alert you to past, present, and potential problems. Later in this chapter, you'll learn how the information contained in these reports can also help you answer the questions of "***What was it?***" and "***What can it be?***"

In addition, the results can help you reach an important goal of performing due diligence: *Gain as much leverage as possible to have the upper hand and be in the best negotiating position to purchase the property.*

Since you are paying for the third-party reports, you are entitled to receive copies of each of the reports. However, most lenders will wait until after closing before remitting a copy to the borrower.

Timing

Because of the strict time constraints in the purchase contract, such as the due diligence period, closing date, mortgage contingency period, etc., it's extremely important for you to have the third-party reports ASAP because they are ground zero for you to start answering the questions "***What is it?,***" "***What was it?,***" and "***What can it be?***"

Unfortunately, in the real world, the third-party reports are often completed too closely to your deadlines. In my LOI, I always try to include a note that the seller will provide the purchaser with copies of any third-party reports they have in their possession, even if they're outdated.

Always notify and alert the third-party consultants of your deadlines. Even if you rely on a mortgage broker to administrate the financing function, keep pressing and keep the pressure on them. Remember, it's your earnest deposit that is at risk.

When the seller first purchased the property, and assuming they performed adequate due diligence, they should have the old property condition report, Phase I Environmental Assessment Report, termite inspection report, appraisal report, etc. that were required at the time of acquisition. This is especially true if financing was involved at the time of acquisition or a subsequent refinance.

Before, or as soon as you receive an executed LOI, request from the seller copies of any property condition reports, Phase I Environmental Assessment Reports, termite inspection reports, and appraisals in their possession even if they are old. Don't wait until the contract is signed and the due diligence period commences.

When you submit your completed application for financing, the lender will generally require a non-refundable deposit from the purchaser which will include the estimated cost of the third-party reports.

<u>Real-Life Example:</u>

If you sign a purchase contract on June 1, the clock on your 30-day due diligence period has started ticking. First, you need to identify the lender you plan to use, and then start assembling the documentation the lender requires. This could take up to two weeks, and then, after you submit it, you need to wait for a written commitment from the lender stating the terms and conditions under which they agree to provide financing. These terms may not be acceptable to you, and the process can be nerve-racking. Many times, upon review of your application, the commitment will contain different terms and conditions than you were first quoted, including, but not limited to, lowering the principal amount of the mortgage, raising the interest rate, requiring a partial or full guarantee of the mortgage, etc.

Additionally, the commitment will generally contain other provisions and contingencies you must meet before final approval for the loan is granted. This includes submitting the results of the third-party reports that may not be completed by the time the commitment is issued.

The actual date you will receive the commitment from the lender or the third-party reports from the consultants is out of your control. In the meantime, the contract may require that you receive a commitment from the lender within 30 days, which is unlikely, especially if you have a mortgage contingency clause in the contract.

The third-party reports can take each outside consultant two to four weeks to complete, depending upon the scope and how busy they are. However, your 30-day due diligence period usually starts before the lender issues a commitment to the purchaser.

Due to the time constraints in the purchase contract regarding the due diligence period, mortgage contingency period, closing date, etc., it is extremely important that the third-party reports are ordered as soon as possible.

Make sure you fully understand the time constraints in the contract. Try to have all your ducks in a row, and always be as prepared as possible. Stay on top of the lender and the third-party consultants like white on rice.

Property Condition Report

To obtain a mortgage, the lender will almost always require that a third-party vendor, chosen by the lender, perform a comprehensive property condition report on the property. This report is at the sole cost of the borrower. Such reports will be addressed to the lender and be entirely for their benefit.

Because of the time it takes to receive the third-party reports, you may not have enough time to adequately review them and determine if the results affect your decision to purchase the property. Therefore, it is common that I, as part of my due diligence, will pay to have a property condition report prepared irrespective of the lender's requirements for my own use. I initiate this as soon as I receive an executed LOI. However, this report will be lesser in scope than the one performed for the lender. My advice is to let the experts do their jobs, even if it costs you money. It is well worth it. Their findings will go a long way in helping you answer the question "*What is it?*"

If you elect to have a property condition report prepared for you, the purchaser, try to obtain an approved list of vendors that the lender will accept. By doing so, the lender can always have the report updated for their benefit which will save on the cost.

A property condition report generally renders an *opinion* on the condition of the various building components and systems based upon non-invasive procedures. No disassembly of systems or building components and no physical or invasive testing is performed. Findings, conclusions, and recommendations included in the report are based on visual observations, municipal information reasonably obtained, information provided by the client, and/or a review of readily available and supplied drawings and documents.

A property condition report generally renders an opinion on the condition of the various building components and systems based upon visual observations, limited research, and non-invasive procedures.

A property condition report will render the company's conclusions and recommendations on the various building components, which include, but are not limited to the following:

Site Conditions:

Topography and drainage, pavement and parking, landscaping, site improvements, and site amenities, municipal services and utilities, and natural hazards.

- Reports any sloping, detriments, or problems, such as ground fractures, settlement areas, or evidence of erosion or chronically standing water, whether there is adequate parking and if it's ADA (Americans with Disabilities Act) compliant, condition of the parking lot, type of materials used, and recommendations of any necessary repairs and/or replacements.

- Reports the current condition of the landscaping, irrigation systems, signage, fencing, dumpster enclosures, handrails, exterior stairs, lighting, observable trip hazards, etc.

- Details the service providers for the property (water and sewer, gas/oil, electricity, etc.). Observes any storm drainage concerns and researches if the property is in a seismic or flood zone.

Building Conditions:

Substructure, superstructure, facades, roofing, basements/attics, ADA accessibility, interior finishings, and components, suspected mold, and moisture.

- Reports current condition of substructure based upon their visual survey, the condition of the building's mechanical systems, slabs, foundations and footings, crawl spaces, exterior and interior walls, and/or columns.

- Reports current condition of interior and exterior finishes and components, subfloors, kitchens, living areas, bedrooms, ceilings, appliances, storage rooms, mechanical rooms, laundry rooms, down units, common areas, trim, exterior doors and windows, exterior paint, roofing, gutters, and downspouts, if ADA-compliant, etc.

Building Systems:

Plumbing, HVAC, building electrical, building and site fire and life safety, elevators, etc.

- Reports current condition, materials makeup, and type of plumbing systems, including, but not limited to boilers, storage tanks, pipes, type of HVAC system, air handlers, condensers, type of electrical system, master or individual meters, type of wiring, circuit breakers, smoke detectors, fire extinguishers, etc.

Material Code Violations:

Examination of building and fire department's records, if available, etc.

Immediate Repairs and Capital Reserves:

The property condition report also gives you details of any immediate and short-term repairs required and recommendations on the number of capital replacements that should be reserved for the future.

Property Condition Report Cover Letters and Condition Reports*

The lender will generally estimate the cost to remediate any immediate repairs and will require at closing one-and-a-half times the estimated cost of the repairs be placed into an escrow account to be held by the lender. Once the repairs have been completed, the lender will do an inspection and then release the funds to the borrower.

The property condition report is a summary of the consultant's observations and recommendations given the limited scope of their engagement. The report will serve to alert you or the lender of existing and potential problems that have been observed. You will then need to ascertain the potential cost to remediate the existing or potential problem and the risk it presents. Many times, the problem can be used as a negotiating tool. Additionally, you may need to hire an expert to provide a more in-depth investigation of the problem.

Rating System

The property condition report uses the following rating system to describe the condition of the various site, building, and system components, as follows:

- Excellent: The component or system is in new or like-new condition, and no deferred maintenance is recommended.
- Good: The component or system is sound and performing its function and/or scheduled maintenance can be accomplished through routine maintenance.
- Fair: The component or system is performing but may be obsolete or is approaching the end of its expected useful life. The component or system may exhibit evidence of deferred maintenance, previous repairs, or workmanship not in compliance with commonly

---

*See Appendix 1 and 2 for examples of Property Condition Report Cover Letters.

accepted standards. Significant repair or replacement may be recommended to prevent further deterioration, restore it to good condition, prevent premature failure, or to prolong its expected useful life.

- Poor: The component or system has either failed or cannot be relied upon to continue performing its original function as a result of having exceeded its typical expected useful life, excessive deferred maintenance, or state of disrepair. The present condition could contribute to, or cause, the deterioration of other adjoining elements or systems. Repair or replacement is recommended.*

Phase I Environmental Site Assessment ("Phase I ESA")

Another third-party report required as a condition for obtaining a mortgage is a comprehensive Phase I ESA Report performed on the property chosen for the benefit of the lender and at the sole cost of the purchaser.

A Phase I ESA Report is intended to satisfy one of the requirements of the Comprehensive Environmental Response Compensation and Liability Act (CERCLA) to protect and limit the liability of prospective property owners.

A Phase I ESA Report is intended to protect and limit the liability of prospective property owners.

Similar to a property condition report, the ESA generally renders an *opinion* on the environmental condition of the property. The focus is on determining if there are any observable hazardous substances, petroleum products, etc. that have or have not been addressed to the satisfaction of the applicable regulatory authorities. Additionally, the analysis will focus on any Historical Recognized Environmental Conditions (HRES) that occurred in the past and whether or not they have been addressed to the satisfaction of the regulatory authorities.

Similar to a property condition report, the Phase I ESA Report simply renders an opinion on the environmental condition of the property. The focus is on determining if there are any observable hazardous substances, petroleum products, etc. that have or have not been addressed to the satisfaction of the applicable regulatory authorities.

While performing the Phase I ESA, no invasive or other tests are generally performed. If a hazardous condition is observed, the report will disclose the issue and render an opinion on how to proceed. For example, Phase I ESAs do not include soil or groundwater testing.

The report will detail their findings and recommendations along with its scope limitations. Their report will include, but not be limited to, a review and analysis of the following:

- Site and Vicinity Historical Review
- Regulatory Agency Records Review
- Regulatory Database Records Review
- Interviews and User-Provided Information
- Site Reconnaissance
- Asbestos-Containing Building Materials\Lead-Based Paint
- Radon
- Mold/Indoor Air Quality Issues

Below is an excerpt from a PSA Report offering their findings and recommendations after completing their analysis on a property.

Conclusions and Recommendations

This assessment has revealed no evidence of recognized environmental conditions (RECs) or historic recognized environmental conditions (HRECs) in connection with the subject property. This assessment has revealed the following evidence of de minimis conditions and business environmental risks in connection with the subject property:

Fluorescent lighting was observed on the subject property. If manufactured prior to 1978, the fluorescent fixture ballasts may contain PCBs. The subject property buildings were reportedly constructed in 1971; therefore, it is possible the ballasts contain PCB oils. XXX considers the presence of potentially PCB-contaminated fluorescent light ballasts to represent a de minimis condition. XXX recommends that during the course of normal maintenance, when replacement of fluorescent light fixture ballasts is required, that the fixtures be inspected for non-PCB content labeling prior to disposal and be disposed of properly (as PCB containing) if no labeling is present.

Phase II Environmental Report (Phase II ESA)

In the event that the Phase I ESA Report reveals that additional investigation is warranted, a more extensive report, known as a Phase II ESA Report, will be required. The Phase II ESA generally requires property sampling and laboratory analysis and is generally a subsurface investigation that can include:

- Soil sampling
- Groundwater monitoring, sampling, and analysis
- Soil vapor/Sub slab soil gas testing
- Ground-penetrating radar
- Characterization of hazardous chemicals

If the Phase I ESA Report reveals that additional investigation is warranted, then a more extensive report known as a Phase II Environmental Site Assessment Report will be required. Such reports generally require property sampling and laboratory analysis and are generally a subsurface investigation.

A Phase II ESA Report is more expensive than a Phase I ESA Report because much more invasive work will need to be performed.

The following are some Recognized Environmental Conditions that may necessitate the need for a Phase II Report:

- Current or former underground storage tanks (USTs)
- Existing USTs past their life expectancy

- Evidence of a release (leaking drum, compactor) or threatened release
- Historical use businesses, such as dry cleaners, metal plating facilities, gas stations, auto repair shops, lumber yards, etc.

Generally, if the property was ever occupied in its history as a business that used potentially hazardous materials, such as a dry cleaner, gas station, auto repair shop, etc. then a Phase II ESA Report will be required.

Termite Inspection Report

Another third-party report required by the lender is a termite inspection report, also called a wood-destroying insect report This report must be prepared by a licensed pest control business. This report's purpose is to inform both the lending institution and the prospective purchaser about termites, termite damage, and other issues related to termites.

The inspection report is a visual, non-invasive examination of the property's condition at the time of the inspection. A standard building inspection typically includes a visual inspection of the property's condition, often including heating and central air systems, interior plumbing and electrical systems, roof, attic and visible insulation, walls, ceilings, floors, windows and doors, and foundation, basement, and visible structures.

Side Note: Termite inspections are important because termites directly affect the building's structure. *However, I like to increase the scope to include other pests, such as bedbugs, cockroaches, and other vermin. Uncovering an infestation of these pests should be uncovered during your due diligence.*

Sometimes an infestation can be the cause for high vacancies and can be used as a negotiating tool. Most times the infestation can be easily remediated.

Property Appraisal Report

The lender also requires that an appraisal of the property is prepared from an independent third-party of their choice at the purchaser's sole cost and expense. Additionally, lenders generally insist that the appraisal should be performed by a company with an MAI (Member of the Appraisal Institute) designation.

Lenders will generally insist that the appraisal should be performed by a company with an MAI designation. MAI stands for Member of the Appraisal Institute, a trade organization that monitors appraisers and holds them to a higher standard than appraisers who are simply licensed and not members of any monitoring organization.

The purpose of this appraisal is to estimate the fair market value of the property. An appraisal should, in theory, represent the most probable price a property should bring in a competitive and open market.

In real life, however, appraisals are extremely subjective because various assumptions are made that can substantially affect the computed value. I have seen appraisals performed for a lender at a much higher value than an appraisal for the same property for the purposes of valuing an estate. Hopefully, the appraiser's value will be in the same range to ensure coverage of the requested mortgage. Appraisals are discussed later in this chapter when answering the question "*What can it be?*"

The purpose of an appraisal is to estimate the fair market value of the property. However, in real life, appraisals are extremely subjective because various assumptions are made in the calculation that can substantially affect the computed value.

Updated Survey

The lender will always require that they are provided with an accurate survey of the property. Generally, the prior owner has a survey in their possession and will provide it to the purchaser. The purchaser will then simply need to have the survey updated which is less expensive than preparing a brand-new survey.

What Was It?

To properly answer this question, you must research and analyze the history of the property. When was it built? By whom? How? Why? What were the property's past uses? Remember that we are looking to uncover *hidden value* and *both existing and potential problems* overlooked by others, so put on your detective hat again.

Some of the best ways to start answering the question, "What was it?" are to (i) review the Phase I ESA Report, (ii) review the property appraisal, (iii) review the title report, and (iv) use the Internet. Put on your detective hat and start interviewing.

Obtain a Copy of the Phase I ESA Report

Unfortunately, in the real world, this report will generally be completed at such a late date that you may not have enough time to properly evaluate it. *This is why you must make every reasonable effort to receive a copy of any Phase I ESA Report that the seller has in their possession, even if it's outdated.* Even an outdated report will provide you with historical information about the property.

The Phase I Environmental Site Assessment Report will provide you with historical information about the property which will bring attention to any *hidden value* and *existing and/or potential problems, including, but limited to the following:*

- Flood Zone Designation and if there is the potential for floods at the property

Comments: If this is the case, the lender may require flood insurance, which can be expensive depending on the risk involved. If the property is subject to floods, there may be ongoing problems with water infiltration into the units or other portions of the property. You may need to install water barriers or other protective devices, which can also be expensive.

Water infiltration generally leads to mold and other problems, which need to be remediated.

- If there are any trees designated as "heritage" trees on the property

Comments: Environmental groups have strong political influence and have been instrumental in changing existing laws in recent years.

Real-Life Example:

In Austin, Texas, if the property has any trees whose circumference is over 50 inches, you can't just cut the trees down. You must make arrangements to find a new location for the tree and pay to move it to a new location, approved by the local officials. If you cut down a heritage tree, you can be fined and/or imprisoned.

- Information regarding demolition permits, the construction/ remodel year of the subject property, and records of permits.

Comments: The permits may indicate a past use that may be grandfathered or contain equipment that can be used by a future tenant.

Real-Life Example:

If a restaurant and/or bar occupied the property, there may be hidden value to salvage. The fact that a bar once operated on the property might prove useful in being granted a liquor license or arguing that the right should be grandfathered. Additionally, if any of the restaurant's infrastructure is intact (i.e. kitchen, venting, sprinkler), it may prove valuable to a new restaurant, leading to a higher rent or obtaining "key money" from a new tenant.

Side Note: The street definition of "key money" is money paid to the land-lord for the valuable "keys" to the premises. Even though the premises are vacant, there may be valuable equipment, furniture, and fixtures, etc. that were left by a former tenant which may prove valuable to a new tenant. In that case, the value can be monetized by increased rent or the payment of key money to the landlord. Generally, equipment or fixtures that are affixed to the premises and left behind by the tenant will become the property of the landlord upon the tenant vacating the space. Examples are ventilation systems, light fixtures, built-in furniture and equipment, etc. Supermarket and restaurant tenants are known to be big players in paying key money for the valuable shelving, equipment, fixtures, etc., left by former tenants.

- If the building or buildings has any historical or landmark designation.

Comments: These designations can cost you a lot of money. For example, you can't make alterations, such as installing new windows or changing the facade of the building, without approval from the federal or local Landmark Commission. These agencies can also force you to use the same type of windows that were historically used, and you may need to go through hoops trying to find similar designs and materials.

Real-Life Example:

The developer Abe Hirschfeld once bought a parcel of buildings, which included a small, dilapidated building inhabited by squatters. Hirschfeld didn't know what to do with the property until his architect informed him that the building was a Stanford White Building. Stanford White was a legendary architect from the turn of the century's Gilded Age. To live in a Stanford White building was the epitome of taste and refinement. If the building could be brought back to even a semblance of its original condition, it would substantially increase in value. This is what Mr. Hirschfeld did, in fact, do.

- Past environmental problems, such as leaking petroleum storage tank facilities, spills, and landfills, if the property was entered into any State Voluntary Programs, etc., or if there are any prior, current, or pending proceedings involving the subject property relevant to hazardous substances or petroleum products.

Comments: This information is *important*. For example, evidence of any potential problems, even if not currently an issue, may become a major problem in the future that can cost substantial funds to remediate.

For example, if a property was ever occupied by a dry cleaner, laundromat, gas station, auto repair shop, lumber yard, or other business dealing with chemicals, you might have to spend hundreds of thousands of dollars cleaning up the site to comply with the new environmental laws. This applies even if the use occurred 20 years ago.

Real-Life Example:

We've owned a neighborhood shopping center since 2010 in Westchester County, New York. Built in 1962, the center has always featured a dry cleaner as a tenant. When we purchased the property, Phase I and Phase II ESA Reports were obtained revealing that no potentially harmful environmental risks existed, even though a dry cleaner was a tenant. However, in 2016, the current dry cleaner decided to replace his outdoor HVAC system. While installing the equipment, the plumber saw what he perceived as hazardous materials and notified the Environmental Protection Agency (EPA) who came to the center armed for battle. The no-nonsense EPA made us remove tons of contaminated soil and install monitoring stations. We were also forced to engage an environmental consultant and subsequently enter the Brownfield Cleanup Program. The EPA determined that toxic chemicals seeped underground and affected the groundwater supply. We have spent over $600,000 on remediation and related costs to date, and the EPA is constantly monitoring the center and requiring more procedures be performed on an ongoing basis.

The point is that Phase I and Phase II ESA Reports didn't disclose any significant problems to us at the time. The only way we could have reasonably found out about this problem was to constantly monitor the actions of the tenant, which is not feasible. And, yes, we had contamination provisions in the tenant's lease. However, the tenant took no responsibility and subsequently went out of business.

Put on Your Detective Hat and Start Interviewing

Shyness can cost you a lot of money. On occasion, I will sit in a neighborhood diner and talk to building residents, people on the street, police officers, and even the town drunk.

Try to identify and interview past owners and occupants of the property to identify historic property uses. Even interviewing adjacent property owners and business operators can be a good source of information. Find out which tenants have lived the longest in the building and ask questions.

Examine the Property History in the Property Appraisal Report

The property appraisal report can also provide historical information about the property which could bring attention to any *hidden value* and *existing and/or potential problems.*

A property appraisal report generally will include the following historical information about a property:

- Historical vacancy and occupancy percentages
- Historical rental rates
- Historical comparable sales schedule
- Historical description of the prior interior and building-wide upgrades and renovations.
- Historical amenities, i.e. type of flooring, kitchen appliances, fixtures, etc. in the units.
- Historical neighborhood description and analysis

It's important to note that the third-party consultants typically don't physically inspect 100% of the units, components, or systems in the building. Generally, only a sample is chosen for physical inspection while other information is obtained to support their findings from credible sources.

Below is an excerpt from an actual property appraisal with regard to prior interior repairs made by the owner of the property.

Approximately 37 (33%) of the 112 units at the subject have been renovated to include stainless-faced appliances, granite countertops, glass top stoves, new bathtubs, two-toned paint, and two-inch faux wood blinds. We note that property management reported that select upgraded units received resurfaced Formica countertops instead of granite and that select upgraded units feature a combination of stainless-faced and black appliances. The exact number of these combinations was unknown, although according to the rent roll all upgraded units per each unit type are receiving higher market rents. None of the units reportedly feature washer/dryer connections, and approximately 50% of all units have built-in stainless-faced microwave ovens.

This historical information about the interior upgrades and/or renovations can provide you with an opportunity to uncover *untapped hidden value.*

For example, assume the rents for the renovated units are $200 per month higher than those of non-renovated units and the renovation cost is $10,000 per unit. The payback period is 4.17 years. However, as you have learned that applying cap rate power to the increased gross income of $2,400 per annum, assuming a 6% cap would translate to approximately $40,000 per unit of additional gross equity. The fact that only 33% of the units have been renovated would indicate that a value-add opportunity exists to substantially increase the NOI and property value.

Examine the Property History in the Title Report

An examination of the existing title policy can reveal a good deal of historical information about the property.

As soon as you receive an executed contract, make sure that your attorney obtains a copy of the existing title report from the seller and provides you with a copy. Your attorney should then order a new title report with the same title company because they have familiarity with the property and any past problems that may have existed.

To ensure that clear title exists, the title company does a complete examination of the property records, known as a title search, in order to ensure that the seller who claims to own the property actually does own the property. The title company searches the historical records of the property and describes in their report the property's title history or chain of title. A title report will generally describe in their report the following historical information that will help you answer the question, "*__What was it?__*"

- If any royalty, surface use, or mineral rights leases or agreements exist.
- If there are any deed restrictions on use.
- History of any liens.
- If any memorandum of leases exists.
- History of any current and prior mortgages on the property.
- History and disclosure of any oil and gas or other easements.
- History and identification of any environmentally suspect historical owners of the property, such as a gas station or dry cleaner.

Side Note: Use the internet. Google or other search engines can provide you with a tremendous amount of historical information about the property. There are services you can subscribe to, such as Property Shark, which provide you with both current and historical information. I also find Wikipedia to be a good source of information.

Real-Life Example:

Cannon Restaurant & Bar Supply Co. operated a restaurant and bar supply business for many years from a one-story building located in the Bowery section of Manhattan. Cannon's owner decided to open a new business division to manufacture pizza ovens. The new venture would require more working space and storage than presently existed. They decided to dig out the basement. While using a jackhammer to bang out the floor, a worker was unexpectedly startled as the floor broke open, revealing a 15-foot drop. After gutting and cleaning out the new space, an elevator was installed to lead from the ground floor to the new basement. Incredibly, as the men were digging the jack-hammer again broke through the floor, revealing another large drop as the floor beneath them crumbled. While cleaning out the new space, they found old newspapers, menus, and other artifacts. That space had been the home of the once-famous Sammy's Follies, a nightclub from 1934 to 1969. Sammy's Follies originally occupied three levels of the building and represented approximately 15,000 SF of space. Cannon was utilizing only 5,000 SF. Besides solving Cannon's immediate need for additional space, the value of the building was substantially increased. If fact, the estimated current value is approximately $15 million.

At one point, approximately 10 to 12 years ago, before the discovery was made, Cannon's owner wanted to sell the property and move to a larger space. Imagine how he would have felt if the new owner would have asked and answered the question, "*What was it?*"

What Can It Be?

To properly answer this question, you must uncover information that will enable you to determine what actions you can take to maximize the prop-erty's value. This generally has to do with such factors as zoning laws, location, the existing footprint, building structure, etc. For example, many properties' valuation is based upon the amount of "buildable" SF that can be constructed on the site, rather than the NOI, especially if condominiums can be built on the property.

In most circumstances, the largest increase in value can be achieved when the existing zoning permits more density or additional construction allowed on the property. This means the potential for a significant increase in rentable SF should translate into a significant increase in net operating income and property value. Whenever a municipality makes a change to allow more density on the site, they effectively give the owner a winning *concrete lotto ticket* to become an instant millionaire.

I recommend that you review Chapter 3 which analyzes the zoning for the Dallas Arms Apartments. These notes explain the various factors that determine the type of building and improvements that can be legally constructed on a property, given the local district's existing zoning regulations. These factors include, but are not limited to, the following:

- Lot Size: Represents the number of acres and square footage of the lot.

- Density: Represents the maximum number of units that can be built on the site.

- Zoning: Represents a specific classification for allowing construction in the zoning district the property is located in. For example, in the case of the Dallas Arms Apartments the MF-2(A) classification means Residential Multifamily - Low Density.

- Height Restriction: Represents how high and therefore how many floors or stories are permitted to be built on the site.

- Other factors: Accessibility rules, parking requirements, setbacks, etc.

"***What can it be?***" refers to what appraisers generally describe as the "highest and best use" of the property. The Appraisal of Real Estate, Tenth Edition, defines "highest and best use" as *"the reasonably probable and legal use of vacant land or an improved property, which is physically possible, appropriately supported, financially feasible, and that results in the highest value."*

Highest and Best Use

Many times, an existing building on a site *does not* represent the highest and best use of the property. However, the existing use generally continues even though the value of the land, as *further improved* or as *vacant*, exceeds the existing value of the property. This situation creates a great opportunity for a purchaser to uncover hidden value in properties.

Arriving at a determination of the highest and best use of a property involves considering the following four criteria:

1. Legal and/or Probable Uses

Those uses which are permitted under the current zoning laws or for which there is a reasonable chance that the zoning may be changed and for which there are no deed restrictions.

a. Certificate of Occupancy (C of O)

A good way to ascertain what legal uses are permitted for the property is to examine the property's certificate of occupancy. A certificate of occupancy is a document issued by a local government agency, usually the building department, certifying that the building is in compliance with all building codes and laws that make the building suitable for occupancy.

Additionally, the C of O will generally describe the legal uses that the property can be used for, such as residential, including single-family and multi-family properties, retail, commercial, industrial, or mixed-use. This classification is to prevent the property from being used in a way it was not intended.

b. Deed Restrictions

Another way of determining if the use of the property has any limitations or restrictions is to examine the title policy. For example, a title policy will disclose if the property is a participant in any affordable income program which may limit the amount of rent that can be charged.

Real-Life Example:

We own a small shopping center in Texas. The center is an out parcel of a larger adjacent center built by the same developer. The developer put in a deed restriction on the title so our center can never lease the space to a hamburger, ice cream, or liquor business.

While answering the question "What can it be?," always examine the Certificate of Occupancy and the title report to find out if there is any use or other restrictions on the property.

2. Physically Possible Uses

Those uses which the site can physically accommodate, taking into account the site's size, shape, topography, frontage, etc. as well as the availability of public utilities.

Real-Life Example:

Assume that the existing zoning and C of O for a 50-unit building permits you to add another three floors to it (another 25 units). Are the conditions at the site (structure, frontage, adequate light, etc.) able to support the additional floors and units? Maybe not.

Once the site meets the first two criteria above, then there are financial considerations.

3. Financial Feasibility

Those uses that are legal and physically possible, which produce a positive return.

<u>Real-Life Example:</u>

Assuming a property meets the criteria of it being both legally and physically possible. Now ask: does it make economic sense? Just because the zoning will allow another three floors to be built, will the increase in net income justify the construction cost?

4. Maximally Productive (Highest and Best Use)

Of the uses which are financially feasible, which produces the highest rate of return? For example, an apartment building's use is one that may be *physically possible, legally permissible, and financially feasible* which will yield the *highest net return.*

After considering the answers to the above-mentioned criteria of (i) *Legal and/or Probable Uses, (ii) Physically Possible Uses and (iii) Financial Feasibility,* the appraiser will use the information to render an opinion of which of the uses represents the *"highest and best use" of the property."*

Appraiser's Methods to Value Property

The three basic methods typically used by appraisers to value a property are (i) the Cost Method, (ii) the Income Capitalization Method, and (iii) the Sales Comparison Method.

Below is a very general description of each of these methods.

The Cost Method:

This method is based upon the reasoning that the value of a property can be determined by the current cost to build a replacement property on the site. Generally, this method is used to value newer properties.

The Sales Comparison Method:

This method is based on the reasoning that a prospective purchaser wouldn't pay more for a property than the cost to acquire a property with the same structure and amenities. The comparables are adjusted according to the terms of sale, age, location, size, financing, and physical characteristics of the comparable as compared to the subject property.

The Income Capitalization Method:
This method involves a computation of anticipated current and future net operating income and then applying a cap rate to determine the value. The NOI income streams are then "capitalized" or discounted to determine the value.

My opinion is that appraisals aren't a very accurate method of determining property value. I consider, but don't rely too much on (i) how much per unit the property is selling for or (ii) the comparable sales schedules. Remember, no two properties are the same, and each property has its own personality.

Property Valuation Example

Consider the following scenario:

- A property is a 250-unit Class C apartment complex located in a Class B+ area.
- The property sits on 7.0472 acres and consists of 18 separate buildings, a total of 186,000 net rentable SF.
- The buildings were constructed in the '60s and are considered to be in fairly good condition with minimal updating taking place since its construction. The complex is 98% occupied at an average rental rate of $693 per unit per month ($0.93/SF).
- The current assessment is $7,431,300, current taxes are $202,000, and the NOI with taxes of $202,000 is approximately $711,000.
- The neighborhood is in transition with several older properties being purchased for redevelopment. The subject's current density of 35 units per acre is well below the MF-2 (Multiple-Family) District's maximum dwelling unit density of 60 units per acre.

Given the age and minimal updating of the property, as well as the allowable density per acre, the question becomes: *Does the property's current use as an apartment community represent the best use of the property?* A professional appraiser's answer would be no! They would issue an opinion that the existing apartment community does not represent the property's *"highest and best use."*

An appraiser's opinion would be based on the fact that the allowable density of 60 units per acre can potentially allow for a new apartment community to be built consisting of approximately *423 units* (7.0472 x 60) which is far greater than the current *250 units* on the site.

In other words, the site is *under-built* by approximately 173 units (423 units - 250 units) or by 69%, (173 units/250 units).

If we assume the market value for vacant land in the immediate area is $44 per SF, then the property's value would not be based upon the NOI of $711,000 but rather on the vacant land or *"dirt"* (an industry term) of 307,258 SF *(7.0472 acres x 43,600 SF per acre).*

Since the market value of the dirt is $44 per SF, then the value of the property as a development site would be approximately *$13,519,352,* ($44 x 307,258 SF).

The Value as an Existing Apartment Community

If we assume the cap rate for similar properties is 6%, a *fatal mistake* would be to compute the value based on the *current* NOI which would equate to a property value of *$11,850,000,* ($711,000/6% cap rate). *But this valuation would be computed before adjusting for the impact of the post-closing reassessment.*

The potential increase in the post-closing assessment and resulting real estate taxes must be considered when determining property value. Not considering this factor could prove to be disastrous!

The current assessment is $7,431,300. However, my general rule of thumb is, *"The projections should include underwriting the post-closing assessment and corresponding real taxes calculated at 80% of the purchase price."*

Therefore, the above purchase price of $11,850,000 (*see above*) should be further adjusted by estimating the post-closing assessment at 80% of this amount or $9,480,000. Assuming a tax rate of 2.71%, the estimated real estate taxes on $9,480,000 would be $256,908.

Since the current taxes are $202,000, we should *reduce* the NOI by $54,908 ($256,908 - $202,000) or from $711,000 to *$656,092* ($711,000 - $54,908).

Applying the 6% cap rate to this amount would value the property at only *$10,934,855* ($656,092 NOI/6% cap rate), not $11,850,000 before the adjustment.

Please be aware that if you didn't understand this concept and paid $11,850,000 for the property, your real cap rate would be only 5.54% ($656,092 NOI/$11,850,000 purchase price) representing a loss in property value of *$915,145* ($11,850,000 - $10,934,855).

An appraiser would conclude that the *highest and best use* of the property would be as vacant land. In this case, the seller would probably realize the highest price for the property by selling it to a developer rather than a purchaser looking to operate the property as an apartment community.

Please be advised that all of the above categories (lot size, density, zoning class, and height restrictions) must be considered to determine the potential for additional construction on the site. This is the job of the zoning attorney and other consultants you will need to engage.

To determine the correct zoning for a property, lot size, density, zoning class, and height restrictions must all be considered in determining the potential for additional construction on the site.

My General Methods to Value a Property

The first thing I ask myself is where do I believe the property's finances and value will be in five years? I need to consider many factors, including, but not limited to, the potential to significantly increase the rent roll and decrease the operating expenses, increase the amount of rentable SF, etc. As you will see in Chapter 7, my opinion is that there are four ways to increase NOI and property value that must be considered.

Street Success Concepts to Remember

1. For all intents and purposes, the comprehensive OM that was created and illustrated in Chapter 3 for the Dallas Arms Apartments is, in effect, an example of a comprehensive property profile for that property.

2. Each and every time you look at a property, ask, answer, and analyze for yourself, the following 3 questions: (i) What is it?, (ii) What was it?, and (iii) What can it be?

3. "What is it" has to do with the actual physical condition of the property and its components at the time you plan to purchase it.

4. As a requirement of obtaining a mortgage, the lender will require that the following reports are obtained from independent third-party consultants of their choice at the purchaser's sole cost and expense: (i) Property Condition Report, (ii) Phase I Environmental Assessment Report, (iii) Termite Inspection Report, (iv) Property Appraisal Report, and (v) Updated Survey.

5. Use your network of contacts to try and obtain copies of third-party reports from other deals. Good sources are the Internet, the third-party consultants themselves, and other real estate professionals. By simply reviewing these reports, you will receive great insight into their purpose and conclusions.

6. Since you are paying for the third-party reports, you are entitled to receive copies of each of the reports. However, most lenders will wait until after closing before remitting a copy to the borrower.

7. Always notify and alert the third-party consultants of your deadlines. Even if you rely on a mortgage broker to administrate the financing function, keep pressing and keep the pressure on them. Remember, it's your earnest deposit that is at risk.

8. Before, or as soon as you receive, an executed LOI, request from the seller copies of any property condition reports, Phase I Environmental Assessment Reports, termite inspection reports, and appraisals in his possession even if they are old. Don't wait until the contract is signed and the due diligence period commences.

9. Due to the time constraints in the purchase contract regarding the due diligence period, mortgage contingency period, closing date, etc., it is extremely important that the third-party reports are ordered as soon as possible.

10. If you elect to have a property condition report prepared for you, the purchaser, try to obtain an approved list of vendors that the lender will accept. By doing so, the lender can always have the report updated for their benefit which will save on the cost.

11. A property condition report generally renders an opinion on the condition of the various building components and systems based upon visual observations, limited research, and non-invasive procedures.

12. The lender will generally estimate the cost to remediate any immediate repair and will require at closing that one-and-a-half times the estimated cost of the repair be placed into an escrow account to be held by the lender. Once the repairs have been completed, the lender will do an inspection and then release the funds to the borrower.

13. The property condition report is a summary of the consultant's observations and recommendations, given the limited scope of their engagement. The report will serve to alert you or the lender of existing and potential problems that have been observed. You will then need to ascertain the potential cost to remediate the existing or potential problem and the risk it presents. Many times, the problem can be used as a negotiating tool. Additionally, you may need to hire an expert to provide a more in-depth investigation of the problem.

14. A Phase I ESA Report is intended to protect and limit the liability of prospective property owners.

15. Similar to a property condition report, the Phase I ESA Report simply renders an opinion on the environmental condition of the property. The focus is on determining if there are any observable hazardous substances, petroleum products, etc. that have or have not been addressed to the satisfaction of the applicable regulatory authorities.

16. If the Phase I ESA Report reveals that additional investigation is warranted, then a more extensive report known as a Phase II Environmental Site Assessment Report will be required. Such a report generally requires property sampling, and laboratory analysis and is a subsurface investigation.

17. Generally, if the property was ever occupied in its history as a business that used potentially hazardous materials such as a dry cleaner, gas station, auto repair shop, etc. then a Phase II ESA Report will be required.

18. Sometimes an infestation can be the cause for high vacancies and can be used as a negotiating tool. Most times the infestation can be easily remediated.

19. Lenders will generally insist that the appraisal should be performed by a company with an MAI designation. MAI stands for Member of the

Appraisal Institute, a trade organization that monitors appraisers and holds them to a higher standard than appraisers who are simply licensed and not members of any monitoring organization.

20. The purpose of an appraisal is to estimate the fair market value of the property. However, in real life, appraisals are extremely subjective because various assumptions are made in the calculation that can substantially affect the computed value.

21. The lender will always require that they are provided with an accurate survey of the property. Generally, the prior owner has a survey in their possession and will provide it to the purchaser. The purchaser will then simply need to have the survey updated which is less expensive than the cost to prepare a brand-new survey.

22. Some of the best ways to start answering the question "***What was it?***" are to (i) review the Phase I Environmental Report, (ii) review the property appraisal, (iii) review the title report, and (iv) use the Internet. Put on your detective hat and start interviewing.

23. Understanding the type of assets and tenant uses that will generate key money is a good way to uncover hidden and potential value.

24. Try to identify and interview past owners and occupants of the property to identify historic property uses. Even interviewing adjacent property owners and business operators can be a good source of information. Find out which tenants have lived the longest in the building and ask them questions. Remember, shyness can cost you money.

25. It's important to note that the third-party consultants typically don't physically inspect 100% of the units, components or systems in the building. Generally, only a sample is chosen for physical inspection while other information is obtained to support their findings.

26. As soon as you receive an executed contract make sure that your attorney obtains a copy of the existing title report from the seller and provides you with a copy. Your attorney should then order a new title report with the same title company because they have familiarity with the property and any past problems that may have existed.

27. While answering the question "**What can it be?**," always examine the certificate of occupancy and the title report to find out if there is any use or other restrictions on the property.

28. The three basic methods typically used by appraisers to value a property are (i) the Cost Method, (ii) the Income Capitalization Method, and (iii) the Sales Comparison Method.

29. The potential increase in the post-closing assessment and resulting real estate taxes must be considered when determining property value. Not considering this factor could prove to be disastrous!

30. To determine the correct zoning for a property lot size, density, zoning class and height restrictions must all be considered in determining the potential for additional construction on the site.

CHAPTER 7

THE FOUR BASIC METHODS TO INCREASE PROPERTY VALUE

BY NOW YOU realize that cash flow and tax benefits are great, but the big money in real estate is made when the value of the property *substantially increases.*

In Chapter 2, you learned to understand the rent roll and how the effect of applying cap rate power to a compounding rent roll translates to substantial increases in property value. You also learned how upgrading and renovating individual units further translates to increases in property value. Now we will discuss additional methods to further increase NOI and property value.

There are four basic methods available to increase property value. They are as follows:

Purchase a Property and...

1. Do *Zippo* (nothing), but pray the value increases

2. Increase the property's revenue

3. Increase the property's amount of rentable square feet (RSF)

4. Decrease the property's operating expenses

Basically, there are four methods to increase property value. They are to (i) do zippo (nothing), (ii) increase the property's revenue, (iii) increase the property's amount of RSF, and (iv) decrease the property's operating expenses.

In this chapter, we will be discussing the first three methods to increase property value. Decreasing operating expenses will be discussed in great detail in Chapter 8.

Purchase a Property and *Do Zippo* (Nothing)

The most common method of many property owners is to simply *purchase a property and do zippo to increase property value.*

This is the riskiest way to own and operate property. Keep the status quo; don't rock the boat; if it ain't broke, don't fix it. Don't be too aggressive, don't raise rents, and continue to operate the property as before. This is *not* the method the pros use to increase property value.

Real-Life Example:

In 2019, we purchased a 112-unit student housing project in Austin, Texas. The property had been owned by a local family for many years. It was in relatively good condition but needed a facelift. Their focus was keeping the property as occupied as possible. To rent the units, they used locators at an annual cost of $90,000 even though the market was strong. They were old school and afraid that changes would jeopardize the occupancy. This is the doing zippo method. We, on the other hand, saw an opportunity to substantially decrease this expense, which would translate to increasing the NOI and property value. After cosmetically upgrading the property, the locator cost since 2010 has been less than $35,000 per year, and we have been 100% occupied ever since.

The real estate wannabes are constantly hearing how great real estate is, but they have no idea why. The newspapers report new record-setting prices for properties. Mabel from Mahjong tells her stories; Frank from golf brags that he made $50,000 flipping a contract. People feel they're missing out on great opportunities. Their mindset becomes, *"I've got to get into real estate before I miss the boat!"*

By the time you read about an area being "hot," it's usually two or more years too late. It's not a healthy market if a property can be purchased at market price, then only *six weeks* later be resold at a price that's $50,000 to $100,000 higher. It is a feeding frenzy based on hype, not on sound real estate fundamentals. At that point, you're just participating in a game of musical chairs.

People can't figure out how to invest the money that's burning a hole in their pockets and get a decent return. Banks offer interest of less than 1%, and they don't even give away toasters anymore. The stock market is both volatile and corrupt. People feel that with real estate, even if the market drops, they will still have bricks and mortar.

Purchasing a property and doing zippo (nothing) is strictly for amateurs and not the method of choice of the pros.

Increases in Base Rent Verses Increases in Operating Expenses

The general belief of these wannabe owners is that base rents will continue to increase, which has been the case for years. The belief is that, given its larger dollar base than operating expenses, the NOI will grow and translate into increased property value over time. Furthermore, since the tenant's rents are covering the debt service payments, purchasers view the amortization portion of the mortgage payment as an additional return on their investment.

If you purchase a property and do zippo (nothing) to increase revenue, you might receive a decent return on your investment, but you will leave a lot of money on the table.

If base rents don't continue to increase at a significantly higher rate than the property's operating expenses it will translate to only marginal increases, and in some cases, decreases in property value.

Beware of Overbuilding in the Area

Many seasoned investors have come to believe that rents will keep increasing. They take it for granted. But who's to say that rents will continue to increase? There are many reasons why rents may actually decrease in an area. The most common reason is due to *overbuilding*.

⇨ *When an area suddenly becomes "hot" and there is an abundance of capital available, developers will quickly scramble to build and/or renovate properties with no end in sight. At some point, supply will exceed demand, and the area will become overbuilt. When an area becomes overbuilt, rents and occupancy will decrease.*

The Domino Effect of Overbuilding

If an owner has trouble renting units in a newly built luxury property located in an overbuilt market, they will be forced to lower rents to avoid vacancies. The difference between the reduced rents for these brand-new properties and the older non-renovated properties in the area may not be that significant. For a little extra cost, especially when roommates are involved, tenants can live in a much nicer property. This causes a domino effect, forcing the owners of older non-renovated properties to lower their rents as well. Owners will also be forced to offer more tenant concessions, incentives, etc.

Real-Life Example:

The student housing market in San Marcos, Texas, has been extremely hot for the past three years. As a result, many new projects have been built, causing the area to become overbuilt. For the pre-covid 2019-2020 semester, the market occupancy is below 75%. Projects with vacant units have substantially lowered rents and have incurred substantial additional costs for marketing, gift cards, concessions, locator fees, etc. as they desperately try to lease their units.

Increased Governmental Oversight

It's not just overbuilding; many markets are concurrently facing new or increased governmental oversight procedures which result in direct increases in operating expenses. These include, but are not limited to, shifting the responsibility for performing repair and maintenance of city-owned streets and walkways to the owner, green energy requirements, increases in issuing non-compliance violations, stricter ADA requirements, etc. Additionally, local taxing districts always look for money, which forces owners to engage attorneys and tax consultants to fight larger assessments of their properties each year.

Real-Life Example:

As a result of increased governmental oversight, city inspectors are visiting our properties in Dallas, Texas, and constantly issuing warnings that we will be assessed penalties if repairs are not made in a timely manner. These inspections resulted in significant increases in operating expenses.

In summary, if your preferred method of ownership is purchasing a property and doing zippo but pray the value increases, your chances of success will be extremely low. However, if you adopt my other methods, such as increasing the property's revenue, increasing the property's amount of rentable square feet, and decreasing the property's operating expenses, your margin of error for success will increase significantly.

Purchase a Property and Increase the Property's Revenue

Make Tenants Want To Live At Your Property

There are many ways to increase the property's gross revenue. Gross revenue is base rent, plus any additional income generated by the property. The potential for increased property value often lies in the growth potential of the NOI. However, before even considering trying to increase the property's revenue, there is one major question: *Do tenants like living at your property?*

Tenants hate taking cold showers, freezing in the winter, sweating in the summer, feeling unsafe, etc. Tenants don't stay long at a property where work orders aren't timely addressed, management is rude and unfriendly, units contain broken appliances, units are infested with rats, mice, cockroaches, bed bugs, bad odors, etc., and where drug deals are made in the open. Tenants want to live in a community that is clean and well-maintained with friendly, responsible management where they feel safe and the building systems all work.

⇨ *Before you even consider trying to increase the property's revenue, answer this question first; Do tenants like living at your property?*

⇨ *A major key to operating any successful property is reducing turnover. Remember that each time a tenant vacates, you will need to hire a cleaning company, repair and/or replace the carpet, pay rental agent fees, offer rent specials, and suffer rent loss until a new tenant takes occupancy. This is not the case when a tenant renews their lease.*

Maintaining and/or Increasing Occupancy

You can't collect revenue from vacant units. It's such a simple concept, but many property owners don't seem to understand the importance of keeping the property as occupied as possible.

If a property experiences low occupancy, you will lose base rent, in addition to any expense reimbursements and other income you may be receiving. These losses will significantly affect the property's NOI and property value.

⇨ *Keep in mind that you can't collect any revenue from vacant units. Always strive for high occupancy, even if it means lowering the rent and giving concessions and monthly specials, etc. You should always be cognizant of the market rent and occupancy percentage in the immediate area.*

<u>Real-Life Example:</u>

We own a student housing community in Austin, Texas. The property has historically been 100% leased. We changed managing agents with the start of the new semester two weeks away. At that point, we had five vacant units. Our leasing agent waited too long to offer rent specials and lower the rents. Now they are scrambling to lease the remaining five units. Meanwhile, our competitors beat us to the punch by reducing rents and offering concessions earlier than we did. We missed the market.

The average rent for each of the five vacant units is $1,500 per month. That means we stand to lose $90,000 per annum if these units remain vacant ($1,500 x 5 units x 12 MO's).

If the leasing personnel had monitored the market better, they might have lowered rents by $200 per month and/or offered a $100 gift card. In that case, our loss would have only been $18,000 ($300 x 5 units x 12 months), and instead of receiving no income, we would receive $72,000 ($90,000 - $18,000). This is in addition to receiving any reimbursements and other income generated. Seems like common sense doesn't it?

Reducing Turnover

⇨ *If your property is transient in nature, you will experience higher turnover rates and substantial higher operating expenses than a property with lower turnover.*

A major key to success is reducing the property's turnover. Always remember that each time a tenant vacates a unit, you will need to incur costly turnover expenses. Your mantra should be to do everything you can to keep the property as occupied as possible. Remember that tenants are your customers and should be treated fairly. I once saw a great sign that said, "*A customer can take years to get but seconds to lose.*" Do everything you can to make tenants want to live at your property.*

Each time a tenant vacates there are substantial turnover costs incurred. Just how much will depend upon the condition of the unit when it's vacated. The vacant unit almost always needs to be repainted or touched-up; the carpets need to be cleaned, dyed, repaired, or replaced; floors need to be repaired or replaced; and resurfacing needs to be done to the bathroom tubs and countertops in the kitchen. Additionally, the kitchen cabinets may need to be repaired and repainted. You won't receive rent while all that is being done, and you may need to offer concessions or incentives to the new tenant. You also may need to engage a collection agency to collect monies owed by the prior tenant.

For our example property, the Dallas Arms, you can assume, on average, approximately $1,565 for interior costs and $1,439 for various re-leasing costs. The estimated average total costs of $3,004 can be higher or lower, depending on various factors. However, if your property is transient in nature, you can expect significant turnover costs, especially for Class C and D type properties.

However, when a tenant renews their lease, there are rarely costs incurred, unless you wish to provide incentives for renewing. I suggest that you do everything you can to obtain renewals. *But it all starts with making tenants want to live at your property.**

⇨ *Remember that tenants are your customers and should be treated fairly. A customer can take years to get but seconds to lose. Do everything you can to obtain renewals.*

---

*See Appendix 1 for examples of the Costs associated with a transient Class C Property.

Example:

Assume a property consists of 100 units. Further assume that 50% of the units turnover each year, and the average turnover cost is $2,500. The annual turnover expense would be $125,000 ($50 units x $2,500). Even if we lower the turnover rate to 30%, the annual cost is $75,000. They are still large numbers. However, in theory, if there was no turnover, the turnover costs would be almost zero. My experience is that for transient Class C and D garden apartment properties, the turnover rate can range from 40% to 60%, depending on various factors. In rare cases, garden apartment properties can have turnover expenses of only 10% to 20% per annum.

⇨ *Excessive turnover expenses will be part of the property's NOI and calculation of property value by financial institutions and prospective purchasers. Therefore, a property that has high turnover expenses can have a devastating effect on property value. On the other hand, this situation is usually due to bad management and can present a great opportunity for prospective purchasers.*

Generally, a community that is desirable should offer tenants a safe and secure environment, convenience, responsible management, various amenities, and functional building systems. Remember, the goal is to make tenants want to live at your property.

Provide a Safe and Secure Environment

Controlled Access Gates:
Having controlled access gates is a great selling point for potential tenants, especially in Class C and D areas. These gates provide tenants with more security by limiting access to the property, thus limiting car theft and damage. It is extremely expensive to install these gates around a property if they don't already exist.

Patrol Service:

Implementing a patrol service is a good way to increase security, especially in communities that are located in Class C and D areas. Garden apartment complexes are usually spread out in different buildings on the property. We usually have a patrol service during the night. A patrol officer walks the property, looking for broken or non-functioning equipment, break-ins, illegal activity, such as drug deals or drug usage, or breaking up loitering by non-tenants.

A patrol service should provide management with a written report on their observations, including the time and date of the report. These reports are extremely helpful in documenting events and alerting management to issues so they can be corrected. Believe me, tenants are aware of these issues and are happy when action is taken by management. Correcting issues in a timely manner helps limit potential liabilities and makes tenants feel safe and secure at the property.

Patrol services are not necessarily a paid outside service. At many of our properties, a group of volunteer tenants patrol and issue reports to management for the good of the community. They serve as another set of eyes and ears watching out for the tenants.

Exterior Lighting:

Exterior lighting is another way to increase security at the property, especially at nighttime. Make sure the lighting is always in working order and change the bulbs on a regular basis. Criminal activity does not usually occur in well-lit areas.

Cameras:

Cameras provide you with a picture record of problems that occur. We have installed cameras at most of our properties, especially in areas that are conducive to damage or are secluded, such as in the gym, laundry rooms, basements, etc. We also installed cameras at various places in our courtyard and parking areas which worked to limit car theft and damage.

Prohibit Dangerous Pets:

Certain breeds of dogs can create a potentially dangerous environment. Nobody wants to deal with loud dogs barking or a large dog jumping on them, especially when children are involved.

We are pet-friendly and allow pets, as long as tenants are willing to submit their pets to a pre-lease interview. At the interview, we take a picture of the pet for the file. Tenants are given rules on unacceptable pet behavior with a warning that violators will be fined and evicted. No reptiles, such as alligators or snakes, or uncaged rodents, etc. are permitted.

We understand that tenants love their pets, and a property that allows pets is very attractive, but safety comes first. At many of our properties, we offer convenient pet parks located throughout the property furnished with refreshment stations, even if it's a water hose and pet waste bags attached to disposal bins.

Get Rid of Troublemakers:

We won't tolerate troublemakers at our properties, and we take immediate steps to evict them from our property. Troublemakers can lead to outright bullying, drugs, and other illegal activities, which causes tenants to become fearful of living at the property.

Take Care of Immediate Repairs:

Repairs that create an unsafe situation are deemed to be life, safety, health, building code violations, etc., and must be corrected immediately. Besides exposing an owner to potential liability, tenants notice these dangerous situations and may no longer want to live at your property. One of my rules is to never ignore any situation that may jeopardize the life and safety of my tenants.

Stressing that your property provides a safe and secure environment is a great selling point for not only attracting tenants but for keeping them as well.

Provide Convenience

Laundry Room:
Having a separate laundry room is a necessity rather than an amenity. Additionally, if the laundry equipment has a card system, it helps to limit theft. One of the most common tenant complaints is that the equipment in the laundry room is not working. Always make sure the equipment is working, and demand that your laundry vendor provides you with the newest state-of-the-art equipment.

Washers and Dryers in Units:
Washer and dryer connections in the units are a plus, especially if the laundry room is small or not nearby. The question is who will bear the equipment cost and the responsibility for maintenance?

Good Schools Nearby with Available Transportation:
Remember, the name of the game for garden apartment communities is to limit turnover and become as non-transient as possible. An important feature I look for in a property is a school system that is highly rated and conveniently located. Good school systems are tremendous draws to a community and lead to much less tenant turnover. Tenants are leery of taking their kids out of school and relocating elsewhere.

Another factor to consider is the distance from the schools, and if public transportation is available nearby. If a bus stop is less than a block or two away, it's a big plus.

⇨ *Good school systems nearby or near readily available public transportation are tremendous draws to a community and lead to much less tenant turnover. Tenants are leery of taking their kids out of school and relocating elsewhere.*

Parking:
One of the biggest complaints from tenants is a lack of available parking at the property for both tenants and visitors. Communities that wish to limit

turnover and become non-transient must offer adequate onsite parking or have adequate street parking available. Parking problems at your property will hurt your leasing efforts and lead to increased turnover. It will be even worse if public transportation is not nearby. Imagine having to walk 10 blocks to the train or bus stop in the freezing cold.

Parking is extremely important and is often overlooked by prospective tenants until they actually become occupants. Then they become extremely unhappy. Nobody wants to come home after a hard day's work in the freezing winter and have to pray for a parking spot to open up.

Parking Ratios:
As discussed in Chapter 3, The Dallas Arms Apartments consists of 60 units with a total of 86 parking spaces, two of which are reserved for handicapped parking. The net number of spaces available for resident parking is 84 spaces, providing a parking ratio of 1.40 spaces per unit.

⇨ *For garden apartment communities, look for a parking ratio of at least 1.25 to 1.50 spaces per unit or higher. The higher the better. However, this will depend upon the unit mix, unit size, and the number of occupant drivers.*

Possible Parking Solutions:

- Try to attract an older tenancy that doesn't drive and is more comfortable using public transportation.
- Offer discounts to tenants who don't own a car.
- Offer discounts to tenants who carpool.
- Monitor the parking and use an outside service to tow illegally parked vehicles.
- Issue assigned parking spots to tenants.
- See if the city will permit you to create additional parking spots on the property by removing grass or paved areas.

At our properties, we generally provide one free space for studio and one-bedroom units and two free spaces for two- and three-bedroom units. There is an additional monthly charge for additional spaces, if available.

⇨ *It is imperative that you become aware of a parking problem at your property and take immediate action to improve the situation. Offer incentives to tenants who don't drive, don't own a car, are more comfortable taking public transportation, or are willing to carpool. Have an outside service tow away illegally parked cars.*

Covered Parking:
Covered parking is a valued amenity, especially in states like Texas where hailstorms are commonplace and can cause damage to the tenant's cars. Installing covered parking is usually cost-prohibitive, so it's a big plus if it already exists.

Adequate Signage:
Inadequate signage may lose many prospective tenants who are looking to rent apartments, especially at night. C and D properties attract prospective tenants who drive by properties looking to rent at non-working hours.

Some years ago, we installed well-lit signage at a property and were amazed at how leasing increased immediately. Signs need to be easily visible to drive-by traffic and should highlight that units are available for rent, along with any specials being offered. Additionally, having signage indicating the location of the leasing office, gym, laundry rooms, pool, storage, etc. make it easier for tenants to locate these areas, especially at night.

Provide Responsible Management

Making people want to live at your property, reducing turnover, increasing revenue, decreasing operating expenses, etc., all depend upon the quality of the property's management. Management makes or breaks you. I have witnessed both good and bad management, and, believe me, it makes a tremendous difference. Good management leads to less vacancy and lower operating expenses. Bad management does the opposite.

⇨ *Making people want to live at your property will reduce turnover, increase gross revenue, decrease operating expenses, etc. It all depends upon the quality of the property's management. Management will make or break you.*

Onsite Leasing/Management Office:
It's best to have a central office onsite as a base for leasing and managing. The property needs a leasing associate onsite to show vacant units, attend to tenant needs, and monitor tenant behavior. Properties that have onsite employees and a central management office are more desirable than those that don't. Additionally, we generally allow tenants the convenience of the facilities at the leasing office such as the copy machine, Federal Express drop off, etc.

For some properties, we converted a studio unit into a small leasing and management office.

Onsite Management Personnel:
Having maintenance and management personnel living onsite at the property is a big plus. Tenants need to easily communicate any problems that occur and have these problems resolved in a timely manner. Tenant problems that are not addressed and resolved will result in lower occupancy and a more transient community. Additionally, tenants will complain to the local regulatory agencies, and your community will develop a bad reputation and may be assessed penalties.

For example, when a tenant complains about a lack of heat or air conditioning or plumbing issues, management issues a work order describing the type of problem then determines who on staff to assign the job to. Sometimes maintenance staff can resolve the problem; other times the problem will require an outside vendor to resolve. Tenants generally understand that building systems sometimes break down, but they will not tolerate a community where management delays resolving problems for weeks or months at a time.

For most of our garden apartment properties with at least 50 units, we have full-time managing/leasing personnel and full-time maintenance personnel. Additionally, at least one of these employees will be given a free apartment or a discount as part of their compensation.

Offering Convenience Can be Dangerous:
Sometimes offering convenience can cause you aggravation and money.

Example:

To streamline the work order process and make it easier for tenants to communicate any issues or problems, a managing agent set up an online work order program. This program allowed tenants to issue their own work orders from their computers. Management would then read the work orders and let the tenant know the estimated time the problem would be fixed. Their good intentions unfortunately backfired. Management was inundated with double the number of work orders and couldn't efficiently service the tenants increased needs.

⇨ *It's human nature that the more convenient it is to complain, the more complaints there will be. Be aware that sometimes offering convenience can cost you aggravation and money.*

Have Friendly, Helpful Employees:
All of our employees are required to act professionally and wear uniforms indicating their name and type of job they have. For example, Jose Lopez, Assistant Maintenance Technician. Unfriendly, rude, and unresponsive employees should be quickly terminated because they will antagonize tenants and ultimately hurt occupancy.

Welcome Package:
A nice touch to start the owner-tenant relationship is to send new tenants a welcome letter and gift package. Gifts such as candy, coffee mugs, etc. with the property's logo should be placed in the unit prior to move-in with an accompanying welcome letter and package from management on the

day of the move-in. The package should include a copy of the resident's paperwork, emergency telephone numbers, contact information for the staff indicating their job descriptions, etc. The package should also include information regarding the resident referral program. The gift and the welcome package will let the tenant know that you value their tenancy.

Provide Amenities

Community Events:

Community events, such as pizza parties, holiday events, and other social activities, may seem like a good idea on the surface. However, my experience is that at a lot of these events tenants start talking about the property's problems, rents they are being charged, any discounts that they weren't offered, etc. For C and D properties, substitute social events with holiday decorations to set a mood at the property. Additionally, my experience is that even if you offer social gatherings, many of the tenants do not attend anyway.

➪ *Staging community events at the property where tenants can congregate may seem like a good idea on the surface. However, always be aware of the possible downside. At these events, tenants are given a platform to voice their complaints to other tenants which include, but are not limited to, discussing the property's problems, rents they are being charged, any concessions they were or weren't offered, and/or to complain about management and the owner.*

Pools:

On the face of it, it seems that having a pool is a big plus, but I don't agree when it comes to smaller Class C and D properties. A pool can be a nuisance, and it can increase your potential for increased liability, especially if children are living at the property. Maintaining a pool in good working order is also expensive. We fill in most of our pools and replace them with barbecue and picnic areas. However, due to the type of tenancy, pools are a must for luxury type Class A and B properties and larger properties.

Curb Appeal:

Impressive curb appeal, such as a freshly painted property that is well-landscaped and clean, attracts more prospective tenants who will lease at the property.

Example:

We own a garden apartment community in Austin, Texas. We are able to obtain rent premiums because of its beautifully landscaped courtyards surrounded by large oak trees that create a special ambiance. It is, however, very expensive to maintain such extensive landscaping. Therefore, you must know what the market demands.

Barbecue Facilities:

People love to barbecue. Therefore, having barbecue facilities on-site featuring grills and picnic-style seating areas is a big plus, especially for Class C and D properties.

Fitness Center:

While not a necessity, having an onsite fitness center is a great amenity that many of your competitors may not have. At one of our properties, we had two laundry rooms. We decided to convert one of them to a small (approx. 500 SF) fitness center. The tenants love the fitness center and use it on a regular basis.

The fitness center should be covered under your general liability policy for the property. Be sure it is! You shouldn't need any separate coverage for this feature.

Provide Functional Building Systems

Building systems should always be serviced on a regular basis to ensure they are in working order. The building systems include boilers, storage tanks, pipes, HVAC and electrical system, air handlers, condensers, master or individual meters, wiring, circuit breakers, smoke detectors, fire extinguishers, etc.

Increasing Revenue

Once you establish your property as a great place to live, then you can look for further ways to increase revenue.

Increasing the Base Rent

When the market is strong and occupancy rates at your property and the immediate area are high, you may want to consider increasing base rents and/or reducing or discontinuing any concessions, monthly specials, etc. that are currently being offered.

Assume your property has been 95% to 100% occupied for the past six to twelve months, and your rents have only increased marginally during this period. You don't have to have a waiting list of prospective tenants before you decide to increase base rents. However, before you start increasing base rents, consider the following:

Prepare a Unit Inventory Schedule

For every property I own, I have a schedule that details the condition of each unit's components and features and rates each unit's pluses and minuses. We call this a unit inventory schedule, and we prepare it after we have walked every unit.

The unit inventory schedule should include, but not be limited to, the following:

- Floor number, unit number, SF
- Current monthly rent and additional charges, i.e.; utilities, parking, etc.
- Appliances: condition of stoves, refrigerators, microwaves, dishwashers, etc. Indicate if replacement needed, if appliances are standard or upgraded.
- Cabinets: type and condition, if replacement or repair needed

- Paint: indicates if full or partial painting needed
- Fixtures: condition, if standard or upgraded, if replacement needed
- Flooring and subflooring: if carpet or plank wood, if replacement needed
- View rating: type of view, i.e. if overlooking landscaped courtyard, pool, or the dumpster
- Location of parking: rates and indicates the distance from assigned parking spot
- Bathrooms: condition and if repair or replacement needed for tubs, countertops, floors, etc.

Preparing a unit inventory schedule will help you quickly identify and compare the attributes of the different units and the rents being obtained. Once this is achieved, you have the information to intelligently develop a specific plan for raising base rents.

For example, assume a tenant vacates a unit. Simply look at the unit inventory schedule and determine the following:

- Are the appliances upgraded?
- Are there plank wood floors, upgraded fixtures, upgraded lighting, etc.?
- Is the unit on the second or third floor? Which is less desirable?
- Is the unit further away from the assigned parking spot?
- What type of view does the unit have?

Other Considerations

If you plan to upgrade the units, you need to determine the amount of the increase for each of the units. Can the increase in base rent be justified to the tenants? For example, will a tenant appreciate that a certain unit's monthly rent is $150 higher because it has new appliances, plank flooring, and two-tone paint?

- Take into consideration any additional rent the tenants will be required to pay such as electric, water and sewer, trash, etc. when comparing base rents in the immediate area.

- Analyze how much the monthly base rent increased over the past six to eight months for new leases at the property. Was the occupancy affected?

- Determine if increasing the base rent can be justified because of any recent property-wide amenities, exterior upgrades, or renovations.

Before increasing base rents, determine where your rent levels are in comparison to the market in the immediate area. Remember to compare apples to apples and take into consideration whether it's an ABP property or if RUBS are charged. Take an inventory of each of the units and indicate each unit's pluses and minuses.

Long-Term Tenants and Renewals

Another matter to consider is how much to increase the base rent for long-term tenants. There is a fine line between a rent increase and the breaking point that makes a tenant move. Chances are their rents have not increased substantially over the years and are, in fact, below market levels. However, they have been loyal tenants who have contributed to the occupancy, and if you bring the rents to market, they may vacate. Then you bear the substantial turnover costs. The following factors should be weighed in your decision to increase their base rent.

- Determine what percentage of the tenants have been living at the property for more than three years. Consider the condition of these units and determine how much below-market the base monthly rent is for these long-term tenants and how much the rents have increased over the last three years. Many managing agents send a renewal lease to the tenant a few months before expiration, indicating a rent increase. Sometimes the increase is enough to shock the tenant, and they start to consider moving. A good procedure to implement is meeting with the tenant a few months before their lease expires and discussing why you feel the increase is justified to see their reaction. At that point, a business decision will need to be made. On various occasions, I have offered tenants upgrades or other concessions to renew. The key is to learn the tenant's intentions before they commit to moving to another property. We have saved countless tenants from moving this way.

- You should also be aware of the mindset of the property's leasing agents. Do the leasing agents earn higher commissions from renewals or when a new tenant is obtained? What is their level of motivation for obtaining renewals. Human nature at work again!

⇨ *A good procedure to implement is a few months before any lease expires, try to meet with the tenant and discuss why you feel a rent increase is justified and see their reaction. Even if there will be no rent increase, management should still meet with all tenants before lease expiration and ascertain what their likelihood of renewing is, so you have a chance of inducing them to renew. The key is to learn the tenant's intentions before they commit to moving to another property.*

Are Your Rents Currently Higher or Lower Than Market?

Survey and analyze the rents and occupancy rates in the immediate area.

Once you determine how your base rent levels compare with the immediate market, you can develop a specific plan for raising rents.

However, be aware that most owners don't want to publicize the actual rents and additional rents they are receiving. Property owners tend to hold their cards very close to the vest. There are many good reasons for this. For example, taxing authorities may use the information to increase assessments or brokers may use the information for comparables in their OM's, which may limit any advantages that owners may have.

⇨ *Please remember that publicized asking rents are often different than the actual rent the tenant will ultimately pay. For example, owners sometimes have a program known as "look and lease." This program offers a prospective tenant a discount if they sign a lease right after seeing the unit.*

It takes more work, but to find out the actual rent being charged, you can actually apply for a unit and see what deals are offered. Factor into your analysis any concessions or other incentives that competitive properties are offering.

Another way to find the actual rent being charged in the area is to pretend you're a prospective purchaser and ask brokers to send you the OM's for similar properties that are for sale in the area. The OM should contain significant information about the nearby property for sale, including an *actual rent roll* for the property. The OM should also include various comparable property information, including the base rents, other charges, and amenities they offer.

Make Sure You Compare Apples to Apples

Remember that no two properties are the same. However, some may be similar. Properties have different locations, unit sizes, amenities, etc. to take into consideration. Make sure you compare apples to apples and not apples to oranges.

⇨ *While performing due diligence on a prospective property I'm considering purchasing, I always look at the rent obtained for the past four to six months to see if there is a steady progression of increases and why. Were increases simply across-the-board increases, the result of upgrades made, or special incentives given? Remember we want to compare apples to apples.*

Will Increasing Rents Potentially Hurt the Occupancy?

Increasing base rents is often one of the managing agent's functions. They are supposed to be constantly monitoring the market. However,

I always want to be involved with the decision to increase or decrease base rents.

⇨ *A lazy managing agent may not be motivated to increase rents when a vacancy occurs since it means physically showing the units to more prospective tenants. Additionally, a more occupied building makes the managing agent look much better in the eyes of the owner. It takes away one of their major complaints: Why are we only 88% occupied?*

- Review the length of time units were vacant and why. Is it a less desirable unit?
- Review the past 90 days of move-outs for lengths of time they stayed. Try to find out why they are leaving.
- Review any pending work orders for vacated units and the length of time until the matter was resolved. Check to see if there were any open work orders when the tenant vacated and how long the work order was not completed. Maybe it's the reason why the tenant vacated.
- Review the next 60 to 90 days of lease expirations and meet with the tenants to ascertain the likelihood of vacating. Try to convince them to renew before their decision is made.
- If the tenant will be moving, see if they will permit you to show the unit before the expiration of their lease.

⇨ *My suggestion is to use a trial and error approach to increase base rents. Use your unit inventory schedule and determine how much each unit should be increased and see what the reaction will be. Upgrade a few units at higher base rent and evaluate the response.*

Are the Property's Base Rents Legal?

For the most part, we have been analyzing the rents for garden apartment complexes located in Dallas, TX. Dallas generally has no rent control laws, except for Section 8 and other subsidized programs. However, many states do have strict rent control laws that limit the amount of annual base rent increases owners can charge tenants.

For example, New York has strict and complicated rent control guidelines that were recently changed. These new laws mostly benefit tenants to the detriment of owners. Other states also have rent control laws that limit the base rent that owners can charge tenants, as well as limiting other charges. Texas recently limited the amount of late fees owners can charge tenants. Be aware that in many states, an owner can't unilaterally decide to charge tenants whatever rent they want.

Billing Tenants for Utilities

Switching the Method of Billing for Utilities:
As you learned, the base rent for garden apartment properties is generally based upon two different methods that have to do with billing for utilities. The two methods are billing on All Bills Paid (ABP), Ratio Utility Billing System (RUBS), or a combination of the two.

All Bills Paid (ABP):
The *owner* pays 100% of the cost for electric, gas, water and sewer, and trash, regardless of the type of meter or HVAC system the property has. Tenants in weaker markets consisting of low- to moderate-income tenants, living paycheck-to-paycheck, are generally more comfortable knowing their fixed monthly obligations ahead of time and strongly prefer an ABP property, even if the rent is higher. The theory behind the ABP concept is that the utilities are built into the base rent.

Ratio Utility Billing System (RUBS):
The cost for either electric, gas, water and sewer, and trash, or any combination of these costs, is billed back to the tenants based upon an allocation formula that takes into consideration the number of occupants and SF of each unit. However, more administrative work is required. Sometimes the

RUBS charges are based on a flat monthly rate without regard to the unit's square footage.

⇨ *One advantage of a RUBS system is that it has proved to promote decreased usage of utilities by the building as a whole because tenants know they are responsible for paying the utility costs.*

⇨ *Depending upon the market and property class, there may be a value-add opportunity to increase revenue by changing from an ABP property to a RUBS program. On the other hand, it may be easier to lease if the property operates as ABP. You need to fully understand the market.*

Again, you must understand the market, but instituting a RUBS system can generally provide you with an opportunity to increase revenue.

Upgrading Units

In Chapter 2, we discussed the economic effects of upgrading units and increasing the base rent and property value of the Ambassador Court Apartments. Upgrading units is one of the best ways to increase base rents and property value, but you must know your market.

Real-Life Example:

A few years ago, we had a small fire at a property that completely destroyed two of the units in the building. The building was a Class C building in a Class A area. The proceeds from the insurance company were sufficient to let us completely gut and renovate these units down to the studs and install top of the line appliances, fixtures, etc. These two renovated units were far superior to any of the other units in the building, but, to our surprise, we could only receive an additional $100 to $150 per month for them. Our asking rents for these units were initially $500 to $600 per month higher than our other units but were above what the market could bear. In this case, the increased rent did not justify the cost. Know your market!

Additional Income Opportunities

Remember, any additional revenue that can be generated from the property will significantly increase the cash flow, NOI, and property value. Below are some samples of additional revenue that you can generate from the property.

Late Fees:

Our policy is that rent is generally due by the 1st of each month, with a grace period until the 4th of the month. In Texas, late fees are limited to a maximum of 10% of the rent. However, in many other states, the late fees are more pro-owner and can be a good source of additional income.

Administrative & Application Fees:

It is customary for garden apartment communities to charge a new tenant an administration fee of $50 to $100 to cover the staff cost, concessions cost, etc. of the transaction.

Application Fees:

In addition to the administrative fee, it's also customary to charge a new tenant an application fee of $50 to $100 to cover the cost of credits checks, staff costs, etc. We sometimes waive these fees if occupancy dips during slow leasing periods.

Risk Fees:

For a tenant's application to be approved, they must have a full-time job, no felonies on their record, and their annual income must meet certain minimum thresholds. The application will be approved, pending the results of a credit report. When a tenant's application is approved, but their credit score is below a certain threshold, the tenant is charged a non-refundable flat fee of $500 which must be paid before occupancy. Some properties also charge an additional $25 to $50 per month for this privilege.

Parking Income:

Depending on the parking situation, additional income can be derived by charging tenants for reserved ($50 per month) and covered parking spaces ($50 to $100 per month extra). Reserved spaces are for specific tenant's use only. Covered parking spaces are coveted, and tenants will willingly pay extra to obtain a covered parking space. Covered parking offers tenants more protection from the elements and thus reduces potential damage to their cars. Installing covered parking is usually cost-prohibitive, but if it exists, it's a big plus.

Key Replacement:

Tenants lose keys on a regular basis. We usually purchase a key-making machine at each property. Tenants who lose their keys are charged $5 per lost key. This is a very small profit center, but it provides a convenience to our tenants who need to get back into their units.

Pet Income:

We charge a pet deposit of $300 ($150 refundable and $150 non-refundable) and a monthly fee of $15 per qualifying pet. There are expenses incurred by allowing pets at the property. For example, a property may offer convenient pet parks located throughout the property furnished with refreshment stations and pet waste bags. Additionally, carpets generally require at least a "pet treatment" in addition to the usual cleaning. In Texas, the TAA lease states that if the tenant has a pet, they "will be charged for de-fleaing, deodorizing, and shampooing."

Bad Check Fees:

Tenants who bounce a rent check are charged a fee of $75. Since the bank charges $25 per bounced check, a small profit is made by charging this fee.

Month-to-Month Fees:

Many times, tenants whose lease has expired are waiting for a new apartment or a house to be built. In these cases, the tenant wants to stay at the property but can't commit to a 12-month lease. We charge such tenants an additional fee of $100 per month for this privilege.

Lease Cancellation Fees and Relet Fees:

Tenants who break their lease by requesting to vacate prior to expiration are charged a fee equal to 75% of their monthly rent, plus two months of rent.

Appliance Upgrade Fee:

We offer a basic appliance package and an upgraded appliance package. The upgraded package is an extra $75 to $100 per month. The updated package usually includes higher-end refrigerators, stoves, microwaves, and dishwashers, costing approximately $1,400 per unit. Even at an additional $75 per month, the payback period is only 1.56 years ($1,400/$900) and is an attractive alternative for prospective tenants.

Storage Income:

Some of our properties offer small storage facilities. We typically charge $50 per month for a 4x4 storage space.

Furniture Rental Fees:

Offering furnished units is a good way of earning additional income, but only for a more upscale tenant group. In transient Class C and D type communities, where it's likely the furniture will be damaged or destroyed, it's a horrible idea. However, for Class A and most Class B communities, especially student housing communities, offering furnished units is a good way of earning additional income.

Example:

Assume you can fully furnish a unit for $3,000 and receive additional rent of $100 per month. The payback period on the investment, assuming no damage, is 2.5 years. Additionally, applying a cap rate of 6% to the additional annual income of $1,200 translates to an increase in gross property value of $20,000. Therefore, the net increase in property value is $17,000 ($20,000 - $3,000) and you still own the furniture. I often find that I can obtain more than $100 per month by offering this amenity.

Vendor Income:

Soda and candy machines at the property provide a convenience for tenants looking for a late-night snack. We contract with an outside vendor service and receive a very small portion of the profit (average of $350 to $500 per annum).

Laundry Room, Washers and Dryers in the Units:

It is possible to get an outside vendor to install and maintain the equipment. However, the owner may receive less than 50% of the net cash flow from the laundry room's operations. Depending on the type of tenancy and other factors, purchasing the equipment may provide an opportunity to obtain additional income, but you must have maintenance staff that can handle the repairs. Also, keep in mind that at some point, the equipment may become obsolete.

Real-Life Example:

At one of our properties, we were receiving approximately $9,000 per annum from the outside vendor which represented 50% of the net cash flow. We decided to purchase the equipment ourselves and have our maintenance employees service the equipment. As a result, we now receive an additional annual net cash flow of $9,000 and total net annual cash flow of $18,000 from the laundry room's operations.

The equipment cost was $22,000. The payback period for our investment is less than two and a half years ($22,000/$9,000). Assuming a 5.75% cap rate, the additional gross property value created is $156,522 ($9,000/5.75%) After subtracting the equipment cost of $22,000 the increased net property value is *$134,522*, plus you have $22,000 of new equipment.

Plank Wood Flooring:

We have found that tenants prefer wood-type flooring and will pay a premium for this amenity. In many of our properties, we charge an extra $50 per month for plank wood flooring. However, sometimes we install carpeting on the upper floors to limit walking noise to tenants living on the floors below.

Upgraded Fixtures and Hardware:

Providing upgraded interior light fixtures, door handles, doors, kitchen faucets, etc. can also generate additional income or be an amenity to provide free to tenants.

Damage Reimbursements:

Security deposits in garden apartment communities are generally low. Tenants who cause damage inside their units and/or to any fixtures, appliances, etc. are charged for the cost of the damage. First, the cost is deducted from their security deposit, then any balance due is the personal responsibility of the tenant. If the tenant skips or refuses to pay for the damage, we send the case to a collection agency. We have been very successful in recovering these costs.

Purchase a Property and Increase the Property's Rentable Square Feet

Another method to increase NOI and property value is to *increase the property's rentable square feet*.

Develop the Building's Roof

The roof of a building represents a portion of the property that is not usually leasable, thus no income is derived from it. However, though there are some risks, rooftop leases are still an excellent source of income, if (i) the lease is written in a way that protects the property and owner, and (ii) the rooftop is properly managed.

In order to place equipment on the roof or facade of a building, plans may need to be filed and permits obtained from governmental authorities. There are also zoning issues, climate issues, and/or other restrictions to consider. In my experience, it is the vendor's responsibility to obtain such approvals.

Billboard ("Signage") on the Roof

If the property is located in a moderate to highly visible area, a property may be able to attract an advertiser who will install a sign on the roof of the building. Depending on the size and visibility to attract potential customers, the income generated can be significant ($500 to $3,000 per month). However, the roof must be able to support the weight of the sign and must be checked with an engineer before installation. Sometimes a small advertisement placed on the facade of a building can generate additional income ($300 to $1,000 per month).

Pitched roofs aren't generally good candidates for signage or cellular antenna installations. It's beneficial for the rooftop to be flat and free of any obstructions, and it's crucial that the roof provides a lot of available space so that the placement and installation and access to the equipment are easy. Many times, buildings will have HVAC equipment installed on the roof. If this is the case, it will make the site less attractive to prospective vendors.

In Manhattan, sign income can generate hundreds of thousands of dollars or more of additional income to an owner, especially in high-traffic areas such as Times Square.

Cellular Antennas on the Roof

Depending on factors such as the building height, location, and roof structure, additional income can be derived by having a cellular communication company lease portions of the roof for installing rooftop antennas. Depending on the roof, it's possible that more than one antenna can generate additional income from the property.

A general rule of thumb is that the site area must be at least 1,200 to 2,000 square feet, with the height of the roof in the range of 35 to 75 feet, or three to seven stories.

⇨ *Generally, the roof and basement of a building represent portions of the property that are not usually leasable and thus no income is derived from these portions of the building.*

Problematic Areas to Consider

The roof protects the rest of the building from the elements, but rooftop structures such as signs and cellular antennas can increase the wear and tear on the roof. Cellular companies are generally required to maintain the equipment but use outside contractors to do the work and rarely if ever inspect the work performed.

- Installation of heavy equipment can pose structural risks and, as a result, can increase insurance premiums.
- The additional income can affect the real estate tax assessment and taxes since additional income is being generated.
- Depending on the financial stability of the cellular or sign company, there is a risk that the equipment will be abandoned, and the owner will incur the cost for removal.
- Owners sometimes don't use an attorney to review the lease agreement and end up signing an egregious agreement that doesn't protect the property and the owner.
- Although studies have been inconclusive, some people believe that cellular antennas may pose a health risk. As a result, some prospective tenants may choose to rent somewhere else.
- Cellular and signage leases usually require that they have 24/7 access to the rooftop, as well as other areas of the building, in order to check and maintain the equipment. As a result, owners and tenants may have to live with employees of the company coming in and out of the building, often without notice. This can cause a security risk since many small owners do not have staff at the building to allow and monitor such access.

⇨ *It is important to note that additional income derived from the roof or facade of a building is discounted for the purposes of underwriting for mortgages or to compute property value. Lending institutions consider these types of income as being less stable in nature. Most contracts for signage and antennas contain cancellation language and are therefore viewed as less permanent in nature. Many prospective purchasers make the critical mistake of including this income in the computation of property value which results in overvaluing the property.*

Convert a Large One B/R Unit to a Small Two B/R Unit

Young professionals today are more willing to rent on a per-bedroom basis rather than on a per-unit or per-SF basis. They are priced out of established neighborhoods and are focusing on more affordable housing options. These segments of tenants are accustomed to shared housing with roommates to pay the rent. Assuming permissible zoning exists, an opportunity arises for an owner to generate a higher rent per SF by changing the configuration of the units.

For example, many garden communities contain units that consist of more space than is cost-effective for tenants. These types of units are harder to rent and usually represent more of the vacancy loss than others. For example, a one-bedroom unit consisting of 600 to 750 SF is more cost-effective and will command a higher rent per SF than a one-bedroom unit consisting of 850 to 1,000 SF. However, if the unit can be changed to a two-bedroom unit of 850 to 1,000 SF, a higher rent per SF can be realized, translating to increased NOI and property value. The additional rent obtained should more than justify the cost to renovate. The larger than needed units in the building, the more potential to reconfigure them and significantly increase NOI and property value.

Develop the Building's Basement

One of the most underdeveloped and underutilized portions of a building is the basement. Some basements can be 600 to 1,000 SF net of mechanical equipment and can be converted to rentable SF. This includes, but is not limited to, the following:

Creating Living Space for a Resident Maintenance Worker

This type of unit is generally given to the maintenance worker as either additional compensation or as an offset against their compensation. An onsite maintenance worker is also considered an amenity for the property. Light and air can be an issue, so owners should first consult with an architect.

Bump-Down to the Basement

We have been very successful renovating and duplexing ground floor units with portions of the basement, sometimes with access to the backyard. Light and air can be an issue, so owners should first consult with an architect. Sometimes if light and air are a problem, we will duplex with the basement and create a recreation room that has fewer requirements than a living unit.

Bump-Up to the Roof

Assume a five-story building is underbuilt, according to the existing zoning regulations. Then you can increase NOI and property value by creating one or two additional bedrooms on the roof and duplexing them with the fifth-floor unit. This creates additional rentable SF. Other alternatives are to create private roof decks or additional common roof deck areas. If zoning regulations limit expansion, an owner should consider simply adding a recreation room that has fewer requirements than a living unit.

Convert Stores to Apartments

Many buildings contain stores which are very hard to lease with rents per SF that are lower than residential rents per SF. On many occasions, we have converted these stores to apartments, and even duplexed with portions of the basement. As a result, vacancy wasn't an issue anymore, and we received a significantly higher rent per SF translating to increased NOI and property value.

Add a Floor to the Building

There are many sites where the permitted zoning ordinance will allow significantly more SF to be built on the property than currently exists. In this case, the property is deemed to be *underbuilt* and there is the potential for additional construction and subsequently more net operating income and property value.

A building we had once owned in Manhattan had the following *original* zoning attributes:

- The property consisted of two connected five-story buildings.
- The lot size of each building is 24 SF wide by 83 SF deep or 1,992 SF times two buildings or a total of 3,984 SF.
- The square footage of each building was originally approximately 9,960 SF for a combined total of 19,920 SF.
- The FAR (floor area ratio) for the property was designated as R10, meaning residential housing can be built ten times the FAR, and there was no density or height restriction.

As a result, assuming the property was completely vacant, the existing zoning would permit the construction of a new building consisting of 39,840 gross SF (total SF of 19,920 x FAR of 10). However, since the building is occupied with rent control and stabilized tenants, it's unrealistic to completely vacant the entire building nor would it be cost-effective.

Since it wasn't feasible to vacate the entire building, we decided to add sixth and seventh floors which would contain eight units with two units duplexed, adding approximately 3,250 of rentable SF to the building. At an average of $4,000 per month in rent, the extra square footage generates additional gross income of approximately $384,000 per annum, significantly increasing NOI and property value.

Side Note: The valuation of many properties is now based upon the amount of buildable square ft. that can be constructed on the property rather than the NOI, especially if condominiums can be built on the property.

The 39,840 SF described above is the maximum amount of SF the existing zoning will permit to be built on the property (1,992 SF x 2 buildings x FAR of 10). The total SF of the building, after adding the two floors, is 23,172, which represents the amount of SF that is now built on the property. If we deduct this amount from the total permissible SF of 39,840, the property still has 16,668 of unused SF or air rights that could be built on the property. However, the building's foundation won't support any additional floors. On top of that, the building doesn't have an elevator. Tenants may feel that a six-and-a-half floor walkup is too much like working out on a Stairmaster to get to their apartment.

Clearly, the 16,668 of unused SF or air rights cannot be utilized for this property. That doesn't mean they're worthless; in Manhattan, unused air rights are transferable under certain limited circumstances. One of these circumstances is if you're lucky enough to have a developer who plans on constructing a luxury high-rise condominium adjacent to the property. They may want additional air rights to add to their planned development. If they can purchase additional air rights, they would be added to the highest and most valuable floors of the building. Therefore, they will be willing to pay handsomely for the extra square footage. Depending on location, air rights are selling for $300 to $500 per SF in Manhattan, so such air rights could potentially be worth $5,000,000 to $8,000,000. However, if there is no willing developer with an adjacent property to develop, the air rights are basically worthless.

Forced Housing

You've heard of low-income housing and affordable housing, and now I want you to add "forced housing" to your vocabulary. Forced housing is housing that shouldn't be built where it is. A house sandwiched between two other houses on a small plot of land is forced housing. As property values and demand for housing increases, forced housing increases. New York City is the mecca of forced housing. You can make lots of money by developing forced housing. This is one way of increasing the gross rental potential of your property. Building two houses instead of one on a plot of land, adding a floor to the roof of a building, building an apartment in the basement, or extending a room into the back yard all are examples of forced housing.

Get the Property Rezoned

In Chapter 3, I introduced you to some zoning terms that I wanted you to become familiar with. The procedures to rezone a property are very complex and too advanced for a detailed discussion in this book; however, I want you to have a working knowledge of the basic underlying concepts behind zoning and rezoning.

Zoning is the division of land into districts. These districts have uniform zoning regulations which include, but are not limited to, land use, handicapped rules, parking requirements, height, setbacks, lot size, density, and floor area ratio (FAR). In other words, every area has strict rules so you can't just build anything you want.

If a property owner can have the zoning changed to more favorable terms, the effect will substantially raise the odds for increased NOI and property value. In my opinion, the ability to rezone a property to allow for more rentable SF, density, height, etc. is the single greatest way to increase property value.

⇨ *The ability to rezone a property to allow for more rentable SF, density, height, etc. is the single greatest way to increase property value.*

Many times, a zoning district will unilaterally rezone certain properties in a district in order to spur development in that area. In these cases, the owners of properties in these areas have been given a winning concrete lotto ticket.

⇨ *You can increase the amount of the properties rentable SF by (i) developing the properties roofs and basements, (ii) converting overly large one-bedroom units to two-bedroom units, (iii) converting less desirable stores into units, and (iv) adding a floor or two to the building, and (v) rezoning the property.*

Street Success Concepts to Remember

1. Basically, there are four methods to increase property value. They are to (i) do zippo (nothing), (ii) increase the property's revenue, (iii) increase the property's amount of rentable square feet, and (iv) decrease the property's operating expenses.

2. Purchasing a property and doing zippo (nothing) is strictly for amateurs and not the method of choice of the pros.

3. If you purchase a property and do zippo (nothing) to increase revenue, you might receive a decent return on your investment, but you will leave a lot of money on the table.

4. If base rents don't continue to increase at a significantly higher rate than the property's operating expenses, it will translate to only marginal increases, and in some cases decreases, in property value.

5. When an area suddenly becomes "hot" and there is an abundance of capital available, developers will quickly scramble to build and/or renovate properties with no end in sight. At some point, supply will exceed demand and the area will become overbuilt. When an area becomes overbuilt, rents and occupancy will decrease.

6. By selecting the method of purchasing a property and doing zippo (nothing) but pray the value increases, your margin of error for success

will _decrease_ substantially. On the other hand, if you adopt the other methods such as increasing the property's revenue, increasing the property's amount of rentable square feet, and, decreasing the property's operating expenses, your margin of error will _increase_ significantly.

7. Before you even consider trying to increase the property's revenue, answer this question first: _Do tenants like living at your property?_

8. A major key to operating any successful property is to reduce turnover. Remember, each time a tenant vacates, you will need to hire a cleaning company, repair and/or replace the carpet, pay rental agent fees, offer rent specials, and suffer rent loss until a new tenant takes occupancy. This is not the case when a tenant renews their lease.

9. Keep in mind that you can't collect any revenue from vacant units. Always strive for high occupancy even if it means lowering the rent and giving concessions and monthly specials, etc. You should always be cognizant of the market rent and occupancy percentage in the immediate area.

10. If your property is transient in nature, you will experience higher turnover rates and substantially higher operating expenses than a property with lower turnover.

11. Remember that tenants are your customers and should be treated fairly. "_A customer can take years to get but seconds to lose,_" Do everything you can to obtain renewals.

12. Excessive turnover expenses will be part of the property's NOI and calculation of property value by financial institutions and prospective purchasers. Therefore, a property that has high turnover expenses can have a devastating effect on property value. On the other hand, this situation usually is due to bad management and can present a great opportunity for prospective purchasers.

13. Generally, a community that is desirable should offer tenants a safe and secure environment, convenience, responsible management, various amenities, and functional building systems. Remember, the goal is to make tenants want to live at your property.

14. Good school systems nearby or near readily available public transportation are tremendous draws to a community and lead to much less tenant turnover. Tenants are leery of taking their kids out of school and relocating elsewhere.

15. For garden apartment community's look for a parking ratio of at least 1.25 to 1.50 spaces per unit or higher. The higher, the better. However, this will depend upon the unit mix, unit size, and the number of occupant drivers.

16. It is imperative that you become aware of a parking problem at your property and take immediate action to improve the situation. Offer incentives to tenants who don't drive, don't own a car, are more comfortable taking public transportation, or are willing to carpool. Have an outside service tow away illegally parked cars.

17. Making people want to live at your property will reduce turnover, increase gross revenue, and decrease operating expenses. All depend upon the quality of the property's management. Management will make or break you.

18. It's human nature that the more convenient it is to complain, the more complaints you will receive. Be aware that sometimes offering convenience can cost you aggravation and money.

19. Staging community events at the property where tenants can congregate may seem like a good idea on the surface. However, always be aware of the possible downside. At these events, tenants are given a platform to voice their complaints to other tenants which include, but

are not limited to, discussing the property's problems, rents they are being charged, any concessions they were or weren't offered, and/or to complain about management and the owner.

20. Before increasing base rents, determine where your rent levels are in comparison to the market in the immediate area. Remember to compare apples to apples and take into consideration whether it's an ABP property or if RUBS are charged. Take an inventory of each of the units and indicate each unit's pluses and minuses.

21. A good procedure to implement is, a few months before any lease expires, try to meet with the tenant and discuss why you feel a rent increase is justified and see their reaction. Even if there will be no rent increase, management should still meet with all tenants before lease expiration and ascertain what their likelihood of renewing is, so you have a chance of inducing them to renew. The key is to know the tenant's intentions before they commit to moving to another property.

22. Please remember that publicized asking rents are often different than the actual rent the tenant will ultimately pay. For example, owners sometimes have a program known as "look and lease." This program offers a prospective tenant a discount if they sign a lease right after seeing the unit.

23. While performing due diligence on a prospective property I'm considering purchasing, I always look at the rent obtained for the past 4 to 6 months to see if there is a steady progression of increases, and why. Were increases simply an across the board increase, the result of upgrades made, or special incentives given? Remember we want to compare apples to apples.

24. A lazy managing agent may not be motivated to increase rents when a vacancy occurs since it means physically showing the units to more prospective tenants. Additionally, a more occupied building makes

the managing agent look much better in the eyes of the owner. It takes away one of their major complaints, *Why are we only 88% occupied?*

25. My suggestion is to use a trial and error approach to increase base rents. Use your unit inventory schedule and determine how much each unit should be increased and see what the reaction is. Upgrade a few units at a higher base rent and evaluate the response.

26. One advantage of a RUBS system is that it has proved to promote decreased usage of utilities by the building as a whole because tenants know they are responsible for paying the utility costs.

27. Depending upon the market and property class, there may be a value-add opportunity to increase revenue by changing from an ABP property to a RUBS program. On the other hand, it may be easier to lease if the property operates as ABP. You need to fully understand the market.

28. Generally, the roof and basement of a building represents portions of the property that are not usually leasable and thus no income is derived from these portions of the building.

29. It is important to note that additional income derived from the roof or facade of a building are discounted for the purposes of underwriting for mortgages or to compute property value. Lending institutions consider these types of income as being less stable in nature. Most contracts for signage and antennas contain cancellation language and are therefore viewed as less permanent in nature. Many prospective purchasers make the critical mistake of including this income in the computation of property value which results in overvaluing the property.

30. The ability to rezone a property to allow for more rentable SF, density, height, etc. is the single greatest way to increase property value.

31. You can increase the amount of the property's rentable SF by (i) developing the property's roofs and basements, (ii) converting overly large one-bedroom units to two-bedroom units, (iii) converting less desirable stores into units, (iv) adding a floor or two to the building, and (v) rezoning the property.

CHAPTER 8

PURCHASE A PROPERTY AND DECREASE THE PROPERTY'S OPERATING EXPENSES

LET ME RE-EMPHASIZE my mantra: *Always* be cognizant of the effect that an increase or decrease in NOI has on property value. This applies from the moment of acquisition on. Whenever employees are seeking raises or I'm renegotiating service contracts, repair items, etc., I always compute what the effect will be on property value.

A $100 *increase in revenue* has the same effect on NOI as a *$100 decrease in operating expenses*. Therefore, if you can legitimately decrease operating expenses, you can increase NOI and property value. When you sell or refinance a property, the sales price or amount of refinancing proceeds will depend upon the NOI of the property.

Realize that a $100 increase in revenue has the same effect on NOI as a $100 decrease in operating expenses. Therefore, if you can legitimately decrease operating expenses you can increase NOI and property value.

In most cases, once the savings are established, those savings will continue to increase the bottom line, year after year.

Management

The best way to decrease operating expenses is by having great management at the property. This is no small order, and even if you have good third-party management, you must provide supervisory management or you could be robbed blind. You must constantly look over their shoulder.

The kind of management you have at your property can make or break you. This applies to both third-party management and self-managed properties.

Human nature tells me that unless someone has a vested interest in the property and skin in the game, they will not be as motivated to increase revenue or control expenses as someone with a vested interest, such as the property owner.

Third-party managing agents do not have a vested interest in the property or skin in the game. As a result, they will not be as motivated to increase revenue or control expenses.

Human nature also tells me that the managing agent may take the path of least resistance. In order to achieve higher rents, they will need to do more showings of the units, which is hard work. It requires less effort to rent the units if they offer below-market rents, and having a higher occupancy makes for a happier owner.

Human nature further tells me that if a managing agent can outsource maintenance tasks that should be performed by in-house personnel, it will require less work for them, but it will be at the expense of the owner.

Day-to-day management has been increasingly difficult. New pro-tenant laws have been passed, and local authorities and lenders are significantly increasing their oversight and monitoring of properties. These increased demands are exhausting available resources and becoming an administrative nightmare for managing agents. As available resources are stressed to the limit, managing agents make more errors that decrease their effectiveness. Generally, I have found that the managing agents for Class C and D properties run them like mills or factories. Managing agent employees used to be assigned to particular properties and oversaw those specific property's operations. They established personal relationships with tenants, contractors, and employees. Today, employees of managing agents must oversee the management of many more properties than in the past. Due to this fact, as well as the growth in specialization, the personal touch will be lost. I think it's only going to get worse as time goes on.

When interviewing a managing agent, you should stress that you are a long-time owner of the property. Managing agents invest time and money to hire, train, and set up a new account's accounting data, vendor accounts, etc. Having good relationships with long-term owners helps to stabilize the managing agent's business. This is a completely opposite approach than dealing with brokers, where you should never stress that you are a long-term owner because, in the broker's mind, it limits their ability to earn future commissions.

Poor Oversight and Supervision

You can lose a fortune if the managing agent's employees are untrained, incompetent, lazy, unmotivated, etc. If these types of employees are involved with running your properties, it's usually the result of a lack of caring and supervision by the owners or the managing agent.

Real-Life Example:

We own a 400+ unit garden apartment community in Dallas, Texas. Over the past few years, expenses for turnover and repair and maintenance have increased significantly. We raised this concern with the managing agent's CFO. He assured us that he would personally do an investigation and provide us with answers. After a week or two had passed, we still hadn't received a response. Meanwhile, we were hemorrhaging money. Finally, we gave him an ultimatum: provide us with answers, or we would look for a new managing agent. A conference call was scheduled. The CFO and the manager blamed the significant increase in expenses on increases in the building's turnover and the fact that the building was getting older and required more repairs. My instinct, which later proved to be true, told me that no investigation was performed, and we were being given lip service.

I asked why there were so many turnovers. He didn't have a good answer. The property was well-staffed with full-time leasing agents, managers, and maintenance personnel. We decided to do our own in-depth investigation. We traveled to Dallas and spent a few days interviewing various building staff and examining invoices and work orders for the past six months. *What we found was very upsetting.* Below is a summary.

With Regard to the Building's Employees, we found that:

- Employees didn't know the names of other staff members.
- Employees were unhappy, unmotivated, unsupervised, and did not have a handle on the property's operations.
- Employee turnover was extremely high.
- Employees lacked a team approach.

In addition, many tasks that could have been performed in-house were instead performed by third-party vendors. This is akin to flushing money right down the toilet.

- Whenever units turned over, outside vendors were used to paint and clean the units. Since no one was watching, employees could be lazy and call an outside service. After all, it wasn't their money. Because of this situation, we wasted approximately $800 to $1,200 per unit. Considering the high turnover, this incompetence cost us approximately $32,000 to $48,000 per annum.

- An outside vendor also completely replaced plank flooring during turnover. There was no need to entirely replace the flooring since damaged strips could be easily replaced. We estimated that waste of money cost us approximately $50,000 to $70,000 per annum.

- To make the in-house staff's work easier, they ordered new appliances when units turned over instead of repairing existing appliances using in-house staff. Our estimate of wasted money was $20,000 to $30,000 per annum.

- A maintenance employee was hired at a higher pay rate because he was certified to repair HVAC units. However, the managing agent still used an outside service to perform this function. We estimated that we wasted $12,000 to $20,000 per annum.

- The costs for outside vendors, such as materials and supplies, painting, plumbing, resurfacing, appliances, etc. were never renegotiated for better pricing.

- Tenant work orders often took months to be addressed.

The high turnover was due in part to *tenants not wanting to live at the property!*

Supervisory Management

Because most of our properties are out of state, we don't have boots on the ground. As a result, we engage third-party managing agents but oversee their efforts with supervisory management. Managing agents aren't often in favor of this but must tolerate our involvement. Overseeing local managing agents is very common with large real estate companies. However, if there is no oversight, it will be a feeding frenzy for local managing agents who have out-of-town property owners. We have weekly conference calls with all our third-party managing agents to review the property's activities and operations. It's amazing how many mistakes were avoided because we jointly found solutions at these meetings.

Property owners should assemble a team and schedule weekly meetings to discuss and review the property's activities and operations. The team should consist of various employees of the owner and managing agent. This is the most efficient way to become aware of existing and potential problems and find timely solutions.

Kickbacks and Conflict of Interest Relationships

Depending on the type of property, third-party managing agents generally charge a fee ranging from 3% to 10% of total cash collections. Generally, the smaller the property, the higher the percentage because it wouldn't be cost-effective otherwise. As part of their fee, the managing agent should be assigning some of their employees as part of their service, i.e.: a regional supervisor.

Historically, there has been widespread speculation that management agents are guilty of kickbacks, overcharges, misappropriation of funds, etc. Based on my experience, *no management company is making money from just their management fee.* In many instances, additional money is made from non-disclosed related company affiliations and/or companies directly or indirectly owned by the managing agent. Other sources of income often result from kickbacks received from various vendors servicing the property.

No management company is making money from just their management fee. Generally, additional money is being made from non-disclosed related company affiliations and/or companies directly or indirectly owned by the managing agent or from kickbacks received from various vendors servicing the property.

As a property owner, you cannot completely eliminate thievery, but you can slow it down. You just have to determine a tolerance level you can live with, but remember this behavior is inflating your operating expenses and hurting your cash flow, and property value because these inflated operating expenses are used to determine NOI. Your job is to monitor and determine how greedy they have become and put an end to it if it goes too far.

Below is a summary of some of the theft I have experienced by managing agents:

- Using the property's employees to work on other properties they own or manage and charging overtime to use their construction company's employees, claiming a shortage of labor to address turnover and work orders.

- Having non-disclosed direct or indirect ownership interests in the construction, flooring, landscaping, snow removal, or building supply company. This may lead to ordering supplies or services that aren't needed for your property.

- Making deals with vendors for a kickback based on a percentage of sales derived from the properties and never depositing the funds into the owner's bank account.

- Charging for installing carpeting and plank flooring that was never installed in the units.

- Showing apartments as vacant while collecting cash rent payments from the tenants.

- Marking up staff payroll.

- Charging for services that should be part of normal management activities, i.e. court appearances, giving expert testimony related to the property, and charging for accounting services for the property and their computer programs, insurance, and mortgage refinancing review, etc.

- Leasing agents charging tenants $300 to be paid in cash to overlook applicants with bad credit and pocketing the money.

When I'm interviewing a prospective managing agent, I ask them to disclose any affiliated relationships they have with vendors servicing the property. This includes any direct or indirect ownership, or profit-splitting relationships, any refund or discounts they will receive, etc. If these relationships are disclosed upfront, you can decide if it's acceptable to you. Additionally, if there are no affiliated relationships disclosed in the management agreement and you later find this untrue, you will have a strong case for a lawsuit and/or a complaint with the state regulatory agencies.

Always have the managing agent disclose in their agreement any direct or indirect ownership or profit splitting relationships, any refund or discounts they will receive, etc. At least if these relationships are disclosed upfront, you can decide if it's acceptable to you.

The following are a few examples of clauses from actual management agreements that I find *acceptable*:

Contracts with Related Parties:
Manager shall not enter into any agreement or arrangement for the furnishing to or by the Property of goods, services, or space with itself or with any entity related to or affiliated with Manager, unless such agreement or arrangement has been approved in advance by the Owner.

Repairs:
Except for emergency repairs, all repairs costing more than $2,500 shall only be undertaken after obtaining competitive proposals from at least three (3) independent contractors and are approved by owner in writing.

Supplies:
On behalf of the Owner, purchase all supplies as shall be necessary to properly maintain and operate the Building; make all such contracts and purchases either in the Owner's name or the Agent's; and credit to the Owner any discounts or commissions obtained for purchases or otherwise.

Expense Reimbursements:

Disbursements for such items as postage, messenger, photocopying (internal and external), courier, long-distance telephone costs, record storage and retrieval costs or overnight delivery expenses (collectively, "Direct Expenses") will be reimbursed to Agent by Owner.

Comments: I have found that many managing companies mark up these costs, i.e.: photocopies, emails, overnight delivery, postage, etc. Make sure that you only pay for the actual cost of the service.

The following are a few examples of clauses from actual management agreements that I find *unacceptable:*

- For services rendered by Agent as a witness or expert witness on behalf of Owner either at Owner's request, or if subpoenaed in person by any litigant, in any arbitration, discovery proceeding (deposition) or court proceeding ("legal action"), by reason of Agent's role as Managing Agent of the Building (a "court appearance"), Agent shall be entitled to a fee of $85.00 per hour for each hour expended by a representative of Agent in addressing a legal action, whether in a court appearance or expended in document production.

Comments: Going to court should be part of their management functions. The need to go to court usually has to do with tenant or local regulatory complaints related to the management of the property. However, the managing agent is entitled to compensation for performing services that are outside the scope of their normal managing activities such as supervising major capital improvements.

- Owner shall pay Agent upon such refinancing a loan coordination fee equal to one-half of one percent (1/2%) of the principal amount of the mortgage.

Comments: Even though disclosed, this fee is without merit and is unacceptable, another way of scamming a fee from the owner. If a mortgage broker is involved, they will be doing most of the work. The only thing the managing agent will need to do is furnish financial records which should be part of their function.

- Agent participates in the commissions received from the placement of insurance with many insurance brokers, and it may receive commissions on the placement of insurance for Owner. Nothing contained in this provision shall be deemed to limit Owner's absolute right to designate any insurance broker to place its insurance.

Comments: Even though it's disclosed, this situation represents a conflict of interest and is unacceptable. Agents need to decide which business they're in and who their complete allegiance is to. The insurance broker should be an independent entity.

- Agent has arranged with several banks and/or other financial institutions ("Cooperating Banks"), to provide services ("Financial Services") to owners of properties managed by Agent, including but not limited to, (i) a lockbox for the collection of the payments by Unit Owners, tenants and others, (ii) maintaining the Operating Account of Owner, and (iii) investment accounts for the deposit of surplus funds of Owner. Agents may receive compensation from the Cooperating Banks related to the Financial Services.

Comments: This one's a joke, and this agent is a pig! They want to make a fee on the float and other routine services that are customarily provided by banks.

- Owner shall reimburse Manager for any off-site maintenance personnel provided by Manager for the benefit of the Property, as follows:

  Work Orders - $50/per hour, Make Ready Labor - $40/per hour

  Ground Services - $32/per hour, After Hours Services - $65/per hour

Comments: This managing agent allocates staff payroll based on the need at the property. Normally, the actual cost for the above services range from $14 to $32 per hour, depending upon each employee's experience and their position. Even if you added payroll taxes and additional employee costs, the cost is substantially marked up. The managing agent is using staffing a property as a profit center, which is completely unacceptable. Not only is the cost higher, but the property will not be getting full coverage. A property needs its own dedicated staff that develops relationships with the tenants. Sending whoever is available to property and left entirely at the sole discretion of a managing agent is akin to giving them a blank check.

There are also good managing companies that perform professionally and try to increase revenue and reduce operating expenses.

Decreasing the Property's Operating Expenses

Be aware that some properties can be so well-managed that their efficiency cannot be matched by other managing agents. Therefore, you may need to make adjustments in your projections depending on the level of competency, purchasing power, etc. that you expect from the managing agent you hire. This fact should especially be considered if you plan on managing the property yourself. You will need to account for the possibility of increased operating expenses, lower rents and occupancy, etc., and this will directly affect the projected NOI you expected to receive.

Investing in Cost-Saving Equipment

Another key to reducing operating expenses is to limit the outsourcing of maintenance tasks by performing repairs and preventive maintenance in-house and by training and utilizing the maintenance staff at the property. However, you may need to purchase some equipment for the maintenance staff. Below are a few examples:

Sewer Machine:

We have a small machine that is used to unclog lines and drains in kitchens and bathrooms, a larger machine to handle larger issues.

Blower:

This is used to blow away leaves and debris in the gutters, patios, parking lots, hallways, etc.

Striping Machine:

This is used to paint the lines of parking spaces and lanes in the parking lot.

Resurfacing Machine:

This machine allows tubs, countertops, sinks, etc. to be resurfaced in-house as opposed to paying $350 to $500 per unit to an outside vendor. Resurfacing is done each time there is a vacancy, so when properties are transient in nature, the cost can be extremely high.

Side Note: An effective way to reduce this expense is to purchase a resurfacing machine for the property and have this function performed in-house by the maintenance staff. While training is required, especially because chemicals are used in the process, it will only take around three hours to complete the work in a unit. Being able to do this in-house can save you a small fortune.

Welding Machine:

This is used to repair metal fencing, gates, stairs, etc.

Paint Sprayer:

This is used to paint units and/or touch up other areas of the property.

Nitrogen and Oxygen Tanks:

These are used to unclog HVAC units.

Put Together a Great Team of Professionals

Decreasing operating expenses starts with putting together a great team of professionals that work together for the benefit of the property. The team consists of the managing agent and its employees and the building's staff. They need to be trained, supervised, and motivated.

Managing agents and staff should be continually renegotiating service contracts and insurance policies, making building-wide improvements to reduce operating expenses, and seeking the lowest prices for building supplies, etc. They must be motivated so they can continually seek to perform tasks in-house rather than calling an outside vendor. It's up to the managing agent to keep the staff focused and motivated to accomplish these goals.

Managing agents do a lot of business with suppliers, service providers, contractors, etc. Because of that, they possess a lot of purchasing power which gives them the ability to obtain much lower prices than small owners would receive. These savings should be passed on to their clients, but, as previously mentioned; sometimes kickbacks get in the way.

Side Note: Additionally, an owner, along with their representatives, should perform supervisory management services which serve to let the managing agent and staff know that somebody is looking over their shoulder to keep them honest.

Authority:
Accountability and internal controls must be in place. Managing agents should determine which staff members have the authority to make decisions and which do not. These include, but are not limited to, ordering supplies, completing work orders, utilizing outside vendors and contractors, etc. You shouldn't have one person in charge of spending an owner's money without supervision or accountability. Checks and balances keep you from being robbed blind. A supervisor needs to approve all staff requests to order supplies or assign outside vendors and contractors to perform work for the property. By putting together a great team of professionals working together for the benefit of the property, you will decrease expenses for repair and maintenance, administrative expenses, turnover, contract services, etc.

General Discussion on Decreasing Operating Expenses

Staff Payroll and Fringes:

Owners often neglect to include additional costs when projecting an amount for payroll costs. These are ones related to having employees, such as Medicare and Social Security taxes, federal and state unemployment taxes, worker's compensation premiums, disability insurance, bonuses, raises, health insurance premiums, etc. These additional costs can be significant. For example, assume an employee's annual base salary is $35,000. Medicare and Social Security for this employee alone are $2,678. Adding in the other costs could increase the total payroll cost by $3,500 to $6,000 per employee.

Medicare and Social Security taxes are federal costs. However, each state has its own requirements for unemployment taxes, disability, worker's compensation, and health insurance. Therefore, you should consult with your accountant to determine what the total cost for staffing the property will be in the particular state the property is located.

Each state has its own requirements for determining the level at which employers are responsible for the cost of health insurance and overtime benefits. In many states, the employer is not required to provide health insurance for part-time employees who work under a certain number of hours per week. Therefore, depending on the state, an owner can save significant money by hiring two part-time workers who are not entitled to benefits instead of one full-time employee who is.

Landscaping:

While a property that is well-landscaped is a great amenity, it is very expensive to maintain extensive landscaping. This is especially true if the property is located in an area that is prone to drought, hailstorms, or other adverse weather conditions. The costs associated with extensive landscaping generally require that a third-party service is hired to cut the grass, water and replace flowers, etc. Additionally, the water cost in some states, such as Las Vegas and Florida, is extremely high.

Because of this, we often use xeriscape as a full or partial solution. Xeriscaping is a form of landscaping that promotes the use of drought-tolerant plants and other gardening techniques that can be maintained with low water levels. Xeriscaping is more popular these days because it doesn't require much maintenance and looks great. It is especially popular in Texas where the climate is hot and dry and prone to hailstorms and droughts, causing plants and flowers to die. However, some local districts may limit the amount of xeriscaping a property can have.

Advertising and Marketing:
This includes all apartment publications, locator and leasing fees, brochures, banners and flags, promotional and hospitality gifts, resident relations, and parties, etc.

Apartment Publications and Internet Sites:
Make sure all social media sites are utilized and info is up to date. Examples are Apartments.com, ForRent.com, ApartmentFinder.com, Craigslist, Zillow, and Facebook. Instagram, etc. These sites are widely viewed by prospective tenants prior to deciding if they want to rent at a property.

Improve the Property's Ratings and Reviews on Social Media Sites:
Tenants will typically post negative reviews on a site if they were unhappy living at the property but tend to be less likely to post positive reviews if they were happy living at the property. Continually review social media sites for posted reviews and information on your property. Protest any negative reviews and postings and try to have them removed from the site. Sometimes competitors purposely post negative reviews to sabotage their competition.

Continually Reevaluate Your Marketing Efforts and Costs:
Are your marketing expenses providing the results you want? Assume you're spending $300 per month on a certain advertising site. Is the site generating the volume of traffic and signed leases that justify the expense? Is the type of traffic being generated from the site meeting the criteria you have

established for the property? Determining the best advertising vehicle for your property is often a process of trial and error.

Locators and Leasing Agents:

Outside leasing personnel are known as locators. Garden apartment communities generally have their own leasing employees at the property. However, sometimes outside locators are also needed. This is often the case with student housing communities. Leasing agents generally receive additional commissions based on whether a new lease or a renewal lease is signed. Commissions received for renewals ($75 per renewal) should be higher than those for new leases ($50 per new lease). Human nature tells me that a leasing agent might be *less* motivated to focus on renewals if they received higher commissions for new leases. The amount of the commissions is meant to obtain as many renewals as possible to limit turnover costs.

Resident Referrals:

If your tenants like living at the property, a great way of attracting new tenants is by offering an incentive to existing tenants if they recommend a new tenant, and a lease is signed. A printed resident referral program should be included in the welcome package, and management should continually advise tenants of the program.

Typically we offer tenants $300 for each referral that signs a lease. The $300 is taken off the tenant's rent 90 days after the referred tenant remains in occupancy and is current with their rent payments.

Marketing to the Neighborhood:

The marketing staff should distribute printed advertisements, such as flyers, to local businesses, churches, restaurants, libraries, colleges, coffee shops, convenience stores, medical offices, schools, day care centers, and other locations to generate traffic and leases. Try to arrange for discounts at local pizza and other stores for tenants at the property and have them also provide flyers for customers.

Model Unit:

For some of our larger and more affluent communities, we have a furnished model unit available for prospective tenants to view. This makes an enormous difference in our leasing efforts at these properties. However, it is my experience that having a model unit is less important for Class C and D properties.

Property Website:

A dedicated website is a great advantage for both prospective and existing tenants. The website should feature information about the property that shows the property's highlights, such as unit floor plans, photo galleries, lists of amenities, rent specials, directions, neighborhood highlights, and online rental applications with the terms and conditions for tenants, etc. If you include a residential log-in feature, it will allow tenants to interact with management and pay their rent online.

Advertising Materials:

Make sure that the management office is stacked with promotional materials to be given to prospective tenants. These include business cards, brochures, and other promotional materials. Additionally, you should have banners and flags showing rent specials hanging from the building's façade in a location where they can be viewed by drive-by traffic.

Utilities

Electric:

Recently many states passed laws to deregulate the state's electricity market. The intent was to increase competition and allow customers to have multiple choices of providers with different options and reduced prices. However, no state's energy market is completely deregulated. The closest is Texas at approximately 85% of the state having the ability to choose their service provider.

My advice is to research the internet to see if the state the property is located in is deregulated. Then find companies that are servicing the area.

Some consultants will determine the best choice for your property. These consultants review the prices and consumption for the property's past six months of electric bills and present you with at least three different bids. Additionally, you can choose to sign a contract to lock in a fixed price for a one- to three-year period. The consultant receives a commission from the markup they receive from the transaction, not from the customer directly, but the cost is built into the price you pay.

If the property operates as ABP (All Bills Paid), the savings will go straight into your pocket. If the property operates a RUBS (Ratio Utility Billing System) program, the tenants will benefit from the savings. You should let the tenants know that you negotiated a low electric rate.

Gas:
To the best of my knowledge, natural gas has not been as deregulated as electricity. As a result, there are fewer providers to choose from and fewer options available. The best way to reduce gas expenses is to install more efficient equipment, i.e. boiler system, HVAC systems, etc.

Water and Sewer:
Water and sewer charges can constitute a large portion of the property's operating expenses, especially in states such as Florida and cities like Las Vegas where water costs are extremely high. Every building is going to have water leaks, but you need to realize how much money can be lost. To sit back and do nothing to correct the problem is akin to throwing money right down the drain.

Multifamily properties generally contain a large number of units that were built at the same time. As a result, plumbing, water heater failures, leaks, etc. tend to occur in batches. Additional problems caused by water leaks can subject owners to more liability, cost, and aggravation.

In many municipalities, sewer charges are directly affected by the amount of water consumption. The sewer bill will be based upon the amount of water consumption multiplied by a fixed factor amount, and that will be the sewer charge.

Water Leaks

Here are some common facts about water leaks:

- A running toilet can waste up to 4,000 gallons of water a day which could translate to up to $22,000 per year in wasted expenses.
- A dripping faucet can waste 3,000 gallons a year. That's as much water as 180 showers.
- A single 1/16" leak can cost $1,160 per year.
- A single 1/4" leak can cost $48,400 per year.
- Even if a tenant hears a hissing sound from a leaking toilet or sees drips coming from sinks, showerheads, faucets, or the outside sprinkler, they rarely report it to management.
- Many water main leaks are caused because the piping is simply too old and thus susceptible to leaks.
- Even a few inches of water caused by a flood can cause mold growth and structural damage to other areas such as the foundation and quickly spread to multiple units, dislodging multiple tenants and causing substantial damage costs for owners.
- Water leaks can subject tenants to significant health risks from mold, mildew, toxins, etc.
- Water leaks can result in an insurance nightmare stemming from multiple claims when one unit's water leak quickly spreads to other units.
- Remediating floods involves draining your resources while handling the cleanup, mold remediation, required repairs, etc.
- Water leaks lead to mildew and bad odors in the units.
- Water leaks create irate owners and tenants.
- When multiple water leaks occur at a property, insurance companies will quickly increase premiums or simply drop coverage.

- In many municipalities, sewer charges are directly affected by the amount of water consumption. The sewer bill will be based upon the amount of water consumption multiplied by a fixed factor amount and that will be the sewer charge, so a water leak directly increases the total sewer charge.
- As temperatures plummet, the risk of pipes freezing and bursting skyrocket. Pipes most at risk are those in unheated interior spaces, such as basements, attics, and garages.

Any unnecessary water usage that is the result of the malfunction or leaks derived from toilets, sinks, showers, pipes behind walls, foundations, pools, irrigation systems, etc. can cost you a fortune. If these inflated water and sewer costs are not corrected, not only will you lose substantial cash flow but your NOI and property value will also be adversely affected.

Observable Signs of Water Leaks or Wasted Water Consumption:

- Visible drips from faucets, showerheads, and toilets
- Hissing sounds from the toilet and the hot water boiler
- Constantly needing to refill the pool
- Curling vinyl floors
- Peeling paint on the walls
- Mold spots
- Over-occupied units

Non-Observable Signs of Water Leaks:

- Foundation leaks: underground pipes are in constant contact with the soil. Electrolysis occurs over the years, causing corrosion of the pipes and leakage.
- Pool leaks
- Broken and/or corroded pipes behind walls
- Timing of the irrigation system

- Equipment with the water off can still leak
- Broken or malfunctioning water meters

Nine out of ten managing agents don't know or care about performing an in-depth investigation to find the exact location of water leaks. Most recommend that you install such water-saving devices as energy-efficient showerheads, aerators in kitchens and bathrooms, and new low flush toilets, but most stop there. While installing water-saving devices can save you a substantial amount, a lot of money will be left on the table if there are water leaks that are hidden from detection.

Simple Water Leak Prevention, Detection, and Solutions:
Finding the exact location of the leak is the challenge. You can't replace a broken pipe when you can't find it, but finding the exact location involves a combination of hide and seek, trial and error, and detective work. You may need to hire a company that provides professional water leak detection services. Unfortunately, my experience is that even the professionals need to play detective, although they have more tools and experience at their disposal. Having a proactive approach in mitigating water damage will help save a property owner thousands to tens of thousands of dollars in wasted water costs and flood damages.

Implement a Water-Savings Training Program:
Implement a water-savings training program for the maintenance staff and do routine preventive procedures. These include but are not limited to the following:

- Periodically advise tenants to immediately notify management of any hissing sounds or visible leaking faucets, showerheads, and toilets. The response is greater for properties using a RUBS system since tenants pay for their water use.

- Periodically check for over-occupied units. During periods of extreme hot and cold weather, power outages, etc. tenants have friends and relatives stay with them. The result is that more water will be used during these periods.

- Advise the maintenance staff that they should check for any hissing sounds or visible leaking faucets, showerheads, and toilets while in the unit after completing a work order.
- A trick to find toilet leaks is to put a few drops of food coloring or dye in the tank and wait about a minute. If color can be seen in the bowl, then there is a leak.
- Install water-saving devices, such as new low flush toilets, more efficient showerheads, and aerators in the kitchen and bathroom faucets. These efficient devices can save approximately 20% of water costs. Many states and cities offer water conservation programs which offer free toilets and fixtures to owners who are responsible for the labor cost to install them. Freddie Mac recently offered a special program that offered a .20 to .30 basis point reduction in the interest rate if water- and energy-saving devices are installed in the property being mortgaged.
- Have the maintenance staff check and repair the caulking around shower doors and bathtubs.
- Check the timing for irrigation to see how many times a day the sprinkler system is on.
- Check the irrigation system for leaks, especially in freezing and extremely cold temperatures.
- Check the pool for leaks. How many times a week does the staff need to add water to the pool?
- Have the maintenance staff check toilets for worn toilet flappers. The flapper is the rubber mechanism located inside the tank that corrodes over time.
- Have the maintenance staff calibrate the water flow of the toilets at an optimal flush rate.
- Periodically have the water meters checked for malfunction. Call the city and ask them to check the meters. Another trick is to have management notify tenants in advance that the water will be shut

off for a two-hour period. Turn the water off and check the meter readings, then check the meters again after the two-hour period. The meter readings should read the same as before the shutoff. If the reading changed, there are probably water leaks. The importance of water monitoring is even more critical in areas where utility meters are often estimated or only read every three months. Additionally, even if the meter readings for a property have been incorrect for years, many cities limit any reimbursement to much shorter periods of time rather than the length of time the problem existed. Therefore, the sooner the malfunction is discovered the better.

- Schedule an annual plumbing inspection. This can inform you of signs of wear and tear to pipes, equipment, etc. so you can be aware of any potential future issues.

- In freezing weather, have management post signs advising tenants to leave faucets dripping, keep the thermostat set to the same temperature during day and night, and set thermostats at no lower than 55 degrees when leaving the unit for extended periods. These measures will help prevent pipes from bursting and floods from occurring.

- Monitor the age of washers and routinely check the appliances in units for cracked or damaged hoses and connections.

- Insulate pipes for sprinkler systems or hot and cold water all year round.

- Extensive landscaping requires a large consumption of water usage. A partial solution is to use xeriscape, as discussed above.

Enter Technology:

Many companies offer affordable technology so owners and property managers can monitor their property's water use in real-time by logging in with any internet-accessible device. These companies also offer alert levels so that potential floods can be remediated before occurring. If a catastrophic leak occurs, the technology will alert you via email and text message, indicating which water line ruptured as well as how much water was lost. Technology is also available that allows users to automatically shut off the water remotely to prevent further damage.

> Side Note: By becoming more knowledgeable about the causes of water leaks and their prevention and remediation, you will put yourself in a position to uncover *hidden value* overlooked by others. For example, while performing due diligence on a prospective property, if you uncover that the water and sewer bills are extremely high, you notice dripping faucets, leaking toilets, and hissing sounds in the units, and you notice that no water-saving devices were installed, then this situation may provide an opportunity to significantly reduce water costs and operating expenses and increase NOI and property value.

Real Estate Taxes

Real estate taxes are generally the largest portion of property's operating expenses.

Texas is known as a "non-disclosure" state. This means that neither sellers nor purchasers need to publicly disclose the purchase price of the property. Each year the taxing authority issues property owners a new *initial assessment* that is supposedly based upon the *estimated* fair market value of the property. It's called an initial assessment because it's subject to change. However, because of Texas's non-disclosure status, the reality is that the initial assessments are based on nothing more than an educated guess since the taxing district is not privy to the actual purchase prices, the income, or the operating expenses and NOI of the property. If the property owner feels the initial assessment is too high, which is almost always the case, they will need to hire an outside consultant to challenge the new initial assessment. The consultant's fee ranges from 20% to 35% of the tax savings. Additionally, you will often also need to file a lawsuit against the district, which costs thousands of dollars. As a result, owners need to play an annoying game with the taxing district each year, with the only winners being the consultant and attorney hired to challenge the assessment.

Owners also need to determine whether or not to challenge the new assessment every year. If your assessment is already low compared to similar properties in the market, you may not want to risk the taxing authority taking another look at the property's numbers. Sometimes the tax authority changes the criteria for determining assessments without the owner having prior knowledge of this fact.

The following assumptions were used in Chapter 3 when discussing the Dallas Arms Apartments real estate taxes:

Current Assessed Value	$1,310,370
Current Tax Rate	2.71%
Current Real Estate Taxes	$35,511
Purchase Price	$3,800,000

Example:

- The current assessment of the Dallas Arms Apartments is $1,310,370, which at the current tax rate of 2.71% translates to real estate taxes of $35,511 ($1,310,370 x 2.71%).

- However, you paid $3,800,000 for the property, which is substantially higher than the current assessment of $1,310,370.

- The new initial assessment could potentially result in increased real estate taxes of $102,980 ($3,800,000 x 2.71%), which is more than double the amount the previous owner paid.

Assume you hire an outside consultant to challenge the assessment, and they are successful in reducing the assessment to $3,000,000. In that case, your real estate taxes would still increase to $81,300 ($102,980 - $21,680) and you would need to pay a consulting fee of $5,420.

Initial Assessment	$3,800,000
Reduced Assessment	($3,000,000)
Decrease in Assessment	$ 800,000
Tax Rate	2.71%
Gross Tax Savings	$ 21,680
Fee Due (25%)	($ 5,420)
Net Tax Savings	**$16,260**

Your net tax savings is $16,260 ($21,680 - $5,420). You may need to go through the whole process again if the taxing district issues another unreasonably high initial assessment next year, which is likely. This would not be the case if the taxing district had a fair and efficient assessment system. These unfair assessment practices cause huge underwriting problems for both sellers and purchasers because there is no real handle on what the reassessment will be after a sale and its effect on NOI and operating expenses.

However, if the current assessment was closer to the purchase price for the property, the problem would be mitigated. There would be much less differential between the new assessment and the previous owner's assessment, in which case you may not even need to challenge the taxes.

We are using a district in Texas for our example. Every state and every taxing district within every state has different methods of determining an assessment. You must find out how the district will determine the post-closing reassessment for a property located in that specific taxing district. Real estate taxes are the largest part of a property's operating expenses, so failing to do so can prove to be disastrous.

Evaluating the current assessment and its relationship to the new purchase price is one of the most important factors to consider when purchasing a property. The closer the current assessment is to the purchase price the better.

Warning: Danger! Danger!

The potential increase in assessment and real estate taxes and its effect on the post-closing value of the property should be considered at the time you are evaluating the OM. Not considering this factor could prove to be disastrous!

The Effect of Increased Assessment on Property Value

- It was previous stated that the Dallas Arms Apartments' NOI is $240,080, and the cap rate is 6.32%. However, these amounts were based on the current real estate taxes of only $35,511.

- If real estate taxes are increased to $102,980 as a result of the new initial assessment or even $81,300 after using the outside consultant, your NOI will be reduced by *$45,789* ($81,300 - $35,511).

- Then your NOI will be reduced to *$194,291* ($240,800 - $45,789), translating to a reduced cap rate of **5.11%** ($194,291/$3,800,000), rather than the 6.32% cap rate shown in the OM.

- Assuming a cap rate of 6.32%, there will be a loss in property value of **$724,509** ($45,789/6.32%), a 19% decrease in property value.

Underwriting the Post-Closing Assessment

I cannot stress enough the importance of checking to see if the financial projections and cap rate presented in the OM take into account what the post-closing assessment and taxes will be. Do not just take the underwriting projections using the current assessment and taxes as fact. If there is no adjustment, then the results will be incorrect and misleading and severely overstate NOI and the cap rate that is shown in the OM.

A rule of thumb is that your projections and the calculation of NOI and resulting cap rate should *include* underwriting the post-closing assessment and corresponding real estate taxes calculated at 80% of the purchase price and not by using the current assessment and real estate tax amounts.

A rule of thumb is that your projections and the calculation of NOI and resulting cap rate should <u>include</u> underwriting the post-closing assessment and corresponding real estate taxes calculated at 80% of the purchase price and not by using the current assessment and real estate tax amounts.

Current Tax Rate (2.710%):
The tax rate, although generally much less volatile than the assessment, is also subject to change. However, be aware that an increase in the tax rate cannot be challenged by the property owner. Part of your due diligence procedures should include examining changes in the district's tax rates over the past five years. In some cases, I have actually seen tax rates decrease or become more volatile.

Tax Abatement Programs:
You should be aware that many cities offer tax abatement programs that can significantly lower real estate taxes. Tax abatements can result in significant reductions or freezing of assessments for periods ranging from one to 30 years, depending upon the program. The terms and conditions of the abatement are established by the taxing authority or governing body granting the abatement. The abatement generally requires the owner and/or the property to meet certain criteria. Additionally, the abatement can be forfeited if the owner and/or property do not comply with the terms of the abatement. In addition to tax abatements, there may be federal, state, or city tax credit programs available for properties that have been or will be developed in certain designated areas.

There may also be tax abatement programs allowing for discounts on your taxes when you make certain qualified capital improvements to a property. Other programs that are potentially available to you may limit benefits to low- to middle-income property owners, but other programs have no income restrictions.

Insurance

The Role of the Insurance Agent

Ensure that you use a competent insurance agent to service the property. A competent insurance agent needs to do the following:

Have extensive access to the various insurance markets:
A smaller agent can only feed so many carriers directly. Therefore, the smaller agent will have to rely on a wholesale agent (who you don't know) to reach the rest of the marketplace. This additional layer often equates to additional cost to you when used unnecessarily. It also puts another company in between you and the carrier in the event of a claim or billing issue that requires special attention to resolve.

Possess leverage by virtue of their purchasing power :
An agent who places a significant number of premiums with a carrier or wholesaler will naturally have more leverage and therefore have a better ability to resolve claims and coverage issues. The larger agent should also have access to expertise to get a complicated issue resolved with a carrier. It's always better to get carrier issues resolved at the agent level without having to hire an attorney.

Always be looking out for the best interests of the insured :
This service should include a free review of insurance and the tricky indemnity sections of agreements you enter into prior to execution.

Always try to obtain the best coverage and lowest premiums possible:
This includes advising the insured of ways to lower premiums while increasing coverage.

Advise the insured of any exclusions from the policy they should be aware of and the cost to have the exclusions removed from the policy i.e.: mold and lead coverage.

Warning—Blocking the Market:

Many insurance brokers wait until a week or even days before a policy expires to present a new insurance quote to the owner. This is often done intentionally in order to *block the market.* Insurance companies generally protect the agent with the first submission from the agent, and their quote will be reserved unless the owner specifically writes a letter requesting another quote from a different agent.

Desk Quotes:

The agent makes up a quote and sends it to the insured. The actual market quote then comes back much higher, requiring the insured to rush into making decisions they may be unprepared for due to the market subsequently becoming blocked.

Co-Insurance:

This is a punitive provision designed to protect the carrier from owners who are underinsured for property insurance. The higher the coinsurance percentage is, the more severe and likely the penalty will be. Ultimately, it is the owner's responsibility to determine the insurable value of the property (replacement cost value). Co-insurance penalties are applied to any loss, no matter the size. The result is always painful and could have been easily avoided. Always try to have co-insurance removed, if possible. If not possible, ask your agent for a Marshal & Swift replacement cost valuation to help validate the proper limits are being carried to avoid the penalty.

Exclusions:

Agents should always explain any exclusions in the policy. They should also advise the insured of the risks and additional cost for coverage to be in effect.

Deductible Amounts:

Pay close attention to how deductibles are worded. Make sure your agent explains exactly how they will be applied, especially with wind/hail deductibles and business income deductibles. Small variances in deductible wording can make a huge difference in how they are calculated.

Property Owners Should Have the Following Insurance Coverages in Effect:

- "All Risks" or "Special Form" property insurance covers casualty losses such as fire, wind and hail, building contents, and rents.

- General Liability covers bodily injury and property damage to others.

- Workers Compensation and Disability apply if the property has employees. Coverage is statutory. The cost depends upon the state where the property is located.

- Auto coverage is for contractor vehicle accidents, i.e. if a contractor's truck hits a tenant, or if you are in an accident while visiting a location and the company is sued as a result.

- Umbrella is any additional coverage over and above the general liability amounts.

- Pollution Coverage covers items generally excluded from basic coverage, including mold, lead, asbestos, underground storage tanks, wind and hail, etc. This is often not required by lenders.

- Owners should require tenants to have a general liability policy to protect for liabilities caused by them, i.e.: a dog bites another tenant or they cause a leak that causes damage to another tenant below them.

Decreasing Premiums and Increasing Companies' Willingness to Insure the Property:

If the property has loss prevention equipment, there should be lower premiums and a wider range of companies willing to insure the property. This equipment includes, but is not limited to, a sprinkler system (30% to 40% less), copper wiring throughout the building (20% to 30% less), and a well-maintained roof that is less than 10 years old.

At the time a property is purchased, insurance companies providing a quote will request a document known as a "loss run" for the property.

The loss run shows the history of any claims, payouts, or settlements made during a certain period of time. Typically, insurance companies only look at the losses for the past five years. The items on the loss runs will have a significant effect on the premiums that are quoted. This means that any losses that occurred before the five-year period will generally fall off and not be considered in determining the new premiums. If loss runs can't be obtained from the seller, a carrier often accepts a letter from the buyer stating they did not discover any losses during their due diligence.

Premiums can also be reduced by remediating chronic issues such as floods, trip and fall claims, etc. You may, for example, hard wire thermostats instead of using ones that are battery-operated, institute flood protection programs such as water leak detection procedures, and install cameras to monitor and document trips and falls.

Each carrier has limits to how much premium credit they can provide through higher deductibles, so your agent needs to know which carriers provide the most credit for high-deductible plans and how to manage those negotiations to your advantage. A property policy has many different types of deductibles that can be adjusted. If you have a high tolerance for risk in general, or for a particular situation, and your lender approves, you should explore higher deductible options.

Contractors, Subcontractors, and Vendors (collectively "Contractors")

By gaining an understanding into the mind of a contractor, you will be in a better position to negotiate with them and decrease expenses. To that end, I want to share some of my observations and opinions about dealing with contractors, subcontractors, and vendors,

An Adversarial Relationship from the Start:
The truth is that contractors and customers have an adversarial relationship by nature. They don't trust each other: the customer thinks the contractor is trying to rip them off, and the contractor thinks the customer will nickel and dime them. Because of this, the contractor will generally submit an inflated proposal believing the customer will always try to negotiate the price downward. The reality is they're both right.

Side Note: On a personal note, I've never met a contractor who would admit that they actually made any money on a job.

Always Get At Least Three Different Bids, Then Have Them Fight It Out:
Always, and I mean always, get different bids from at least three independent contractors. Remember that the managing agent is often getting the bids from contractors they have relationships with. This can be good and bad. On the good side, they can negotiate on your behalf using their purchasing power to obtain better pricing, and they are familiar with the quality of the contractor's workmanship and reliability. The bad side is that the managing agent could have long-term kickback arrangements, so they may lean toward making deals with less-than-reputable contractors for their own profit.

I play one contractor against the other. I share the bids' information, the price quotes, and what's included, and let them fight it out. It's amazing to see how open they become to negotiate for lower prices. Of course, it depends on how busy they are and how much they want the work.

Investigate the Contractor's Reputation and Track Record:
I like dealing with contractors who have a proven track record and are viewed favorably in the business community. I don't want contractors who consistently show up late or not at all, who are rude and nasty, who overcharge for their work, who perform substandard work, etc.

In the event they don't complete the work or if the work is substandard, you might not have any recourse. How can you protect yourself from these potentially unpleasant situations? Below are a few ways.

- Ask the contractor for a list of references, then call them. Remember that shyness can cost you money. Call the references and ask if they had a good experience with the contractor. Ask them if they had to say one bad thing to say about the contractor, what would it be?

- Look online for any complaints or lawsuits the contractor was involved in.

- Ask around about the contractor. Ask brokers, attorneys, managing agents, other contractors, etc. from your network of connections.

- Ask your attorney to perform a litigation and lien search on the contractor. This may cost a bit, but it will disclose information related to the contractor's principals and corporations and show any past or present litigation the contractor was involved in. It may also disclose any other corporations the contractor may be involved in.

Contractors are notorious for setting up shell corporations with no assets to do the work. If they get in financial or legal trouble, they close the company and immediately set up a new one. In this case, you'll most likely be out of luck if you try to recoup any monetary losses.

Price and Service Will Depend on How Busy They Are:
Right now, contractors are extremely busy with more work than they can handle, so they throw out crazy prices and see what sticks. Unfortunately, even though you're paying a higher price than normal, you'll still be serviced by a company with limited resources because of all the jobs they're doing.

- Inquire about how many jobs the contractor is currently working on and how many are in the immediate pipeline.

- Inquire about who will be supervising the work and their background and experience. How long have they been working for the company? Look out for a lot of employee turnover.

A good contractor becomes a bad contractor if they take on too many jobs. Contractors will try to get obscene prices for their work while owners get a contractor who has fewer resources available to service them.

Showing Up Late Is the New Normal:

When you call the cable or telephone company, they tell you someone will be there between 9:00 a.m. and 3:00 p.m. You kill your day waiting for them. Unfortunately, contractors have adopted the same behavior. I call this behavior "contractor time." "*We'll be there when we're there.*" One contractor even had the nerve to charge us for a service call because he came three hours late and nobody had waited for him. Contractors who are on time want to be paid a premium, thinking this is a special service for the customer.

Psychology of A Contractor:

On a few occasions, contractors have told me, "*Look how much money I'm making for you!*" Not only do I not want to hear that, but it shows that the contractor is resentful. When a contractor is resentful of an owner, theft generally follows. Being resentful is human nature, but it also means that they may not have your best interests at heart, and they will take whatever means they can to satisfy their resentment. They can take shortcuts and charge and overcharge you for things you may not need. Try to uncover and ascertain the contractor's attitude and use that to make a determination about their integrity.

Never Let a Contractor Get Ahead of You:

This is rule number one! Some contractors demand an upfront deposit of 30% to 50% before any work is performed. The excuse is usually that materials need to be purchased. An initial 30% to 50% deposit is much more than the actual cost of the upfront materials. It really represents pre-paid labor. Therefore, if you start out by giving a large upfront deposit, the contractor will be ahead of you in terms of receiving payment for work that hasn't been completed. This is not the position you want to be in.

For example, what happens if the contractor disappears or you experience delays and/or problems with their work? You have lost your leverage. By giving the contractor a large deposit, you *let the contractor get ahead of you.* Try your best to never be in this position. I always try to be ahead of the contractor, or at least up to date with the completed work.

As a way of protecting myself, I usually have the payments conditioned upon the architect or managing agent approving progress payments as the work is completed.

Progress Payment Example:

Owner agrees to pay Contractor the amount of Forty-Eight Thousand Seven Hundred Dollars ($ 48,700) Dollars (the "Contract Sum") for the Work, payable as set forth below.

(i) $ 4,870 (10%) upon signing of contract.

(ii) $ 14,460 after 30% of demolition work is completed.

(iii) $ 14,460 after 30% of rough plumbing/electric is completed.

(iv) $ 9,740 after 20% of ceramic tile floors is completed.

(v) $ 4,870 upon completion of job and final inspection and approval of the work by the architect.

The amount of the deposit is negotiable, and you should take the contractor's reputation, financial position, cost of the supplies that will be ordered, etc. into account when negotiating the initial deposit. After the initial deposit, your contract should have a payment schedule that details how much will be paid to the contractor when percentages of the work are completed.

Retention:

After you've hired a contractor and given them a deposit, the last thing you want is for them to walk off the property, leaving the job half-finished or with defective work. One way to limit or eliminate this potential problem is through **retention**. Retention is an acceptable practice in the construction industry. Retention means that the owner holds back, or "retains," a certain percentage (5% to 10%) of the contracted amount until the job is finished. The contractor only gets the retained amount when you're happy with the work they've done. Generally, the architect is used to confirm that the work has been completed.

Contractors are known for robbing Peter to pay Paul and being terrible businessmen and money managers. Try to never prepay the contractor more than the actual work completed, except possibly for verified material costs. In other words, never let the contractor get ahead of you and never pay for prepaid labor.

Always Get Lien Releases from Subcontractors:
I always insert the following language into the general contractor's, subcontractor's, or any other worker's proposal or contract: *Upon request, Contractor will provide Owner with an executed "Release and Affidavit of Subcontractor and/or Vendor" for each Subcontractor who has performed work or furnished materials to XXXXXX.*

When a contractor performs work on a property, they want to make sure they get paid. Contractors hire subcontractors who actually perform the work. If the general contractor doesn't pay the subcontractor, the subcontractor can file what's known as a "mechanic's lien" against the property. This lien gives the lienholder (the subcontractor) some assurance that they will get paid by giving them a claim against the real property.

If the contractor can't or won't pay the subcontractor, the lienholder (subcontractor) will then ask the owner of the property to pay the debt or the lien will not be released. The owner generally isn't aware that the subcontractor wasn't paid since they paid the general contractor. This causes all kinds of problems for the owner. Title will be clouded, which will cause problems with the lender, and the lien will need to be satisfied before the property can be sold or refinanced. Be especially careful if you find that subcontractors aren't being paid. Many times, desperate general contractors will fill out the release of lien form and forge the subcontractor's signature.

I have provided a general discussion of the lien release concept, but *please consult with your attorney regarding protecting yourself for these types of situations.*

If a subcontractor doesn't get paid, they will file a "mechanic's lien" against the property which will cloud the title and cause all kinds of problems for the owner. Additionally, the owner will ultimately be responsible for the amount owed, even if the owner paid the general contractor for the work, but the general contractor didn't pay the subcontractor. The owner's best protection against this occurring is to obtain a signed release of lien forms from each subcontractor.

Find Out If the Work Is Being Subbed Out:
Who will be doing the work? If the company you're contracted with has subcontracted out to perform the work, you will generally be paying more for the work since a middleman has become involved.

Extras Must Be First Approved in Writing by Owner:
"Extras" are charges for work not covered by the proposal or contract. Contractors can make substantial profits on performing extras since they have a higher markup than the contracted work itself. Human nature tells me that this is an area that contractors can abuse, and, unfortunately, some contractors cheat and overcharge their customers. It's imperative that the contractor presents you with a detailed cost proposal and the reason for the extra *before* work has commenced. You will then have the opportunity to review the extra and decide if you approve or wish to get another bid from a different contractor.

I usually insert the following clause in a contractor's proposal and/or contract:

All increases in the Contract Sum or changes in the Work ("Extras") must be approved by Owner in writing. No Extras will be owed or paid to the contractor, unless such extra work is first approved in writing by Sam Liebman. If contractor performs any such extras or furnishes materials without first obtaining written approval from Sam Liebman, contractor does so, for free.

Please realize that many extras can be legitimate. For example, you can't expect the contractor not to charge you for extra work he needs to perform for damage uncovered after a wall is taken down. On many occasions, the owner may want to add to the original scope of work, i.e. deciding on more expensive flooring, appliances, cabinets, etc.

Contractor's Insurance

Before any work commences, require the contractor to provide proof that the following insurance coverages are in full force and will continue to be in force during the entire period the work is being performed.

- General Liability:

  Covers bodily injury and property damage to others. Limits are fairly standard. The cost depends upon the contract value and nature of the work being performed.

- Workers Compensation:

  Coverage is statutory, and it covers work-related bodily injury to the workmen. The cost depends upon the state where the work is performed, and the amount of payroll involved for each job type times a multiplier based on their claims history called the NCCI Modifier (MOD).

  > Side Note: To assess the safety record of a contractor, ask them to provide you with a copy of their MOD number. If the number is under one, they are very safe. If it is between one and a half and two, I would ask them to explain the reason. If it is two or higher, it's a red flag.

- Auto:

  Coverage for contractor's vehicle accidents, i.e. contractor's truck hits a tenant or the building.

- Umbrella:

  Additional coverage over and above the general and auto liability amounts.

- Builder's Risk:

  This is property insurance covering the materials and, for ground up construction, the structure, against fire and wind, etc. For smaller projects, the contractor should carry the insurance. For larger projects, I recommend the owner carrying the insurance since it is your property that is at risk.

- "All Risks" or "Special Form" property insurance:

  The contractor should be solely responsible for insuring their equipment and property for loss or damage.

- Certificate of Insurance:

  The contractor should provide the owner with a certificate of insurance and a copy of all related endorsements evidencing all insurance policies required by the agreement and naming the owner as an additional insured under contractor's general, auto, and umbrella liability policies for ongoing and completed operations. The contractor should be required to maintain the owner as an additional insured for the full period for completed operations in the state that the work is performed.

Other Insurance Tips:

- If your property is located in an area that is prone to large seasonal storm losses (hurricanes, hail, or tornadoes), try to move your renewal date out of the storm season for that area.

- Having a renewal date in the 4th quarter can sometimes be advantageous as you might find an underwriter who is more negotiable that hasn't made their numbers for the year yet. This strategy is best utilized in a soft market when insurance rates are generally flat or down for the year.

The type and amounts of coverage will depend upon the size and nature of the work being performed. *Please consult with your insurance agent to further discuss the insurance the contractor should provide for your protection.*

Capital Improvement Certificate:
Depending on the state the property is located in, contractors should charge sales tax on the labor portion of a capital improvement and not on the material cost of the work. If you make a capital improvement to the property, you should complete a capital improvement certificate and give it to the contractor. The certificate will be kept by the contractor as support for not charging sales tax on the material portion of the work.

Remember, it must be a capital improvement as defined by the state tax code the property is located in, and not simply for repair or maintenance work. For example, installing a new roof is a capital improvement, but appliances such as a refrigerator, washer, and dryer are personal property and are subject to sales tax. Many times, I have found that the managing agent has neglected to complete and give a capital improvement certificate to the contractor for qualifying work. In that case, the owner will have paid sales tax they shouldn't have. You should consult with your accountant about sales and use tax requirements in the state the property is located.

Contract Termination:
Never sign a contract that contains language stating, *"The term will automatically renew under the same terms and conditions upon expiration, unless written notice is given within 90 days prior to expiration."* This can be a death sentence!

Assume a contract has an initial term of five years and expires on December 31, 2020. However, you neglected to provide written notice within the

90-day window that you wish to terminate the contract. The contract will then be in effect for another five-year term.

Acceptable language would be, *"If written notice of termination is not received then the contract will renew on a month-to-month basis."* Then you can terminate the contract by giving 30 days written notice.

Never sign a contract that contains language stating, "The term will automatically renew under the same terms and conditions upon expiration unless written notice is given within a certain period of time." This can be a death sentence! Acceptable language would be, "If written notice of termination is not received then the contract will renew on a month-to-month basis." In this case, you can terminate the contract by giving 30 days written notice.

Street Success Concepts to Remember

1. Realize that a $100 increase in revenue has the same effect on NOI as a $100 decrease in operating expenses. Therefore, if you can legitimately decrease operating expenses you can increase NOI and property value.

2. The kind of management you have at your property can make or break you. This applies for both third-party management and self-managed properties.

3. Third-party managing agents do not have a vested interest in the property or skin in the game. As a result, they will not be as motivated to increase revenue or control expenses

4. When interviewing a managing agent, you should stress that you are a long-time owner of the property. Managing agents invest time and money to hire, train, and set up a new account's accounting data, vendor accounts, etc. Having good relationships with long-term owners helps stabilize the managing agent's business. This is a completely opposite

approach than dealing with brokers, where you should never stress that you are a long-term owner because, in the broker's mind, it limits their ability to earn future commissions.

5. You can lose a fortune if the managing agent's employees are untrained, incompetent, lazy, unmotivated, etc. If these types of employees are involved with running your properties, it's usually the result of a lack of caring and supervision by the owners of the managing agent.

6. Property owners should assemble a team and schedule weekly meetings to discuss and review the property's activities and operations. The team should consist of various employees of the owner and managing agent. This is the most efficient way to become aware of existing and potential problems and find timely solutions.

7. No management company is making money from just their management fee. Generally, additional money is being made from non-disclosed related company affiliations and/or companies directly or indirectly owned by the managing agent or from kickbacks received from various vendors servicing the property.

8. Always have the managing agent disclose in their agreement any direct or indirect ownership or profit-splitting relationships, any refund or discounts they will receive, etc. At least if these relationships are disclosed upfront, you can decide if it's acceptable to you.

9. Be aware that some properties can be so well-managed that their efficiency cannot be matched by other managing agents. Therefore, you may need to make adjustments in your projections depending upon the level of competency, purchasing power, etc. that you expect from the managing agent you hire. This fact should especially be considered if you plan on managing the property yourself. You will need to account for the possibility of increased operating expenses, lower rents and occupancy, etc., and this will directly affect the projected NOI you expected to receive.

10. Decreasing operating expenses starts with putting together a great team of professionals that work together for the benefit of the property. The team consists of the managing agent and their employees and the building's staff. They need to be trained, supervised, and motivated.

11. Each state has its own requirements for determining the level at which employers are responsible for the cost of health insurance and overtime benefits. In many states, the employer is not required to provide health insurance for part-time employees who work under a certain number of hours per week. Therefore, depending on the state, an owner can save significant money by hiring two part-time workers who are not entitled to benefits instead of one full-time employee who is.

12. If the property operates as ABP (All Bills Paid), the savings will go straight into your pocket. If the property operates a RUBS (Ratio Utility Billing System) program, the tenants will benefit from the savings. You should let the tenants know that you negotiated a low electric rate.

13. In many municipalities, sewer charges are directly affected by the amount of water consumption. The sewer bill will be based upon the amount of water consumption multiplied by a fixed factor amount, and that will be the sewer charge.

14. Any unnecessary water usage that is the result of a malfunction or leaks derived from toilets, sinks, showers, pipes behind walls, foundations, pools, irrigation systems, etc. can cost you a fortune. If these inflated water and sewer costs are not corrected, not only will you lose substantial cash flow but your NOI and property value will also be adversely affected.

15. Evaluating the current assessment and its relationship to the new purchase price is one of the most important factors to consider when

purchasing a property. The closer the current assessment is to the purchase price the better.

16. The potential increase in assessment and real estate taxes and its effect on the post-closing value of the property should be considered at the time you are evaluating the OM. Not considering this factor could prove to be disastrous!

17. A rule of thumb is that your projections and the calculation of NOI and resulting cap rate should include underwriting the post-closing assessment and corresponding real estate taxes calculated at 80% of the purchase price and not by using the current assessment and real estate tax amounts.

18. A good contractor becomes a bad contractor if they take on too many jobs. Contractors will try to get obscene prices for their work, while owners get a contractor who has fewer resources available to service them.

19. Contractors are known for robbing Peter to pay Paul and being terrible businessmen and money managers. Try to never prepay the contractor more than the actual work completed, except possibly for verified material costs. In other words, never let the contractor get ahead of you and never pay for prepaid labor.!

20. If a subcontractor doesn't get paid, they will file a "mechanic's lien" against the property which will cloud title and cause all kinds of problems for the owner. Additionally, the owner will ultimately be responsible for the amount owed, even if the owner paid the general contractor for the work but the general contractor didn't pay the subcontractor. The owner's best protection against this occurring is to obtain signed release of lien forms from each subcontractor.

21. Never sign a contract that contains language stating, "The term will automatically renew under the same terms and conditions upon

expiration unless written notice is given within a certain period of time." This can be a death sentence! Acceptable language would be, "If written notice of termination is not received then the contract will renew on a month-to-month basis." In this case you can terminate the contract by giving 30 days written notice.

CHAPTER 9

UNDERSTANDING WHY CAP RATES CHANGE

AS YOU LEARNED, even a small cap rate swing of 1% can increase or decrease property value substantially. Large cap rate swings can make property values increase by amounts that defy logic and traditional real estate fundamentals.

⇨ *When the fundamentals of real estate investing are compromised or no longer apply, then purchasing real estate becomes more akin to gambling than investing.*

We will now discuss factors that have directly caused cap rates to drastically change from a high cap rate environment in 1991 to an extremely low cap rate environment in 2019. The change in market cap rates is the most dynamic force that affects property values. Unfortunately, unlike increasing the rent roll or decreasing operating expenses, your ability to control the change in market cap rates is limited, but when you fully understand the underlying factors that cause these changes, you should be able to become aware of the warning signs that substantial changes may be on the horizon. This knowledge will enable you to determine if it's time to buy, sell, or sit back and do nothing. As Kenny Rogers sings in "The Gambler," "*You got to know when to hold…know when to fold.*"

⇨ *Understanding why cap rates change will help you identify the warning signs early so that preventive action can be taken.*

This book so far has dealt primarily with garden-style apartment communities located in *non-rent-regulated areas* where, for the most part, property owners could increase rents without governmental oversight or limitation. Further increases were generally determined by the strength or weakness of the local market or supply and demand, even if the property was upgraded. For the purposes of the following discussion and analysis of understanding why cap rates change, we are going to use New York City as our model. New York City has very strict rent regulations and will provide a good introduction to the effects that rent control can have on Cap rates.

A Narrative of the Changes in Cap Rates: 1991 to 2019

⇨ *The higher the cap rate, the lower the purchase price. The lower the cap rate, the higher the purchase price.*

Let's examine the various factors and the environment that existed during the "High Cap Rate" years. During this period, my partners and I purchased over 35 buildings in New York City.

The High Cap Rate Years: 1991 to 1996

Simply put, during the high cap rate years of 1991 to 1996, there was *too little money chasing too many deals, as opposed to a low cap rate environment where there is too much money chasing too few deals.* The New York City real estate market was very depressed. Many properties were in a state of foreclosure, crime was rampant, and many viewed New York City as a "city in decay." Interest rates offered by lending institutions to purchase multi-family properties were in excess of 9%. Additionally, banks were not lending for new construction projects. Real estate was not considered an attractive place to invest, especially in New York City. Banks were inundated with foreclosures and concerned about potential liabilities inherent with property ownership. Banks were neither prepared nor equipped to manage property. These reasons, combined with other factors, meant banks were more than willing to write off their losses and move on. For example, it wasn't uncommon for banks to write off losses from a $3,000,000 defaulted mortgage by selling it at a 30% to 50% discount.

⇨ *During high cap rate years, there is generally too little money chasing too many deals, as opposed to too much money chasing too few deals during low cap rate years.*

High interest rates and attractive alternative investment opportunities contributed to a tremendous supply with little or no demand from buyers. Why purchase real estate when you could receive 5% to 6% interest on a certificate of deposit without doing anything? Marginal, as well as prime, multi-family residential properties were selling at 8% to 12% cap rates with purchasers realizing cash-on-cash returns ranging from 10% to 15%, even with mortgage interest rates above 9%. Sellers were offering concessions, and the properties available held tremendous potential for increased value since the buildings contained many low paying rent-controlled and/or stabilized tenants, and brokers were pleased to receive any offers. There wasn't much demand for real estate during these years, which made it a great time to buy, but not a very good time to own real estate.

⇨ *In a high cap rate environment, sellers are willing to be flexible when negotiating to sell their property. Negotiating leverage is greatly in favor of the purchaser.*

The conditions and factors that existed during the high cap rate years can be summarized as follows:

Supply and Demand:
High supply and low demand for properties, low supply of capital chasing too many deals, lowering of purchase prices and rents, maintenance, and other steep concessions offered to prospective purchasers of co-ops and condominium apartments.

Banks:
Inundated with foreclosures, willing to restructure and/or sell mortgages at deep discounts, willing to accept and write off losses, fearful of potential liabilities from owning and operating property, unwilling to lend, high interest rates for mortgages, and unwillingness to give mortgages for new construction projects.

Sellers:
Readily willing to grant generous due diligence periods, accept lower contract deposits, cure existing violations, provide more representations, provide purchase money mortgages, willing to meet face-to-face to negotiate a deal.

Brokers:
Extremely motivated to quickly sell property and make deals as quickly as possible, pleased to receive any offers. Higher brokers fees charged due to excess supply and less demand.

Potential Purchasers:
Can receive very high cash-on-cash returns on investment due to the high cap rates, even with paying high interest rates. Many properties available to choose from, etc.

Alternative Investments:
Generally high interest rates available on money market and certificates of deposit accounts.

Political:
Unfriendly real estate environment, few if any available incentives offered for real estate investment.

General:

Usually, crime increases and buildings become in disrepair during high cap rate environments.

The Start of a Comeback: Cap Rates Decrease 1997 to 2000

Between 1997 and 2000, property values started to increase. Crime was down, and blighted areas such as Times Square were experiencing a transformation. A new administration led by Mayor Rudy Giuliani rejuvenated the city and made it vibrant again. *Vacancy decontrol* regulations introduced in 1994 and favorable tax abatement programs, as well as other special benefits and incentives, were offered by various government agencies to encourage real estate investment. As a result, property values steadily increased while market cap rates steadily decreased. Led by the Disney Corporation, enormous sums of capital were earmarked to restore Times Square to the entertainment capital of the world. As large investments in other parts of the city followed, real estate investment became attractive again, and the city became vibrant. Apartment rents increased substantially, adding to increased property values.

During this period, interest rates on mortgages began to drop from 8% in 1997 to 7% in January of 1999. Between 1995 and its peak in March 2000, the Nasdaq Composite stock market index increased over 400%, and investors were fearful of the bubble bursting, which soon became a reality. Investments in savings accounts, certificates of deposits, etc., were yielding lower interest rates. Real estate was starting to become the popular investment choice again.

Cap Rates Continue to Decrease: 2001 to 2015

By the end of 2015, real estate values had skyrocketed to unbelievable proportions. Property owners started believing the hype created by brokers who bombarded owners with artificially high expectations. Property owners started second-guessing themselves about if they should sell or hold. Fueled by the benefits of 1031 tax exchanges and low interest rates, the decision was easy. Keep the property unless you receive an "offer you can't refuse" or refinance the mortgage. Since interest rates were lower owners could pull out substantial equity and have the monthly payment remain the same or become even lower. Because many properties were held long-term and refinanced so many times, a sale of the property would not generate enough net proceeds to pay the resulting capital gain taxes that would be due. As the values of the properties continued to escalate, this problem was mitigated or disappeared.

Interest rates were continuously dropping, and the Federal Reserve was giving mixed messages about the future of interest rates. Banks and other financial institutions had so much money to lend and pressure to put the money out on the street that the standards for lending went out the window. Almost anybody could get a loan to purchase income-producing property. Properties in blighted areas like the Bronx and parts of Queens were being financed with only a 10% to 15% down payment. I heard of instances where banks lent money at 110% of the purchase price based upon an appraisal.

The conditions and factors that existed during the comeback years can be summarized as follows:

Supply and Demand:
Rising purchase prices and rents, lower supply and higher demand for properties, higher supply of available capital targeted for real estate acquisition, much less need for sellers to offer maintenance and other concessions to prospective purchasers of co-ops and condominium apartments.

Banks:
Cleaned up much of their inventory of foreclosures, less willing to restructure and/or sell mortgages at deep discounts, less fearful of potential liabilities from owning and operating property, more willing

to lend, and lower interest rates now available for mortgages. More willing to give mortgages for new construction projects due to increased demand.

Sellers:

Started believing the hype created by brokers who bombarded owners with artificially high expectations, causing an attitude among sellers of believing they held gold. Less willing to grant customary due diligence periods, demanded higher contract deposits, less willing to cure existing violations, provide customary representations, provide purchase money mortgages, or meet face-to-face to negotiate a deal, etc.

Brokers:

Much less motivated to sell the property, more patience to obtain many offers and the highest price.

Potential Purchasers:

Lower cash-on-cash returns on investment due to higher purchase prices, even with paying lower interest rates. Fewer properties available to choose from.

Alternative Investments:

Interest rates had decreased on money market and certificate of deposit accounts.

Political:

New vacancy decontrol laws and favorable tax abatement programs in addition to other special benefits and incentives now offered by various government agencies to encourage real estate investment.

General:

Led by the Disney Corporation, enormous sums of capital were earmarked to restore Times Square to the entertainment capital of the world. As large investments in other parts of the city followed, real estate investment became attractive again.

Narrative of the Cap Rate Years 2016 to 2019

By 2016, there was too much money chasing too few deals. That's it in a nutshell. Due to various factors, the current real estate market had been experiencing an unprecedented suppression of cap rates. This is evidenced by the astronomical sales prices realized in the market. I had never before experienced such insanity in the real estate market. I saw more purchasers taking on more risk for less reward than ever before. With the dramatic increase in the price of land and the cost of construction, developers were faced with the prospect of personally guaranteeing construction loans for double the amounts required five to ten years ago. Additionally, the amount of equity required by banks and other financial institutions had almost doubled. Contractors who were too inundated with jobs were operating beyond capacity, causing delays in completing projects. As a result, developers were offering bonuses to contractors for completing the project earlier than projected because they feared missing the market. In Manhattan, properties were being sold at negative cap rates, which meant that the purchaser would need to invest additional capital simply to pay the operating expenses and debt service on the property. Investors were effectively buying property for the next generation.

Real estate prices in Manhattan and throughout the country were at record highs, and there seemed to be no end in sight. An amazing statistic had been brought to my attention "a quarter of the new condominiums being constructed will never be lived in." These units were not built to fill a shortage of housing but rather to fill the demands of speculative investors and investors engaged in the business of "flipping." Purchasing a condominium for $2,000,000 that is worth $2,500,000 to $3,000,000 or more in less than a year is not the sign of a normal growth pattern. This was a great time to own but a very dangerous time to acquire property.

⇨ *The best time to purchase property is when purchase prices are low and interest rates are high or in a high cap rate environment.*

Acquiring real estate at these super-low cap rates is more akin to a game of musical chairs. The question is, when will the music stop? Nobody knows, but you can study the different factors that contributed toward both high and low cap rate environments and be aware of the warning signs.

Factors Contributing to the Current Low Cap Rate Environment

During the past 10 to 15 years, real estate has been the beneficiary of a perfect storm. Some of the key factors that contributed to the current low cap rate environment where real estate prices are at all-time highs include:

Seller's Attitudes

⇨ *A key difference between high and low cap environments is the difference in seller's attitudes from willing to unwilling. In low cap rate environments characterized by tremendous demand for property, sellers are less willing to be flexible when negotiating to sell their property. Clearly, negotiating leverage is greatly in favor of the seller.*

For example, generally in a *low cap rate* environment, properties are being sold "as is" with sellers *unwilling* to grant customary due diligence periods, cure existing violations, pay for contamination remediation, or sell subject to proposed zoning changes. Additionally, sellers demand all-cash deals and are unwilling to meet face-to-face to negotiate. Brokers inventory bona fide offers and try to turn the purchasing process into an auction with prospective purchasers sometimes bidding against themselves without knowing it. Owners with no intention of selling are flooding the market with property listings at nonsensical asking prices, further confusing legitimate sellers about the value of their property. Due to extreme competitiveness to find deals, sellers are asking for contract deposits to go hard on day one before a purchaser has a chance to perform their due diligence. If the deal closes, the seller will credit the contract deposit price to the buyer. If the deal doesn't close, the purchasers forfeit their contract deposit. Sounds crazy, but many hedge funds consider the loss of their contract deposits as the cost of doing business.

⇨ *In real estate, you make money on the buy which means buying right. The purchase price is a permanent cost; it cannot be changed. However, interest rates are a temporary cost which can be changed to more favorable terms over time.*

Political Climate

Another key factor that contributes to a low cap rate environment is the political climate. The political views of the incumbent president along with the House and Senate have a direct effect on the real estate industry. For the past 10 to 15 years, real estate has enjoyed a series of tremendous benefits due to a continued favorable administration along with the various lobbying groups supporting the real estate industry. The policies of the Federal Reserve have kept interest rates low, and the encouragement of foreign investment by President Obama's Jobs Act is a reflection of the political climate that has contributed to the current low cap rate environment.

Starting in 2017, the Trump administration passed new laws that drastically changed the tax structure for property owners, corporations, and individuals. While some of these new laws are very favorable to the real estate industry, many are not. For example, in **many** blue states, real estate taxes and state and city income taxes are now limited to a total deduction of only $10,000. Homeowners living in these states lost a very valuable deduction. This new policy has had an adverse effect on the residential housing market in these states. However, the new laws are very favorable for multi-family property owners, allowing even more accelerated deductions and lower tax rates than existed before. Property owners can deduct large expenditures for capital improvements in the year expended rather than depreciating them over much longer periods, significantly decreasing the amount of a property owner's taxable income. Additionally, there are other pro real estate tax benefits available under the new laws, such as the significantly reduced tax rate on pass-through entities which are generally used by property owners to hold title to their real estate. In NYC, politics were one of the most dominating factors in increasing property values. *Politics Matter!*

Available Capital Investment

⇨ *In a low cap rate environment, there are massive amounts of capital and financing available for real estate investment. In a high cap rate environment, there is generally little capital or financing available for real estate investment.*

Hedge Funds and Retirement Plan Investment:

The growth of 401Ks and other retirement plans, coupled with unattractive alternative investment opportunities and the desire for investment diversification, has made real estate a viable alternative investment for retirement plans. A large part of hedge fund's compensation is in the form of various fees; hedge funds have large overhead costs and large amounts of capital to invest. On many occasions, I have found that they will **overpay** for property due to the pressure they are under to earn fees to maintain their overhead. Generally, capital contributed by investors to the hedge fund earns some sort of preferred return, but if capital isn't invested, not only will the hedge fund not earn their fees, but they will need to start accruing a preferred return on the investor's capital contributions without any offsetting income from the investment. Unattractive alternative investments, coupled with the constant pressure of having a large overhead, usually translates to a much higher tolerance for risk, causing capital to be placed in more risky investments than normal.

Massive Amounts of Foreign Investment in the U.S.:

A relatively new factor that contributed to the astronomical rise in real estate prices is the tremendous amount of foreign investment targeted at the United States' real estate. Due to the volatile governments in China, Russia, and other countries, many foreigners are using United States real estate as a safe haven (*a brick safety deposit box*) for their money. A weak U.S. dollar had made investing in the U.S. attractive because it allows foreigners to purchase property at a discount because their foreign dollars were worth more than U.S. dollars. Foreigners were the leading purchasers of expensive condominiums in Manhattan, with many holding them vacant rather than renting them out. These investors are just happy to own U.S. bricks. Foreigners are also purchasing office buildings, hotels, and residential communities across America.

⇨ *Foreign investment targeted at the U.S. is directly affected by the strength of the U.S. dollar, the current administration's foreign policies, and the volatility of foreign governments.*

The EB-5 Program:
Another relatively new factor had also contributed to the massive amounts of foreign capital available for real estate projects in the U.S. In 1990, the United States Congress' Immigration Act created a government program known as EB-5. Large developers such as Silverstein Properties, the Durst Organization, and Extel Development were literally lining up to obtain cheap capital and/or debt through this program.

This program allows wealthy foreigners and their families to become U.S. residents in return for making a $1,000,000 investment ($500,000 in special areas) in a U.S. business that creates a minimum of 10 new jobs for each green card issued to an investor. Because of this "low" barrier to entry, the number of applicants is now so great that the government might reach its full quota for the year in January. (*Please note that the rules and criteria for this program are constantly changing.*)

The opportunities in America were extremely attractive. A green card offers a way for wealthy foreigners to send their children to our colleges, to escape pollution and corruption in their country, and to enjoy our freedoms and our ability to cater to foreign cultures. Approximately 80% to 85% of EB-5 visas were issued to Chinese investors, with the balance going to South Korea, Taiwan, Iran, and Venezuela. The EB-5 Program has provided an important alternative source of financing, benefiting many real estate projects such as Brooklyn's Atlantic Yards real estate development, the Gem Tower in Manhattan, and the Marriott International Hotel in Seattle, to name just a few.

Obama's New JOBS Act:

Another new government-sponsored program that contributed to the massive amounts of capital available in the investment market is the Jumpstart Our Business Startups Act or JOBS Act. It is a law intended to encourage the funding of United States small businesses by easing various securities regulations that have been in place for over 50 years. It was signed into law by President Obama on April 5, 2012. This new law basically opened the floodgates to a new group of potential investors who historically have been deemed unqualified to invest in certain types of investments because of their risk, given their incomes and financial position. In summary, the Act, (i) lowers the criteria for becoming an Accredited Investor, (ii) lifts the ban on "general solicitation" and advertising, (iii) allows those seeking money to advertise investment opportunities on TV or via Facebook or Twitter - wherever, including at crowdfunding sites, and (iv) creates a new vehicle ("Crowdfunding") allowing investment by the masses.

It sounds great in theory, but I believe that the new law will encourage more Ponzi and financial schemes. Easing regulations for an industry filled with corruption doesn't seem like a great idea to me. In my opinion, the new laws sell out investor protections in return for allowing large amounts of new capital to enter the United States' investment market.

⇨ *A vital sign to monitor is the increase or decrease in foreign capital available for real estate investment. If this source of capital dries-up or even softens, the results to the real estate industry could be disastrous.*

Interest Rates for Mortgages

For the past five to seven years, interest rates have been artificially low. Traditionally, a high demand for money should result in a high interest rate, and a low demand for money should result in a low interest rate. However, even though there was a large demand for the past five or so years, interest rates for mortgages have been so low that banks are practically giving money away for free. Fannie Mae and Freddie Mac had been providing non-recourse financing for as much as 80% of the purchase price at sub 4% interest rates for multifamily apartment communities. Furthermore, the government is faced with a Catch-22 situation; if interest rates are increased, then the bond market and the economy could collapse.

⇨ *I believe the odds of interest rates increasing are much greater than the odds of them remaining constant or decreasing.*

Alternative Investments Opportunities

Another factor of a low Cap rate environment is unattractive alternative investment opportunities, such as bonds and savings accounts. Banks were offering interest rates as low as .01% to .08% on savings accounts. No more toasters for a $100,000 deposit. U.S. Treasury Bills are paying almost 0% interest. In fact, in the near future, banks may charge a fee just for the privilege of having a bank account. The stock market is at an all-time high with companies valued at ridiculous multiples of earnings. Many investors were leery of the stock market after years of volatility. In this type of environment, billions of dollars of investor funds had been redirected toward real estate investment.

Banks and Financial Institutions

Willingness to Lend:
Under President Clinton, the Gramm-Leach-Bliley Act repealed the Glass-Steagall Act in 1999. This new act allowed banks to use deregulated

derivatives, which substantially contributed to the 2008 financial crisis (a.k.a. the sub-slime mortgage crisis).

On July 21, 2010, President Obama signed into law the Dodd-Frank Wall Street Reform and Consumer Protection Act. The Act is a direct result of the 2008 financial crisis. It was specifically written to prevent another financial crisis. Before the law, the financial system lacked oversight, resulting in a broken system that allowed banks to take risks without understanding the consequences. Furthermore, since the government had no authority to do anything about it, high-risk lending, hiding fees, and misguiding borrowers became standard practice. Dodd-Frank regulated the financial markets to make another economic crisis less likely, which is exactly what Glass-Steagall had achieved after the 1929 stock market crash. The Dodd-Frank Wall Street Reform and Consumer Protection Act is a law that places significant regulations on financial institutions to prevent unnecessary risk-taking and abusive lending practices.

⇨ *As a result of the 2008 financial crisis, President Obama passed into law the Dodd-Frank Wall Street Reform and Consumer Protection Act. As a result, banks and financial institutions are now under constant scrutiny by outside regulators and compliance officers with many more hoops to be jumped through before loans are approved.*

Bailout Money

Another factor to be aware of is that during the Obama administration's first term, banks were getting bailout money from the government as long as the troubled loans remained on their books. If they wrote off the loans, they would receive less bailout money from the government. Banks played a game with the borrower known in the industry as *"extend and pretend"* whereby the borrower's loan would be restructured to more favorable terms rather than the bank foreclosing on the loan. This way the bank kept the defaulted loan on its books and continued to receive bailout money, and the borrower was able to weather the storm. When the sailing got smooth, the borrower was able to keep their property and was rewarded for their bad behavior with tremendous profits as properties appreciated over the next five years. I asked a friend of mine who owned an office building during that time how his office building was doing. He replied with a grin, "*First or second time around?*"

Many banks offered defaulted mortgages for sale on various websites. However, it wasn't real: The bank just needed to show the government it was making an effort to get these loans off their books. In reality, the banks had no incentive to do so because it would jeopardize the bailout money they received.

Another factor that determines a bank's willingness to lend is its concentration of loans in a particular submarket or type of real estate in its loan portfolio. Harsh regulations, coupled with constant oversight by regulators, play a major role in a bank's ability or willingness to lend. For example, if a bank has too many outstanding loans in a particular submarket, such as shopping centers or new construction projects, it will be less willing to lend to this group of borrowers.

Creative Financing

As financial institutions have become more creative and sophisticated, many favorable financing alternatives have become available in the market. I have seen amortization periods for as long as 40 years, something that didn't exist in the 1990s. Fannie Mae and Freddie Mac offer 30-year amortization periods and interest-only periods of one to ten years. Interest-only mortgages allow property owners to significantly increase cash flow and their cash-on-cash return on investment; however, prepayment penalties have become more painful. Instead of declining penalties as loans mature, there are now penalties based on yield maintenance or defeasance which can cause prepayment to be prohibitive.

⇨ *A scary reality to keep in mind is that these days the strength of the U.S. dollar is not backed by gold or silver but only by our way of life. Another reality is that only 10% of the money supply is in currency. The rest is electronic debits and credits.*

Change in Valuation to Buildable SF

During the early 2000s, a new valuation method for determining property value was becoming the new norm, especially if the property had development potential. The air above a building became monetized and known as the building's "Air Rights." That, plus an increase in condominium construction, propelled property values into the stratosphere, especially in New York City. Properties began to be valued based upon the buildable SF (length x width x permissible height) of the site instead of the traditional method of basing property value on net operating income (NOI).

⇨ *In New York City, the monetization of air rights caused a change in valuation from a cap rate basis to a buildable SF basis. This factor, coupled with an increase in condominium construction, propelled property values into the stratosphere.*

Property Value Using Traditional Method

Example:

Under the traditional method, if the property had a Net Operating Income (NOI) of $ 300,000 and the market cap rate was 5%, the property would be valued at approximately $6,000,000 (Property Value = Net Operating Income ("NOI")/Cap Rate).

When the traditional method went out the window, the NOI became irrelevant. Instead, the footprint of the property and its permissible zoning became the factors in determining property value. The permitted FAR (Floor Area Ratio) is now the key factor.

Property Value Using Buildable SF Method

Example:

Assume the footprint of the property in the above example is 75 feet wide and 100 ft. deep for a land area of 7,500 sq. ft. Further assume that the zoning permits construction of a 10-story building containing a total of 75,000 sq. ft. (75 x 100 x 10). In today's Manhattan real estate market, properties in good areas sell for $500 to $800 or more per buildable SF which translates into values of $30,000,000 and $60,000,000, respectively.

*Those numbers are quite different from valuing the property based on its NOI, which translates to a property value of $6,000,000. This represents an increase in property value of $24,000,000 to $54,000,000, simply because of the monetization of the air rights. Sounds unbelievable, but I assure you it's true. Many long-term owners in Manhattan and the outer boroughs have made millions of dollars because the potential buildable SF of their property became monetized. Many property owners received "**concrete lotto tickets**," courtesy of the City of New York who recently up-zoned many areas such as Chelsea, Williamsburg, and Downtown Brooklyn. Multi-millionaires were created overnight simply by being at the right place at the right time.*

Real Estate Brokers' Hype

⇨ *Sellers who don't list their property for sale on the open market to save the broker commission are fools. Furthermore, purchasers who use a broker to acquire property without being aware of their tricks are also fools.*

Real estate brokers also played a key role in contributing to a low cap rate environment. Real estate brokers are a necessary evil because they possess the most knowledge about the market and the ability to market to a vast number of prospective purchasers. My experience is that there are good, bad, and really bad brokers. Due to greed and extreme competition to obtain listings, the new generation of brokers have engaged in behaviors that border on, or are in fact, unprofessional and illegal in order to obtain listings. Over the past 10 years, brokers have been known to:

- Bombard property owners with solicitations to sell their property promising astronomical selling prices that defy logic.

- Offer owners a free detailed appraisal of their property in order to get their foot in the door and try to establish any sort of relationship.

- Inventory legitimate offers from prospective purchasers and use them as leverage to further drive up selling prices.

- Encourage owners with no intention of selling to flood the market with property listings at asking prices that further confuse legitimate sellers about the value of their property.

- Form in-house capital-raising facilities to buy the property themselves, thereby allowing for a first look before putting the property on the market.

- Offer in-house mortgage facilities with properties being offered with pre-approved financing.

- Try to shift the responsibility for paying the broker's fee to the buyer, even though the broker is representing the seller in the transaction.

- Offer properties for sale using a bidding process without showing a purchase price. Purchasing real estate has become an auction, just like eBay. A prospective purchaser can wind up bidding against themself without ever knowing it.

- Lower their commissions, which were 5% to 6% in high cap years, to 1% to 3% dependent on the sales price.

- Receive commissions from both the seller and the buyer without providing any disclosure.

There are also excellent professional brokers. These brokers try to be realistic with prospective sellers about the value of their property and will prepare a professional marketing package that shows comparable properties that were recently sold in the immediate area.

⇨ *Brokers generally enter into an exclusive sales agreement with the seller. The broker's first choice is to sell the property themselves and earn a full commission. However, many deals are made with the assistance of an outside or co-broker who will share in the overall commission.*

I have learned two important lessons when dealing with brokers, especially in a low cap rate environment.

⇨ *Assume a broker has two acceptable offers: one that earns them a full commission and one they need to split with another broker. Be aware that the broker is more likely to try to sway the seller to take the offer that yields a full commission.*

⇨ *Never tell a broker that you plan on keeping the property long-term. Always tell the broker that your holding period is only one to three years. In a broker's mind, a long-term purchaser is a one-shot deal for a commission. A short-term purchaser may give the broker another bite at the apple.*

New Laws for Rent-Regulated Apartments

Rent regulations vary based on state politics, but they provide regulations as to how much a tenant's rent can increase upon the expiration of their lease and the allowable rent increase upon a vacancy.

In New York City, there are three different apartment designations. The apartment is subject to the laws of *rent control* or *rent stabilization* or the apartment is *decontrolled.*

Various changes in the rent regulations in New York City from 1997 to 2017 greatly favored property owners, allowing increases in appreciation and property value as never seen before. In my opinion, the change to vacancy decontrol in New York City was the single factor most responsible for the astronomical increase in property value that transformed the city into a low cap rate environment.

Tax Benefits: Before Trump's New Tax Laws in 2017

The following discussion of tax benefits is general in nature and is for illustration purposes only. There are other factors to consider regarding the full deductibility of the various depreciation deductions and real estate losses. The reader should contact their own tax advisor before making a decision with regard to their own situation.

The Trump Administration's Tax Cuts and Jobs Act

As previously mentioned, in December 2017, the Trump Administration signed into law the Tax Cuts and Jobs Act which made drastic changes to the existing laws that, in my opinion, increased benefits for the real estate industry. Most of these changes went into effect on January 1, 2018. You don't need to be a CPA or tax attorney to understand the various concepts in the tax law that affect property owners. However, you do need guidance, and you do need to read and educate yourself about these laws. Although it may be frustrating and difficult at times to fully understand them, you must learn the fundamentals. By reading, re-reading, and asking questions you will eventually get it.

⇨ *If you can learn and understand the fundamentals of the tax benefits for real estate, you can learn to plan and defer and/or save yourself tremendous amounts of money. Tax savings, as opposed to tax deferrals, can be viewed as an additional return on your investment.*

Tax Laws that Benefit Property Owners

The following section is not meant to teach you tax law, but instead, its sole purpose is to make you aware of the factors that contributed to the changing from a high cap rate environment in 1991 to a low cap rate environment in 2019. We will focus primarily on the laws and benefits that existed prior to Trump's Tax Cuts and Jobs Act of 2018.

These are advanced concepts, so don't worry if you don't fully understand them at this time.

⇨ *The theory behind tax planning can be summed up by the concept that a tax deduction today is worth more than a tax deduction tomorrow, or a dollar today is worth more than a dollar later.*

Besides the traditional tax benefits of capital gain treatment and depreciation attributable to real estate investment, there were many other *non-traditional* tax benefits available to property owners. These relatively new benefits have contributed to the current low cap rate environment. The following tax benefits currently available to owners of real property are akin to participating in a legalized tax shelter. *Owners of real property are not only allowed one or two of these benefits but are allowed all of these benefits.* These tax benefits include, but are not limited to, the following:

- Properties Qualifying for 1031 Exchanges
- Cost Segregation Study
- Bonus Depreciation
- New IRS Rules for Capitalization and Depreciation
- Safe Harbor for Routine Maintenance
- The Real Estate Professional Tax Loophole
- Real Estate Tax Abatement

Properties Qualifying for 1031 Exchanges

The 1031 Exchange has been considered one of the most powerful wealth-building tools available to taxpayers. The skyrocketing demand for properties qualifying for the 1031 Exchange has substantially contributed to the low cap rate environment.

Besides deferring capital gains, other benefits to a 1031 Exchange include allowing for a less management-intensive property to be acquired and giving the seller the ability to unlock their equity and purchase a more expensive property with greater cash flow, potential appreciation, and a larger mortgage to amortize.

<u>Real-Life Example:</u>

We owned a small eight-unit mixed-use apartment building in New York City. The rent roll was $300,000, and my partner and I were receiving annual cash distributions of approximately $60,000 each, $120,000 in total. In 2015 we sold the building for $6,350,000. The capital gain was approximately $5,750,000. We subsequently used the net cash proceeds from the sale of $5,500,000 to purchase over $20,000,000 of property in Texas. Our new annual distribution increased significantly to approximately $250,000 each, $500,000 in total. Besides deferring tax on the $5,750,000 capital gain, we are amortizing a much higher mortgage of approximately $14,500,000 over 25 years. Furthermore, we are receiving a much larger depreciation deduction due to the increased cost basis of the new property acquired.

The problem with doing a 1031 Exchange is the strict time limits that must be obeyed. Among other rules, a taxpayer has only 45 days from the closing date to identify an exchange property and must close on the exchange property within 180 days from the day of the closing. In my opinion, these dates should be reversed. It is extremely hard to find a viable new property within the 45-day window. As a result, many sellers are under extreme pressure to find a new property to purchase and will **overpay** to acquire a new one. I can't tell you how many times a broker has called me with the opening line of, *"I have a 1031 Buyer who is desperate because their time is running out and will overpay for your property."*

⇨ *A 1031 Exchange allows a taxpayer who sells a property to postpone (defer) the capital gain from the sale by purchasing another qualified property within a certain time frame. Generally, both federal and state taxes gain can be postponed until the new property is sold or can potentially be postponed forever as long as the IRS rules are followed. This is a smart tax and investment strategy as well as an estate planning tool.*

The following benefits are based on the fundamental principle that *a tax deduction today is worth more than a tax deduction tomorrow.* When an asset's life is shortened, depreciation expense is accelerated, and tax payments are decreased during the early stages of a property's life. This, in turn, releases cash for investment opportunities or current operating needs.

Cost Segregation Study

Cost segregation has been in existence since 1954. However, it wasn't until the Hospital Corporation of America sued the IRS in 1997 and won that cost segregation was approved as a viable tax-saving strategy allowed by the IRS.

A cost segregation study identifies and reclassifies portions of the building into different categories that have *shorter tax lives,* thus accelerating depreciation deductions. These shorter tax lives are typically five, seven, and 15 years, rather than 27.50 years for residential real property or 39 years for nonresidential real property. A cost segregation study is most efficient for new buildings under construction, but it can also uncover retroactive tax deductions for much older buildings.

A cost segregation study examines and segregates into different useful lives (i) the building's HVAC, plumbing, electrical systems, etc., (ii) land improvements such as concrete paving, sidewalks, landscaping, site lighting, etc., and (iii) specific equipment such as, break room sinks, courtyard railings, etc.

Cost segregation provides property owners with additional accelerated depreciation deductions. Remember, *a tax deduction today is worth more than a tax deduction tomorrow.*

The following tax benefits were not available during the high cap rate years before 2000.

Bonus Depreciation:

Bonus depreciation was created in 2002 to encourage investment by small businesses and stimulate the economy. Under certain circumstances, it also applies to real estate for qualified capital expenditures. Bonus depreciation allows a deduction in the first year for a large portion of eligible assets cost in the year acquired, rather than having to deduct depreciation over longer periods of time. The allowable percentages have changed many times since 2012, from 30% to 100% of the eligible cost allowed to be deducted in the first year.

Trump's Tax Cuts and Jobs Act was passed in 2017 and injected steroids into the law. It doubled the bonus depreciation deduction for qualified property, as defined by the IRS, from 50% to 100%. More importantly, it extended bonus depreciation to cover **used** property under certain conditions while it previously only applied to new property purchasers. This new law gave property owners an even greater benefit.

Bonus depreciation is only available for the *first year* the asset is placed in service. Bonus depreciation is a method of accelerating depreciation deductions for the first year with less depreciation available in later years. Bonus depreciation is only available for federal tax purposes and certain states. However, it still represents additional accelerated depreciation deductions for property owners. And remember again that *a tax deduction today is worth more than a tax deduction tomorrow.*

⇨ *Bonus depreciation is another tax benefit available for property owners. Bonus depreciation currently allows a deduction in the first year for 100% of an eligible asset's cost in the year acquired, rather than having to deduct depreciation over longer periods of time. It also applies to used property under certain conditions.*

Safe Harbor Election (De Minimis Election):

In 2015, the IRS released new regulations regarding the deductibility or capitalization of tangible property costs. The final regulations provide an important tax benefit for taxpayers. A taxpayer can make a **_Safe Harbor Election, known as the de minimis election,_** that allows them to immediately expense certain property that would otherwise have to be capitalized. For 2016, the Safe Harbor Election allowed taxpayers to deduct an expense whose invoice was less than $2,500. The election is made on the taxpayer's tax return.*

⇨ *A taxpayer can make a Safe Harbor Election, known as the de minimis election, on their tax return. The election allows taxpayers to immediately expense certain property whose invoice is under $2,500 rather than having to capitalize and depreciate the cost over a longer period of time.*

Safe Harbor for Routine Maintenance:

Another tax benefit of the new IRS Rules for Capitalization and Depreciation is the *Safe Harbor for Routine Maintenance*. Under the new rules, building maintenance qualifies for the routine maintenance safe harbor if, when you placed the building or building system into service, **_you reasonably_** expected to perform such maintenance more than once every ten years. You don't even actually need to do the repair; you only have to reasonably expect that you will need to do the repair more than once every 10 years.

Example:

Assume you purchased a residential property with 100 parking spaces in 2015. At the time of purchase, the parking lot was in disrepair, and you knew that extensive repairs, repaving, and restriping would be needed immediately. You also *reasonably expected that you would need*

---

*See Appendix 1 for the benefits of the Safe Harbor Election (De Minimis Election).

to perform similar repairs over the next 10 years. In 2016, you made all the necessary repairs at a cost of $250,000. The entire $250,000 is deductible. Under the old law, the $250,000 cost would need to be capitalized over a 27.50-year period, and the depreciation deduction would only be $9,091 per annum.

The Real Estate Professional Tax Loophole

If you are simply a passive real estate investor (one that is not actively involved), the current deductibility of your net real estate loss is limited, phased-out, or not deductible at all. In 2019, if your income is less than $100,000, your net real estate loss is limited to $25,000 per year against your other income. If your income is between $100,000 and $150,000, the amount of allowed loss phases out with no allowable losses for income over $150,000. Unallowed net real estate losses can be carried forward to future years and be offset against other passive gains.

A Real Estate Professional overcomes the assumption that all rental activities are passive, thus allowing their losses to be deducted without limitation. Additionally, Real Estate Professionals are exempt from the additional 3.8% surtax on investment income. As a result, it has never been more desirable for a taxpayer with rental activities to meet the Real Estate Professional qualifications.

Real Estate Professional is a status designation given by the IRS based on the number of hours that you work in real estate activities versus other activities. This could include being a real estate agent, or it could mean that you spend time locating, renovating, leasing, or otherwise developing your own real estate portfolio. *Please consult with your tax advisor about the requirements to be a real estate professional.*

⇨ *If you qualify as a Real Estate Professional, you can take an unlimited number of real estate paper losses against your other income, no matter how much you make or how much the real estate loss is.*

Real Estate Tax Abatement

Many municipalities offer real estate tax abatement and/or tax exemption benefits to developers whose sites create affordable units or were vacant, underutilized, or had a nonconforming zoning use. Under the program, owners are exempt from paying the increase in property taxes that result from the new construction. Exemptions and abatement programs range from three- to 30-year periods.

Example:

Assume the following.

- *A tax rate of 2.62% of the taxable assessment.*
- *A developer purchases a parcel of land for $2 million, and the taxes at the time of purchase are $52,400 ($2 million x 2.62%).*
- *A new building is constructed, and the post-construction assessment increases to $15 million because of the improvements and the resulting increase in value. Additionally, assume the taxes due on the building portions assessment is $340,600 ($13 million x 2.62%).*
- *The post-construction assessment of $15 million will have two parts: the land portion of $2M, and the improved building portion of $13M. The developer receives a 10-year tax exemption which freezes the pre-construction assessment and phases in the post-construction assessment on the improvements at the rate of 20% every two years throughout the 10-year exemption period.*
- *As part of the tax exemption, the developer will be required to pay the taxes on the $2 million cost of the land, or $52,400, throughout the 10-year exemption period. Additionally, these taxes are subject to any annual tax rate increases in the future.*
- *Each year, the increased assessment of $13 million will be phased in at the rate of 20% every two years, until the assessment reaches 100% after year 10.*

The real estate tax abatement in our example will save the developer or subsequent property owner $1,236,296 over the 10-year term of the exemption.

A Road Map to Understanding These Awesome Tax Benefits

The following is a road map to help you understand what a windfall these tax benefits can be for property owners. Below we will illustrate, step by step, each of the tax benefits so you can see firsthand the economic windfall they present for property owners.

The following tax benefits, for the most part, weren't available during the high cap rate years. As these new tax laws became available, they became factors as cap rates started to decrease.

The Awesome Power of Combining the Tax Benefits of...

- Cost Segregation
- Bonus Depreciation
- Safe Harbor Election (De Minimis Election)
- The Real Estate Professional Loophole

Road Map Assumptions:
Purchase of a Residential Garden Apartment Complex
Purchase Price: $5,000,000
Cost Basis for Depreciation (80%): $4,000,000

Prior to the Above Tax Benefits:

Example:

Assume the above-mentioned garden apartment complex was purchased on January 1, 1995, for $5,000,000. Further assume that the land has an assessment of $1,000,000 or 20% of the purchase price. Only the building can be depreciated since land is not a depreciable asset. Therefore, the building's cost basis for depreciation is $4,000,000 ($5,000,000 - $1,000,000).

In 1995, residential buildings could be depreciated over a period of 27.50 years. As a result, the property owner received a depreciation deduction of $145,455 ($4,000,000/27.50 years) each year until the building was fully depreciated in 27.50 years. Assuming a 30% federal tax bracket, this would translate to an annual tax savings of $43,637 ($145,455 x 30%). Although there were some accelerated methods available, this scenario is a typical example of what tax benefits were

Now Let's Start Adding the Above Tax Benefits to the Equation

Cost Segregation Study:

First, we'll start by performing a cost segregation study, which was first approved in 1997 as a viable tax-saving strategy allowed by the IRS. Using the same road map assumptions, except instead of 1995, move it to 2017, and the owner performs a cost segregation study for the new property.

Appendix 2 shows that the annual depreciation deduction has increased by *$110,493.* a 76% increase in the deduction. The depreciation deduction has been accelerated due to the shorter useful lives of portions of the building from 27.50 years to five, seven, and 15 years.*

Before cost segregation, the property owner's depreciation deduction would be a consistent $145,455 per annum or $727,275 over a five-year period (Appendix 1). Using cost segregation increases, the total deduction to $255,948 per annum, *$1,279,740* over a five-year period. If we assume a 30% federal tax rate, this translates to a tax savings over the five-year period of *$383,922* ($255,948 x 5 years x 30%).

These added deductions represent a timing difference. You are simply trading accelerated deductions in exchange for a reduction or expiration of

---

*See Appendix 2 for the benefits of a Cost Segregation Study.

these deductions in the near future. But remember, *a tax deduction today is worth more than a tax deduction tomorrow.*

A Fully Depreciated Building Component:

Now let's discuss the building component re-categorized as 5-year property by the cost segregation study. At the end of five years, the property owner would have received total depreciation deductions over the five-year period of $600,000 ($120,000 x 5 years). Since the allocated depreciable cost basis determined by the cost segregation study was $600,000, and total depreciation deductions were also $600,000, the component became *fully depreciated* and no further depreciation deductions would be allowed in future years for this component of the building. The same would hold true for the seven-, 15-, and 27.50-year components as their useful life ends.

Bonus Depreciation: Injecting Depreciation with Steroids:

In later years, the IRS introduced a new accelerated deduction known as bonus depreciation. Bonus depreciation allows property owners to deduct a large percentage of the cost of five-, seven-, and 15-year building components in *the first year* a building component is placed into service. rather than depreciating them over various periods of years. The building whose useful life is 27.50 years is not eligible for bonus depreciation. This extremely valuable benefit was not available during the high cap rate years.*

Depreciation Deductions Using the Bonus Depreciation Method:

In 2016, bonus depreciation was equal to 50% of the cost basis of the asset, (increased in 2019 to 100%). There is a requirement that the depreciable basis must be reduced by the amount of the bonus depreciation taken, and the balance can be depreciated over the remaining useful life of the asset. The effect of bonus depreciation is to cause an accelerated depreciation deduction of 50% of the cost basis of the asset in the first year it is placed into service. If the property is held long-term, the depreciation deduction

---

*See Appendix 2 for the benefits of Bonus Depreciation.

in later years will be significantly reduced. But *a tax deduction today is worth more than a tax deduction tomorrow.*

Appendix 2 shows, the bonus depreciation deduction alone is a whopping *$478,000* for 2016 (50% of the cost basis of the assets, excluding the 27.50-year component). After reducing the remaining cost basis by 50%, the property owner is also entitled to depreciate the balance over the remaining shorter useful lives of the assets.

This amount is $183,319. Therefore, the total depreciation deduction for 2016 is a whopping *$661,319* ($478,000 + $183,319). Under the prior IRS rules that existed during the high cap rate years, the property owner would have been limited to depreciation deductions of only $145,455. This represents an additional **first-year** depreciation deduction of *$515,864 ($661,319 - $145,455).*

The total depreciation deduction for Year 1 would be $661,319. Assuming a 30% federal tax bracket, this would translate to tax savings of *$198,396* ($661,319 x 30%). Keep in mind that bonus depreciation can also be taken on any other five-, seven-, or 15-year property you purchase, such as HVAC units, plank floors, appliances, etc.

Comment: The above example assumed a bonus depreciation rate of 50% of the cost of the asset. In 2019 the bonus rate was increased to 100% of the asset cost. In 2019, the bonus depreciation would have been double or $956,000 instead of $478,000. As a result, the taxpayer would receive whopping bonus depreciation deduction for the full cost of the asset in year one and the asset would be then be fully depreciated and no further depreciation deductions would be available in future years.

Trump's Tax Cuts and Jobs Act of 2017 doubled the bonus depreciation deduction from 50% to 100%, effective for assets purchased in 2018. The new law also made bonus depreciation benefits eligible for older assets for the first time. What a loophole for the real estate industry. But we're not finished yet!

New IRS Rules for Capitalization and Depreciation:
After considering the tax benefits of cost segregation and bonus depreciation, one might say that enough is enough. How much better can it get for the real estate industry? **Well, it gets better. Much better!**

Safe Harbor Election (De Minimis Election):
Let's add another recent tax benefit to our example, one that wasn't available during the high cap rate years. As discussed above, under the new rules a taxpayer could make a Safe Harbor election, known as the de minimis election that allowed for immediate expensing of certain property that would otherwise have to be capitalized. This election allows for a deduction as an *operating expense*, rather than as a depreciation expense. For 2016, The Safe Harbor election allowed a taxpayer to deduct an expense whose invoice is less than $2,500.*

Let's add another recent tax benefit to our example, one that wasn't available during the high cap rate years. As discussed above, under the new rules a taxpayer could make a Safe Harbor election, known as the de minimis election that allowed for immediate expensing of certain property that would otherwise have to be capitalized. This election allows for a deduction as an *operating expense*, rather than as a depreciation expense. For 2016, The Safe Harbor election allowed a taxpayer to deduct an expense whose invoice is less than $2,500.*

The Real Estate Professional Tax Loophole:
Another tremendous tax benefit that didn't exist during the high cap rate years is the Real Estate Professional designation. If you qualify as a Real Estate Professional, you can take an unlimited number of real estate losses against your other income, no matter how much you make or how much the real estate loss is. Taxpayers who don't have this status are significantly limited in deducting losses from real estate activities, but for Real Estate Professionals, this is one powerful tax benefit.**

---

*See Appendix 3 for benefits of the Safe Harbor Election (De Minimis Election).
**See Appendix 4 for benefits of Real Estate Professional.

The bottom line is that because of the *combination* of these tax benefits, each partner (as described in Appendix 4) could offset their other income by a whopping $215,410, either reducing or completely wiping out the taxes that would otherwise be due.

Additionally if the result of these deductions resulted in a personal taxable loss the taxpayer could carry the loss back and possibly receive a refund or carry the loss forward for use in future years.

These tax deductions are akin to a legalized tax shelter, or maybe even better! What a present from the government!

Please keep in mind that the illustrations and examples presented above only considered ownership of **one single property**. Many property owners have five, 10, 15, or more properties. Can you imagine the aggregate amount of tax benefits they have been given? In theory, if a property owner takes full advantage of the new tax laws, they could avoid paying taxes for the next five to 20 years or forever. This does not even include the many other tax benefits not discussed in this chapter.

Let me remind you again to consult with your tax advisor for the requirements to be a Real Estate Professional.

Street Success Concepts to Remember

1. When the fundamentals of real estate investing are compromised or no longer apply, then purchasing real estate becomes more akin to gambling than investing.

2. Understanding why cap rates change will help you identify the warning signs early so that preventive action can be taken.

3. The higher the cap rate, the lower the purchase price. The lower the cap rate, the higher the purchase price.

4. During high cap rate years, there is generally too little money chasing too many deals, as opposed to too much money chasing too few deals during low cap rate years.

5. In a high cap rate environment, sellers are willing to be flexible when negotiating to sell their property. Negotiating leverage is greatly in favor of the purchaser.

6. A key difference between high and low cap environments is the difference in seller's attitudes from willing to unwilling. In low cap rate environments characterized by tremendous demand for property, sellers are less willing to be flexible when negotiating to sell their property. Clearly, negotiating leverage is greatly in favor of the seller.

7. In real estate, you make money on the buy which means by buying right. The purchase price is a permanent cost; it cannot be changed. However, interest rates are a temporary cost which can be changed to more favorable terms over time.

8. In a low cap rate environment, there are massive amounts of capital and financing available for real estate investment. In a high cap rate environment, there is generally little capital or financing available for real estate investment.

9. Foreign investment targeted at the U.S. is directly affected by the strength of the U.S. dollar, the current administration's foreign policies, and the volatility of foreign governments.

10. A vital sign to monitor is the increase or decrease in foreign capital available for real estate investment. If this source of capital dries up or even softens, the results for the real estate industry could be disastrous.

11. The odds of interest rates increasing are much greater than the odds of them remaining constant or decreasing.

12. As a result of the 2008 financial crisis, President Obama passed into law the Dodd-Frank Wall Street Reform and Consumer Protection Act. As a result, banks and financial institutions are now under constant scrutiny by outside regulators and compliance officers with many more hoops to be jumped through before loans are approved.

13. A scary reality to keep in mind is that these days the strength of the U.S. dollar is not backed by gold or silver but only by our way of life. Another reality is that only 10% of the money supply is in currency. The rest is electronic debits and credits.

14. In New York City, the monetization of air rights caused a change in valuation from a cap rate basis to a buildable SF basis. This factor, coupled with a boom in condominium construction, propelled property values into the stratosphere.

15. Sellers who don't list their property for sale on the open market to save the broker commission are fools. Furthermore, purchasers who use a broker to acquire property without being aware of their tricks are also fools.

16. Brokers generally enter into an exclusive sales agreement with the seller. The broker's first choice is to sell the property themselves and earn a full commission. However, many deals are made with the assistance of an outside or co-broker who will share in the overall commission.

17. Assume a broker has two acceptable offers: one that earns them a full commission and one they need to split with another broker. Be aware that the broker is more likely to try and sway the seller to take the offer that yields a full commission.

18. Never tell a broker that you plan on keeping the property long-term. Always tell the broker that your holding period is only one to three

years. In a broker's mind, a long-term purchaser is a one-shot deal for a commission. A short-term purchaser may give the broker another bite at the apple.

19. If you can learn and understand the fundamentals about the tax benefits for real estate, you can learn to plan and defer and/or save yourself tremendous amounts of money. Tax savings, as opposed to tax deferrals, can be viewed as an additional return on your investment.

20. The theory behind tax planning can be summed up by the concept that *a tax deduction today is worth more than a tax deduction tomorrow*, or a dollar today is worth more than a dollar later.

21. A 1031 Exchange allows a taxpayer who sells a property to postpone (defer) the capital gain from the sale by purchasing another qualified property within a certain time frame. Generally, both federal and state tax gains (depending on the state) can be postponed until the new property is sold or can potentially be postponed forever as long as the IRS rules are followed. This is a smart tax and investment strategy as well as an estate planning tool.

22. Bonus depreciation is another tax benefit available for property owners. Bonus depreciation currently allows a deduction in the first year for 100% of an eligible asset's cost in the year acquired, rather than having to deduct depreciation over longer periods of time. It also applies to used property under certain conditions.

23. A taxpayer can make a Safe Harbor Election, known as the de minimis election, on their tax return. The election allows taxpayers to immediately expense certain property whose invoice is under $2,500 rather than having to capitalize and depreciate the cost over a longer period of time.

24. If you qualify as a Real Estate Professional, then you can take an unlimited amount of real estate paper losses against your other income, no matter how much you make or how much the real estate loss is.

A NOTE FROM SAM LIEBMAN

I HOPE YOU enjoyed this book and it significantly increased your knowledge of real estate. That was my goal! I tried to provide you with a little bit of everything but with a focus on the real-life concepts and fundamentals you need to build upon to achieve lasting wealth.

This book was intended to get you started on your path, not for you to be able to go out and start purchasing property immediately. Your real estate education is still a work in progress and must be built upon before you are ready to start purchasing property.

Just as a building with a weak foundation will ultimately crumble, so will your chances for success if you mistakenly look for shortcuts and focus more on getting out there and purchasing property. Instead, focus on mastering the basic core fundamentals.

One of the most important concepts I want to leave you with is that by mastering the fundamentals, you will drastically reduce, manage, or eliminate *fear,* which is the number one stumbling block to success.

Thinking outside of the box, finding out what goes on in the real world, and using street knowledge is what the pros do. Be a sponge and learn from as many sources as you can. Remember, you need to combine street knowledge with a traditional education to become successful.

GOOD LUCK!

APPENDIXES

Chapter 2

Appendix 1: Example of the Actual Monthly Rent Roll for Ambassador as of January 1, 2018

Unit No.	Type	Sq. Ft.	Resident Name	Move In Date	Lease Start Date	Lease End Date	Monthly Base Rent
1	3 B/R, 1 BTH	970		2/21/08	9/1/17	8/31/18	$899
2	2 B/R, 1 BTH	836		2/1/15	6/1/17	5/31/18	$810
3	2 B/R, 1 BTH	836		11/22/17	11/25/17	11/30/18	$829
4	3 B/R, 1 BTH	970		3/1/18	3/1/18	2/28/19	$929
5	2 B/R, 1 BTH	836		5/1/06	3/1/18	2/28/19	$829
6	2 B/R, 1 BTH	836		9/1/12	4/1/18	3/31/19	$829
7	2 B/R, 1 BTH	836		5/1/12	7/1/17	6/30/18	$799
8	2 B/R, 1 BTH	836		11/2/16	11/1/17	10/31/18	$829
9	2 B/R, 1 BTH	836		6/1/11	6/1/17	5/31/18	$804
10	2 B/R, 1 BTH	932		2/1/18	2/1/18	1/31/19	$880
11	2 B/R, 1 BTH	836		6/10/16	6/1/17	5/31/18	$739
12	2 B/R, 1 BTH	932		10/6/17	10/6/17	10/31/18	$800
13	1 B/R, 1 BTH	509		5/31/17	6/1/17	5/31/18	$639
14	1 B/R, 1 BTH	435		1/28/17	1/1/18	12/31/18	$649

Unit No.	Type	Sq. Ft.	Resident Name	Move In Date	Lease Start Date	Lease End Date	Monthly Base Rent
15	1 B/R, 1 BTH	509		1/2/17	1/1/18	12/31/18	$669
16	1 B/R, 1 BTH	435		7/12/17	10/1/17	9/30/17	$649
17	2 B/R, 2 BTH	660		11/1/17	11/1/17	10/31/18	$729
18	1 B/R, 1 BTH	435		7/1/11	8/1/17	7/31/18	$639
19	1 B/R, 1 BTH	435		5/5/17	5/5/17	4/30/18	$639
20	1 B/R, 1 BTH	435		1/4/18	1/4/18	1/3/19	$669
21	1 B/R, 1 BTH	435		6/1/16	6/1/17	5/31/18	$609
22	1 B/R, 1 BTH	509		3/20/17	33/1/18	5/31/18	$639
23	1 B/R, 1 BTH	435		11/2/17	11/1/17	10/31/18	$669
24	1 B/R, 1 BTH	509		2/1/18	2/1/18	1/31/19	$669
25	1 B/R, 1 BTH	450	Vacant - F.M.V.	N/A	N/A	N/A	$669
26	1 B/R, 1 BTH	450		1/6/16	1/6/16	12/31/16	$670
27	1 B/R, 1 BTH	450		3/1/18	3/1/18	2/28/19	$669
28	1 B/R, 1 BTH	450		10/13/17	10/13/17	9/30/18	$669
29	1 B/R, 1 BTH	450		10/26/15	12/1/17	5/31/18	$585
30	1 B/R, 1 BTH	450		1/30/17	2/1/18	1/31/19	$669
31	1 B/R, 1 BTH	450		5/1/15	4/1/18	3/31/19	$669
32	1 B/R, 1 BTH	465		2/28/18	3/1/18	2/28/19	$669
33	1 B/R, 1 BTH	409		1/26/18	1/26/18	1/31/19	$669
34	1 B/R, 1 BTH	465	Vacant - F.M.V.	N/A	N/A	N/A	$669
35	1 B/R, 1 BTH	409	Vacant - F.M.V.	N/A	N/A	N/A	$669
	Total SF	21,131				Total Base Rent	$25,120
			Total Annual				$301,440

Appendix 2: Example of Increase in NOI in 5 years

	Beginning of Yr. 1	End of Yr. 1	End of Yr. 2	End of Yr. 3	End of Yr. 4	End of Yr. 5
Base Rent Increases @ 3% Per Annum	$301,440	$310,483	$319,798	$329,392	$339,273	$349,452
Cumulative Increase in Base Rent						$48,012
Less: Operating Expenses @3%	$150,000	$154,500	$159,135	$163,909	$168,826	$173,891
Cumulative Increase in Operating Expenses						$23,891
Net Increase in NOI						$24,121

Appendix 3: Example of the economic effects of how capitalization causes a compounding effect on the annual base rent increases each year during the five-year period

* Assume Base Annual Rent at Beginning of Year 1 was $301,440

	Beginning of Yr. 1	End of Yr. 1	End of Yr. 2	End of Yr. 3	End of Yr. 4	End of Yr. 5
Base Annual Rent	$301,440	$310,483	$319,798	$329,392	$339,273	$349,452

	Beginning of Yr. 1	End of Yr. 1	End of Yr. 2	End of Yr. 3	End of Yr. 4	End of Yr. 5
End of Year 1						
APPLY A 3% ANNUAL INCREASE	$9,043	**Becomes Capitalized**				
TO BASE RENT OF $301,440						
New Base Rent - Jan 1 - Year 1	**$310,483**					
Beginning of Year 2						
APPLY A 3% ANNUAL INCREASE		$9,315	**Becomes Capitalized**			
TO BASE RENT OF $310,483						
New Base Rent - Jan 1 - Year 2		**$319,798**				
Beginning of Year 3						
APPLY A 3% ANNUAL INCREASE			$9,593	**Becomes Capitalized**		
TO BASE RENT OF $319,798						
New Base Rent - Jan 1 - Year 3			**$329,392**			

	Beginning of Yr. 1	End of Yr. 1	End of Yr. 2	End of Yr. 3	End of Yr. 4	End of Yr. 5
Beginning of Year 4						
APPLY A 3% ANNUAL INCREASE				$9,882	Becomes Capitalized	
TO BASE RENT OF $329,392						
New Base Rent - Jan 1 - Year 4				**$339,272**		
Beginning of Year 5						
APPLY A 3% ANNUAL INCREASE					$10,179	**Becomes Capitalized**
TO BASE RENT OF $339,272						
New Base Rent - Jan 1 - Year 5					**$349,452**	
Annual Increase in Base Rent	$9,043	$9,315	$9,593	$9,882	$10,179	
Cumulative Increase in Base Rent	**$9,043**	**$18,358**	**$27,951**	**$37,833**	**$48,012**	

Appendix 4: Example of property value increases or decreases as cap rates increase or decrease, assuming NOI of $150,000.

PROPERTY VALUE = $150,000/**8%** =$1,875,000

PROPERTY VALUE = $150,000/**7%** =$2,142,857

PROPERTY VALUE = $150,000/**6%** =$2,500,000

Appendix 5: Cumulative Increase in Property Value in 5 Years

	Beginning of Yr. 1	End of Yr. 1	End of Yr. 2	End of Yr. 3	End of Yr. 4	End of Yr. 5
Gross Base Rent @ 3% Annual Increases	$301,440	$310,483	$319,798	$329,392	$339,273	$349,452
Less: Total Operating Expenses @ 3% Increases	$150,000	$154,500	$159,135	$163,909	$168,826	$173,891
Total Operating Expenses	**$150,000**	**$154,500**	**$159,135**	**$163,909**	**$168,826**	**$173,891**
Net Operating Income (NOI)	**$151,440**	**$155,983**	**$160,663**	**$165,483**	**$170,447**	**$175,560**
Property Value @ a 6% Cap	**$2,524,000**	**$2,599,720**	**$2,677,712**	**$2,758,043**	**$2,840,784**	**$2,926,008**

	Beginning of Yr. 1	End of Yr. 1	End of Yr. 2	End of Yr. 3	End of Yr. 4	End of Yr. 5
Cumulative Increase in Property Value	$0	$75,720	$153,712	$234,043	$316,784	$402,008

Appendix 6: Example demonstrates the cumulative effects on Base rent of upgrading 18 units

	Beginning of Yr. 1	End of Yr. 1	End of Yr. 2	End of Yr. 3	End of Yr. 4	End of Yr. 5
After Upgrading 18 Units						
BASE RENT BEGINNING OF PERIOD	$301,440	$323,040	$332,731	$342,713	$352,995	$363,584
ADD: $100 PER MONTH, PER UNIT OR $100 X 18 UNITS X 12 MONTHS	$21,600	Becomes Capitalized				
New Base Rent - Jan 1 - Year 1	$323,040					
YEAR 2 - APPLY 3% RENT INCREASE		$9,691	Becomes Capitalized			

	Beginning of Yr. 1	End of Yr. 1	End of Yr. 2	End of Yr. 3	End of Yr. 4	End of Yr. 5
TO BASE RENT AT THE END OF YEAR 1						
($323,040 X .3%)						
New Base Rent - Jan 1 - Year 2		**$332,731**				
YEAR 3 - APPLY 3% RENT INCREASE			$9,982	**Becomes Capitalized**		
TO BASE RENT AT THE END OF YEAR 2						
($332,731 X .3%)						
New Base Rent - Jan 1 - Year 3			**$342,713**			
YEAR 4 - APPLY 3% RENT INCREASE				$10,282	**Becomes Capitalized**	
TO BASE RENT AT THE END OF YEAR 3						

	Beginning of Yr. 1	End of Yr. 1	End of Yr. 2	End of Yr. 3	End of Yr. 4	End of Yr. 5
($342,713 X .3%)						
New Base Rent - Jan 1 - Year 4				**$352,995**		
YEAR 5 - APPLY 3% RENT INCREASE					$10,589	**Becomes Capitalized**
TO BASE RENT AT THE END OF YEAR 4						
($352,995 X .3%)						
New Base Rent - Jan 1 - Year 5					**$363,584**	
Annual Increase in Base Rent	$21,600	$9,691	$9,982	$10,282	$10,589	
Cumulative Increase in Base Rent	$21,600	$31,291	$41,273	$51,555	**$62,144**	

Appendix 7: Example demonstrates the effects on property value of upgrading 18 units

	Beginning of Yr. 1	End of Yr. 1	End of Yr. 2	End of Yr. 3	End of Yr. 4	End of Yr. 5
Base Rent - with Upgrades & 3% Annual Increases	$301,440	$323,040	$332,731	$342,713	$352,995	$363,584
Operating Expenses - @ 3%	$150,000	$154,500	$159,135	$163,909	$168,826	$173,891
Net Operating Income (NOI)	$151,440	$168,540	$173,596	$178,804	$184,168	$189,693
Cumulative Net Operating Income (NOI)	$0	$17,100	$22,156	$27,364	$32,728	$38,253
Property Value @ a 6% Cap	$2,524,000	$2,809,000	$2,893,270	$2,980,068	$3,069,470	$3,161,554
Cumulative Increase in Property Value	$0	$285,000	$369,270	$456,068	$545,470	$637,554

Appendix 8: Statement of Net Cash Flow-Ambassador Apartments

Income	End of Year 1
Gross Potential Income	$301,440
Plus: Electric Reimbursements	$40,000
Subtotal	$341,440
Less: Vacancy & Collection Loss @ 5%	($17,072)
Less: Concessions	($2,000)
Total Rental Income	$322,368
Other Income	
Laundry Income	$2,500
Application Fees	$1,500
Late Fees	$3,000
Miscellaneous Income	$1,350
Total Other Income	$8,350
Effective Gross Income	$330,718
Operating Expenses	
Payroll & Fringes	$30,000
Repair & Maintenance	$9,000
Turnover Expense	$7,000
Contract Services	$8,000
Administrative	$4,500
Advertising & Marketing	$750
Utilities	$55,000
Real Estate Taxes	$24,000

Income	End of Year 1
Insurance	$7,500
Management Fees	$9,922
Total Operating Expenses	$155,672
Net Operating Income (NOI)	$175,046
Less: Capital Reserves	$10,600
Net Cash Flow Before Debt Service	$164,446
Less: Debt Service	$43,457
Net Cash Flow	$120,989

Chapter 3

Appendix 1: Comprehensive Pro-forma OM
for a *fictional* garden apartment community

Offering Summary	Proforma
Sales Price	$3,800,000
Apartment Community Name	Dallas Arms
Street Address	2609 N. Fitzhugh
City, State, Zip	Richardson, Texas 75211
Price Per Unit	$63,333
Offered Free and Clear	Yes

Site Description	
Lot Size	2.29 Acres
Building Size	62,500
Parking Surface	Asphalt
Parking Spaces	86
Parking Spaces - Handicapped	2
Parking Ratio	1.28 Spaces Per Unit
Covered Parking	No
Landscaping	Mature Trees & Xeriscaping

Building Information	
Building Type	Garden Apartments
Building Class	Class C
Area Class	Class A
Number of Buildings	5
Number of Floors	2
Number of Units	60
Average Unit Size	951 SF
Average Current Rent Per Unit	$937

Offering Summary	Proforma
Year Built	1962
Current Leasing Percentage	98%
Current Physical Occupancy	95%
Current Area Occupancy	95%
Net Rentable Square Feet	57,066
Cap Rate	6.25%
NOI	$240,080
Renovated	Yes
Last Date Renovated	2012 - 2015
Average Rent Per Square Foot	$0.95

Construction

Style	Garden
Foundation	Concrete Slab
Framing	Wood, Concrete
Exterior	Stucco, Brick Veneer, Hardieboard Siding
Roof	Pitched, Shingles

Mechanical

HVAC	Individual Units
Electrical	Individually Metered
Hot Water	One Gas Boiler
Fire-Protection	Battery Operated Smoke Alarms
Electrical Wiring	Aluminum

Utilities

Electricity	Paid By Tenant
Water & Sewer	Paid By Landlord
Gas	Paid By Landlord

Offering Summary	Proforma
Telephone	Paid By Tenant
Cable	Paid By Tenant
Internet	Paid By Tenant
All Bills Paid/RUBS	Mixed

Amenities

Laundry Room	Yes
Washer & Dry in Units	No
Leasing/Management Office	Yes
Controlled Access Gated Community	No
Pool	No
Other	No

Tax Information

Current Assessed Value	$1,310,370
Current Tax Rate	2.710%
Current Taxes/Tax Year	$35,511

Zoning

Lot Size	2.29 Acres
Density	27.39 Units Per Acre
Zoning	MF-2(A)
Height Restriction	30 SF

Schools

	Name
District	Fort Worth ISD
Elementary School	John T. White Elem School
Middle School	Meadowbrook Middle School
High School	Eastern Hills High School
Transportation	Bus service, 1 block Away From the Property

Appendix 2: Rent Comparable Schedule

Floorplan	Units	SF	Avg. SF Subtotal	Percent of Units	Current Monthly Rent	Current Rent Per SF	Current Total Monthly Income	Proforma Monthly Rent	Proforma Rent Per SF	Proforma Total Monthly Income
1 BED/1 BATH	24	684	16,416	29%	$750	$1.10	$18,000	$825	$1.21	$19,800
2 BED/ 1.5 BATH	11	1,000	11,000	19%	$840	$0.84	$9,240	$915	$0.92	$10,065
2 BED/ 1.5 BATH	8	1,100	8,800	15%	$885	$0.80	$7,080	$960	$0.87	$7,680
2 BED/ 2 BATH	10	1,175	11,750	21%	$885	$0.75	$8,850	$960	$0.82	$9,600
3 BED/ 2 BATH	7	1,300	9,100	16%	$950	$0.73	$6,650	$1,025	$0.79	$7,175
Total/Average	**60**	**951**	**57,066**	**100%**	**$937**	**$0.87**	**$49,820**	**$937**	**$0.95**	**$54,320**

Chapter 4

Appendix 1- Example of a comprehensive LOI

Rolling Cash Realty, Inc.
1430 Broadway - 14th Floor
New York, NY 10018
Tel: xxx-xxx-xxx
Email: xxxxxxxxxx

[date]

By: Email - xxxxxxxxxxx
[Recipient's Address] Broker or Seller

Re: *[Name and Address of Property]*
Dear _____:

This Letter of Intent (the "**Letter of Intent**") will outline the terms and conditions under which **Rolling Cash Realty, Inc. 1430 Broadway - 14th Floor New York, NY 10018** (the "**Purchaser**") is interested in negotiating for a definitive written agreement (the "**Contract**") to purchase from **XXXXXXXXXXXX LLC** (the "**Seller**") the fee simple title to the land and the improvements thereon and the appurtenances thereto, and all personal property owned by Seller and used or useful in connection with the operation and maintenance of the improvements, referred to as **XXXX XXXX Ave. Dallas, TX 75214 a.k.a, XXXXXXX Apartments** (the "**Property**"). Based upon information previously made available to Purchaser and our preliminary evaluations, and subject to the satisfaction of conditions precedent set forth herein, the Purchaser is prepared to negotiate for a definitive transaction with respect to the Property and to proceed to consider this transaction on the following terms.

I. **Purchase Price**. The purchase price for the Property shall be $12,000,000 (the "Purchase Price"). Purchaser shall acquire the Property free and clear of any mortgage or other indebtedness or liens. The Purchase Price, plus or minus proration, shall be paid by wire transfer on the Closing Date (as hereinafter defined).

II. Closing Date. The date which is thirty (30) days after the expiration of the Due Diligence Period (or such earlier date as both parties may mutually agree) (the "Closing Date"), provided that if such date is not a business day in Dallas, Texas, the Closing shall be held on the next business day thereafter. Buyer may extend the Closing Date for one (1) additional period of thirty (30) days, by written notice to Seller on or before the originally scheduled Closing Date and the deposit of Additional Earnest Money of $50,000 with the Escrow Agent

III. Real Estate Commission. Seller shall be responsible for all commissions that may be payable to brokers and shall indemnify, defend and hold harmless Purchaser therefrom.

IV. Earnest Deposit. $150,000 shall be deposited in a segregated interest-bearing escrow account (together with earnings thereon, the "Earnest Deposit") with **XXXXXX** Title Company, or any other title company as determined by Purchaser, ("Title Company"), within 3 business days after acceptance of the Contract. The Earnest Deposit shall be held by the Title Company and applied toward the Purchase Price at closing, or remitted to either Seller or Purchaser prior to closing, as specified in the Contract. The Earnest Deposit shall be fully refundable prior to the expiration of the Due Diligence Period (as hereinafter defined). After the Due Diligence Period, any refund of the Earnest Deposit shall be determined pursuant to the Contract.

V. Closing Costs. Seller shall be responsible for all basic title charges of Purchaser's owner's policy of title insurance, updating of existing survey expenses, transfer fees, documentary stamp taxes, recording fees, transfer taxes, escrow fees, costs incurred to repay any liens and all other expenses due or incurred in connection with the transaction. Purchaser and Seller shall each pay the fees and expenses of their respective legal counsel incurred in connection with the transaction. Any interest, taxes, rents, service contracts, operating expenses, etc. will be prorated as of the date of the closing as is customary for commercial real estate transactions in Austin, TX

VI. Inspection of the Property. After the acceptance of this Letter of Intent and through the Closing Date, the Purchaser and its agents and consultants shall have access to the Property and the books and records relating to the ownership and operation of the Property and shall be permitted to make, at Purchaser's sole cost, such inspections, studies, reports, tests, copies and verifications as they shall deem necessary or appropriate to determine, in Purchaser's sole and absolute discretion, whether the Property is satisfactory. The Purchaser agrees to indemnify and hold Seller harmless from and against any claims or damages arising by reason of such inspections, provided that such indemnity and hold harmless obligations shall not extend to (a) the mere discovery of any condition at the Property (e.g., existing environmental conditions), or (b) any claim or damage arising from any act or omission of Seller.

VII. Due Diligence. The Purchaser shall undertake a due diligence review with respect to the Property. To facilitate such review, Seller shall, within ten (10) business days from the date hereof, provide to Purchaser the information listed on Exhibit A hereto. As a condition precedent to closing the Contract, Purchaser shall have approved, among other things:

a. The condition of title to the Property.

b. The form of title insurance policy and the company issuing the same; the policy shall contain, to the extent available, such endorsements and affirmative coverage's as may be required by Purchaser or its lender. The Title Company shall also deliver to Purchaser or its counsel copies of all recorded documents affecting or relating to the title to the Property.

c. The survey of the Property, which shall be a current TLTA survey or ALTA survey.

d. Leases, service contracts, warranties, licenses, permits and all other agreements relating to the Property.

e. "As-built" plans and specifications for the Property.

f. The condition of the improvements and the machinery, equipment and other personal property owned by Seller and used in connection with the ownership and maintenance of the Property.

The Purchaser shall notify Seller in writing of its approval or disapproval of the results of its due diligence review of the Property within *forty five (45)* days after execution of the Contract (said *45-day* period is called the "Due Diligence Period") provided that if such date is not a business day in Dallas, Texas, the Due Diligence Period shall be on the next business day thereafter. The obligation of the Purchaser to complete its due diligence review within the Due Diligence Period shall be contingent on the Purchaser's timely receipt of all required information. The Due Diligence Period shall be extended for an additional thirty (30) days to the extent a material issue has been identified by Purchaser during the initial *[forty five (45)]* day period. If Purchaser does not elect in writing to move forward with the transaction on or prior to the last day of the Due Diligence Period, then Purchaser shall be deemed to have elected to terminate the Contract and receive a refund of the Earnest Deposit.

VIII. Financing Condition. The obligation of Purchaser to close the acquisition of the Property is conditioned upon Purchaser receiving third party financing for no less than 75% of the Purchase Price on terms and conditions satisfactory to Purchaser. In the event Purchaser fails to receive third party financing satisfactory to Purchaser at or prior to the closing (hereinafter defined), Purchaser may, in Purchaser's sole discretion, terminate the Contract by written notice to Seller delivered at or prior to the Closing.

IX. The Contract. In addition to the items set forth above, the Contract shall provide, among other things, the following conditions precedent to the Purchaser's and Seller's obligation to consummate the transaction:

a. There shall be no material adverse change in any of the items approved by the Purchaser during the Due Diligence Period.

b. Seller shall deliver to Purchaser a current estoppel letter, satisfactory to Purchaser, from all tenants. Each tenant listed on the rent roll will be in occupancy of the Property and in full compliance with the terms and conditions of its lease.

c. On the Closing Date, unless otherwise required by Purchaser, all management and leasing agreements with respect to the Property shall be terminated and Seller shall be solely responsible for any termination fees, if any, due to the manager, all leasing commissions owing, and any accounts payable.

d. After the execution of the Contract, Seller or its agents shall not amend or modify any lease or other material contract and shall not enter into any new lease, material contract or obligate the Property for any capital commitment, without the Purchaser's prior written approval, which approval shall not be unreasonably withheld if Purchaser receives the written request therefore during the Due Diligence Period, and which approval otherwise may be withheld in Purchaser's sole discretion. Further, after the expiration of the Due Diligence Period, Seller shall not modify or enter into any service contracts or maintenance agreements or other licenses without the prior written consent of Purchaser (which consent may be withheld in Purchaser's sole discretion).

e. Withdrawal of Property from Market. During the term of this Letter of Intent and thereafter while the Contract remains in effect,

Seller agrees not to market or show the Property for sale or enter into any agreement with respect to the sale of the Property.

f. Assignment. Purchaser shall have the right on or before the Closing Date to assign its rights and obligations hereunder and under the Contract to an affiliate of Purchaser.

g. Non-Binding Agreement: Term. This Letter of Intent is only intended to set forth general understandings and agreements of the parties and to provide the basis for negotiating the Contract. This Letter of Intent is not a binding commitment or agreement between the parties to purchase or sell the Property until the Contract, which must be in form and content satisfactory to each party and its counsel, has been executed by the parties. This Letter of Intent does not obligate either party to proceed to the completion of an agreement. Further, this Letter of Intent does not obligate the parties hereto to negotiate, in good faith or otherwise, toward the execution and delivery of the Contract. If the parties fail to enter into the Contract on or before twenty (20) business days from acceptance of this Letter of Intent, this Letter of Intent shall be of no further force or effect.

XIII. Confidentiality. Buyer and Seller shall at all times keep this LOI and the negotiations and subsequent agreements relating to the Property confidential, except (i) to the extent necessary to comply with applicable laws and regulations, and (ii) for consultation with either party's legal counsel or accountants. Any such disclosure to third parties shall indicate that the information is confidential and should be so treated by the third party. No press release or other public disclosure may be made by either party or any of its agents concerning this letter or the negotiations and subsequent agreements regarding the Property without the prior written consent of the other party.

If the provisions of this Letter of Intent are acceptable to you, please indicate by causing the enclosed duplicate original copy hereof to be signed by an authorized signatory of Seller and returned to the undersigned on or before xxxxxxx, 2010.

Sincerely,

Rolling Cash Realty Inc.

By: Sam Liebman, President

Agreed this   day of August, 2010

Seller: _____

By:_____ Title: _____

Chapter 6

Appendix 1: Property Condition Report Cover Letter Examples

Example of a *cover letter* for a property condition report prepared for the benefit of the **purchaser**.

- The purpose of this report was to observe and document readily visible materials and building system defects that might significantly affect the value of the property, and determine if conditions exist which may have a significant impact on the continued operation of the facility during the evaluation period. The report is intended to provide the client with information regarding the physical condition of the property at the time of the survey and related maintenance issues over a ten-year loan term with a twelve-year projection.

- The intention of this report is to assist *XXXX (purchaser)* with the evaluation of the XXXX Apartments property in preparation for acquisition and rehabilitation. The report has no other purpose and should not be relied upon by any other person or entity. Reliance upon this report does not extend to existing property owners or entities or other individuals interested in purchasing the subject property.

===

Below are excerpts from sections of an actual property condition report prepared for the sole benefit of the *lender*.

- The exclusive purpose of this Property Condition Report (the Report) is to assist *XXX (Lender)* in its underwriting of a proposed mortgage loan on the Subject Property described in this Report. This Report has no other purpose and should not be relied upon by any other person or entity. Reliance upon this Report does not extend to property owners, or entities or individuals interested in purchasing the subject property.

- The information reported was obtained through sources deemed reliable, a visual site survey of areas readily observable, easily accessible, or made accessible by the property contact, and interviews with owners, agents, occupants, or other appropriate persons involved with the Subject Property. Municipal information was obtained through file reviews of reasonably ascertainable standard government record sources, and interviews with the authorities having jurisdiction over the property. Findings, conclusions, and recommendations included in the Report are based on visual observations in the field, the municipal information reasonably obtained, information provided by the Client, and/or a review of readily available and supplied drawings and documents.

- No disassembly of systems or building components or physical or invasive testing was performed. XXXX renders no opinion as to the property condition at un-surveyed and/or inaccessible portions of the Subject Property. XXXX relies completely on the information provided during the site survey, or provided or obtained during the writing of the draft Report, whether written, graphic or verbal, provided by the property contact, owner or agent, or municipal source, or as shown on any documents reviewed or received from the property contact, owner or agent, or municipal source, and assumes that information to be true and correct. XXXX assumes no responsibility for property information or prior reports withheld or not provided during preparation of the Report for any reason whatsoever.

- The contents of the Report are *not* intended to represent an in-depth acquisition analysis of the Subject Property, including, but not limited to, facades, roof, paving, mechanical, elevator, sprinkler, fire safety, and electrical systems or components. Anyone wanting information about the condition or characteristics of these property systems or components should consult the appropriate professional.

- Immediate Repairs as may be identified during the survey are typically limited to life, safety, health, building code violations, or building or property stabilization issues observed at the Subject Property. Routine operational, normal or customary annual maintenance or preventative maintenance items are not reported or included in this Report as they are not considered life, safety, stabilization, or code issues, but deferred maintenance repairs.

Appendix 2: Property Condition Problems and Recommendation

Below are a few examples from actual reports on the condition of a few building components obtained from various property condition reports.

Roofing

Description:
The Subject Property has pitched and gabled architectural-grade shingle roof systems that are conventionally wood framed with plywood sheathing. The roofs are flashed with metal flashing. The roof systems are estimated to be approximately 8 years old,

Observations/Comments:
The architectural grade asphalt-shingle roof systems appear to be in good condition overall. Roofs of this type typically have an average useful life of approximately 30 years, depending on the property's location, material type and quality, quality of installation, roof maintenance and exposure, amount of roof traffic, and regional climatic conditions. Based on the reported ages, current conditions, and expected useful lives, the roofs are expected to reach their life expectancy after the analysis term.

Pavement, Curbing and Flatwork

Description:
The open parking areas and travel lanes consist of asphalt pavement. According to observations made during the property visit, the subject property is improved with approximately 285 parking spaces. Extruded asphalt speed bumps are also provided within the apartment community travel lanes to control traffic flow. Cast-in-place concrete treads and painted wood risers and handrails systems provide access to the upper levels of the apartment buildings. The upper-level apartment units are accessed by elevated walkways composed of plywood pans filled with lightweight concrete and painted wood trim and handrail systems.

Observations/Comments:
The paved areas are in poor to fair condition and damaged or significantly weathered asphalt pavement was observed throughout the travel lanes and parking areas on site. Based on the conditions observed during the property survey, Immediate Repairs are recommended for the replacement of approximately 2,800 square feet of damaged asphalt pavement as well as the replacement of the damaged and weathered speed bumps within the travel lanes. In addition, the Project Consultant recommends that the significantly weathered asphalt payment is seal-coated and restriped as Immediate Repair Items. Replacement reserves are also recommended for future repairs, seal coating, and restriping during the analysis term due to normal wear, and estimated costs are included in Table 2 - Replacement and Reserve Analysis provided in Section 4.0.

The concrete walkways range from poor to good condition across the property. The following deficiencies, needs, and recommended actions were noted during the inspection of the concrete walkways on site:

- Replace the isolated areas of uneven and broken concrete observed along the walkways throughout the apartment development,
- Level the isolated trip hazards along the concrete sidewalks on site,

- Replace the cracked, un-level or damaged entry landings observed at the main entrance to the leasing office,
- Repair the trip hazard existing along the parking areas where the cast-in-place concrete curbing has pushed above the adjacent concrete walkways - these conditions were observed near apartment buildings 7 and 11,

Repair of these areas is recommended as an Immediate Repair (sections removed, repaired, replaced, or ground to smooth transition). Estimated costs for the Immediate Repairs have been included in Table 1 - Immediate Repair Items.

Additionally, management should perform minor repairs, replacements, and seal non-displaced cracks during the term as part of routine maintenance.

Chapter 7

Appendix 1: Example of the Costs associated with a transient Class C Property

Category	Estimated Cost per Unit	Average Cost per Unit	Comments
Cleaning	$65 - $85	$75	Outside Cleaning Service - Tubs, Toilets, Kitchen,
			Appliances, Blinds, etc.
Painting	$200 - $250	$225	Outside Service - Full Painting Plus Cost of Paint
			If Only Touch Up Needed - $75 - $100 Per Unit
			Tubs, Countertops, Bathroom Countertops, Kitchen, Countertops, Tile Surround - $150 ea.
Carpet Cleaning	$50 - $75	$65	Carpet Dying, Replacement, Wood Floor Repairs
Replace Blinds	$20 - $75	$50	Assume Needs to Be Done 50% of the Time
			Depends on Type of Blinds
Cabinet - Painting & Restoration	$350 - $450	$400	Assume This Needs to Be Done 50% of the Time
Subtotal		**$1,565**	
Re-Leasing Costs			
Vacancy Cost		$800	Assume only one month

Category	Estimated Cost per Unit	Average Cost per Unit	Comments
Concessions		$299	Leasing Special
Leasing Commissions		$50	Given to Onsite Leasing Agent
LEGAL/ COLLECTION	$175 - $250	$215	Assume Needs to Be Done 50% of the Time
SUNDRY		$75	Hardware, Plumbing, Cleaning Supplies, etc.
Subtotal		**$1,439**	
Estimated Total Cost		**$3,004**	

Chapter 9

Appendix 1: Benefits of the Safe Harbor Election (De Minimis Election)

Let's assume a building contains 75 units, and during 2016, we replaced the carpeting in 35 apartments with plank wood floors (**with removable strips**) at a cost of $900 per apartment, $31,500 in total. Additionally, we upgraded each apartment with new HVAC units (cost $450), appliances (cost $1,200), blinds (cost $75), and interior doors (cost $75). Total cost per apartment $2,700, *$94,500* for 35 apartments.

Under the IRS regulations, **some** flooring is not easily removable. Therefore, the IRS considers it part of the building and depreciable over a period of 27.50 years. HVAC Units, appliances, blinds, and interior doors have a useful life of five years. Under the **old** law, the taxpayer incurred $94,500 in capital improvements and received a depreciation of only $13,745 for 2016.

Under the Old Law- Available in the High Cap Rate Years

Capital Improvement	Per Apartment	Total 35 Apartments	Useful Life Under Old Law	Annual Depreciation
Plank Wood Floors	$900	$31,500	27.5 Years	$1,145
HVAC Units	$450	$15,750	5 Years	$3,150
Appliances	$1,200	$42,000	5 Years	$8,400
Blinds	$75	$2,625	5 Years	$525
Interior Doors	$75	$2,625	5 Years	$525
Total	**$2,700**	**$94,500**		**$13,745**

Under the New Law - Available in the Low Cap Rate Years

Capital Improvement	Per Apartment	Total 35 Apartments	Useful Life Under New Law	Annual Depreciation	Annual Operating Expense Deduction
Plank Wood Floors (with removable strips)	$900	$31,500	N/A	N/A	**$31,500**
HVAC Units	$450	$15,750	N/A	N/A	**$15,750**
Appliances	$1,200	$42,000	N/A	N/A	**$42,000**
Blinds	$75	$2,625	N/A	N/A	**$2,625**
Interior Doors	$75	$2,625	N/A	N/A	**$2,625**
Total	**$2,700**	**$94,500**			**$94,500**

*Notice that $63,000 of the entire cost of $94,500 is deductible as an <u>operating expense</u> rather than having to be capitalized and depreciated.

By electing the Safe Harbor De Minimis Election, the taxpayer incurred $94,500 in capital improvements and received an *operating expense deduction* of $94,500 for 2016.

Assuming a 30% federal tax bracket, this would translate to a tax savings of $28,350 ($94,500 x 30%).

The result would be an *additional* deduction for 2016 *in the form of an operating expense deduction rather than a depreciation deduction* of $80,755 ($94,500 - $13,745).

The ability to claim the Safe Harbor De Minimis Election has continued to be in effect each year through 2020.

Appendix 2: Benefits of a Cost Segregation Study

Category	Cost Segregation Allocation	Useful Life	Annual Depreciation	Comments
5 - Year Property	$600,000	5 Years	$120,000	$120,000 Deduction Per Year, Next 5 Years, Then No Further Deduction
7- Year Property	$20,000	7 Years	$2,857	$2,857 Deduction Per Year for Next 7 Years, Then No Further Deduction
15 Year - Property	$336,000	15 Years	$22,400	$22,400 Deduction Per Year for Next 15 Years, Then No Further Deduction
27.50 Year Property	$3,044,000	27.5 Years	$110,691	$110,691 Deduction Per Year for Next 27.5 Years, Then No Further Deduction
Total	**$4,000,000**		**$255,948**	

Depreciation Expense - **With** a Cost Segregation Study	$255,948
Depreciation Expense - **No** Cost Segregation Study	$145,455
Increase in Annual Depreciation Deduction	**$110,493**

Appendix 3: Benefits of Bonus Depreciation

Category	Cost Segregation Allocation	Bonus Depreciation 50%	Less: Basis Adjustment	Adjusted Depreciation Basis	Useful Life in Years	Regular Annual Depreciation	Total First Yr. Depreciation
5 - Year Property	$600,000	$300,000	($300,000)	$300,000	5	$60,000	$360,000
7- Year Property	$20,000	$10,000	($10,000)	$10,000	7	$1,429	$11,429
15 Year - Property	$336,000	$168,000	($168,000)	$168,000	15	$11,200	$179,200
27.50 Year Property	$3,044,000	$0	$0	$3,044,000	27.5	$110,691	$110,691
Total	$4,000,000	$478,000	($478,000)	$3,522,000		$183,319	$661,319

Appendix 4: Benefits of a Real Estate Professional

Let's Summarize the Deductions Discussed Above;

Bonus & Regular Depreciation Deduction	$661,319
Safe Harbor Election Operating Expense Deduction	$94,500
Total Tax Deductions	**$755,819**

If the taxpayer qualifies as a Real Estate Professional. the taxpayer would be able to also offset their other non-real estate income against their real estate losses often resulting in negative taxable income.

Example:

Assume a taxpayer is a 50% partner in a partnership that owns a garden apartment community. Further assume that the properties net taxable income before deducting depreciation is $325,000. After deducting bonus and regular depreciation and the Safe Harbor Operating Expense deduction the partnership has a net taxable loss of ($430,819).

Note: the Safe Harbor Operating Expense deduction would ordinarily be part of the properties operating expenses. However, for illustration purposes we have showed it as other deductions.

At the Partnership Level

Net Operating Income (NOI) of the Property	$525,000
Less: Mortgage Interest	($200,000)
Net Taxable Income	$325,000

Other Deductions

Bonus & Regular Depreciation	($661,319)
Safe Harbor Election Operating Expense Deduction	($94,500)
Total Deductions	($755,819)
Net Taxable Loss	**($430,819)**

Each Partner will receive a K-1 form from the partnership showing a real estate loss of ($215,410) to report on their personal income tax returns.

Assume partner 1 personally has interest, dividends, and management fee income of $450,000.

On Partners 1's Personal Tax Return

Interest, Dividends, and Management Fees	$450,000
Less: Net Taxable Loss From the Property (Per K-1)	($215,410)
Net Taxable Income	$234,590

ABOUT THE AUTHOR

Sam Liebman is currently the founder and CEO of WealthWay Equity Group LLC, a New York based private equity and real estate Development Company (**www .wealthwayequitygroup.com**). He has owned substantial interests in over 70 properties during the past 30 years, ranging from **multifamily communities, office buildings** and **shopping centers** to the ground up construction of **a luxury 21-story condominium development in Manhattan. Liebman has extensive** experience in finance, property management, acquisition, and development.

He is also the chief executive officer of Rolling Cash Realty, Inc., a real estate management company, as well as a partner in Tepper & Co., a certified public accounting firm. From 1983 to 1986, Mr. Liebman served as the chief financial officer of Mountain Development Corp., a leading New Jersey real estate development company. Liebman has extensive experience representing owners, choosing properties for acquisition, and subsequently negotiating their purchase and sale. He has overseen new building construction and interfaced with renovation and operational staff, architects, engineers, and contractors.

In 2008, he formed a fund that turned $9,000,000 in capital into a portfolio of 20 properties with an aggregate market value that has grown to over $120,000,000.

After decades of experience, he's now committed himself to teaching others how to build lasting wealth through real estate. His promise is to teach his students the fundamentals and tricks of the trade so that *their knowledge of real estate will increase exponentially!*